英美司法案例选读

主编　焦洪宝

参编　黄影　陈桂华　严飞行

王岩华　白明华　翟文喆

南开大学出版社

天　津

图书在版编目（CIP）数据

英美司法案例选读 / 焦洪宝主编. —天津 ：南开
大学出版社，2017.8(2024.7 重印)
ISBN 978-7-310-05428-2

Ⅰ. ①英… Ⅱ. ①焦… Ⅲ. ①司法－案例－英国②司
法－案例－美国 Ⅳ. ①D956.1②D971.2

中国版本图书馆 CIP 数据核字(2017)第 169023 号

英美司法案例选读
YINGMEI SIFA ANLI XUANDU

南开大学出版社出版发行
出版人:刘文华
地址:天津市南开区卫津路 94 号　　邮政编码:300071
营销部电话:(022)23508339　营销部传真:(022)23508542
https://nkup.nankai.edu.cn

天津创先河普业印刷有限公司印刷　全国各地新华书店经销
2017 年 8 月第 1 版　　2024 年 7 月第 2 次印刷
260×185 毫米　16 开本　8.25 印张　202 千字
定价:39.00 元

如遇图书印装质量问题,请与本社营销部联系调换,电话:(022)23508339

目录

（Content）

一、宪法案例

纽约时报公司诉沙利文案
The New York Times Co. v. Sullivan（1964）

【选读理由】（Selected Reason）

在美国社会中，新闻媒体被称为"无冕之王"。由于有美国宪法第 1 条修正案的保驾护航，它不仅不是政府的喉舌，反而是监督政府的重要力量。1964 年 3 月 9 日美国最高法院做出判决的纽约时报公司诉沙利文（*The New York Times* Co. v. Sullivan）一案，就是因政府官员控告《纽约时报》构成诽谤而引发的一个重大民事诉讼案件。本案的判决意见从宪法的高度为新闻媒体批评政府与公职官员的权利和自由提供了法律保障，使其成为美国宪政史上的一个里程碑式的判决。

【案件事实】（Facts）

Respondent's complaint alleged that he had been libeled by statements in a full-page advertisement that was carried in *The New York Times* on March 29, 1960. Entitled "Heed Their Rising Voices," the advertisement began by stating that "As the whole world knows by now, thousands of Southern Negro students are engaged in widespread non-violent demonstrations in positive affirmation of the right to live in human dignity as guaranteed by the U.S. Constitution and the *Bill of Rights*." It went on to charge that "in their efforts to uphold these guarantees, they are being met by an unprecedented wave of terror by those who would deny and negate that document which the whole world looks upon as setting the pattern for modern freedom..." Succeeding paragraphs purported to illustrate the "wave of terror" by describing certain alleged events. The text concluded with an appeal for funds for three purposes: support of the student movement, "the struggle for the right-to-vote," and the legal defense of Dr. Martin Luther King, Jr., leader·of the movement, against a perjury indictment then pending in Montgomery.

被申请人沙利文起诉称他受到了 1960 年 3 月 29 日刊载在《纽约时报》上整版广告的诽谤。这篇题为《倾听他们高涨的呼声》的广告文章在一开篇写道："今天，全世界都知道了。美国南方数以千计的黑人学生，正在发起一次和平示威游行，宣布黑人同样受美国宪法和《权利法案》保护，并享有人格尊严和生存权利。"接下来这篇广告控诉称"在维护这份保障的努力过程中，他们遭遇了前所未有的粗暴对待，施暴者蔑视并践踏了这份在全世界看来将确立保护现代化自由模式的宪法文件……"。接下来的段落描述了一些所谓的事件来佐证这一"恐怖浪潮"。文章最后表达了三项诉求：支持学生运动，为选举权而奋斗，为马丁·路德·金博士在蒙哥马利受到的伪证罪指控做法律辩护——他是此次运动的领袖。

Of the 10 paragraphs of text in the advertisement, the third and a portion of the sixth were the basis of respondent's claim of libel. They read as follows:

Third paragraph:"In Montgomery, Alabama, after students sang 'My Country, 'Tis of Thee' on the State Capitol steps, their leaders were expelled from school, and truckloads of police armed with shotguns and tear-gas ringed the Alabama State College Campus. When the entire student body protested to state authorities by refusing to re-register, their dining hall was padlocked in an attempt to starve them into submission."

Sixth paragraph:"Again and again the Southern violators have answered Dr. King's peaceful protests with intimidation and violence. They have bombed his home almost killing his wife and child. They have assaulted his person. They have arrested him seven times—for 'speeding,' 'loitering' and similar 'offenses.' And now they have charged him with 'perjury'—a *felony* under which they could imprison him for *ten years...*"

广告文本共有 10 段，其中第 3 段和第 6 段的一部分是本案被申请人主张诽谤索赔的依据。第三段写道："在亚拉巴马州蒙哥马利的州议会厅前，当学生们唱完《我的国家，也是你的》这首歌后，学生领袖随即被校方开除。成卡车的警察拿着枪和催泪瓦斯，包围了亚拉巴马州立学院的校园。当全体学生反对在州当局办理重新注册后，他们封锁了学校食堂，试图用饥饿迫使他们就范。"

第六段写道："南方违宪者一次又一次地用恐吓和暴力回答了金博士的和平抗议。他们已经炸毁了他的家，差点杀死他的妻子和孩子。他们殴打他，他们以超速、闲逛和类似的违章为由 7 次逮捕他。现在他们又以伪证罪指控他——这是个能将他投入监狱 10 年以上的重罪。"

Although neither of these statements mentions respondent by name, he contended that the word "police" in the third paragraph referred to him as the Montgomery Commissioner who supervised the Police Department, so that he was being accused of "ringing" the campus with police. He further claimed that the paragraph would be read as imputing to the police, and hence to him, the padlocking of the dining hall in order to starve the students into submission（Respondent did not consider the charge of expelling the students to be applicable to him, since "that responsibility rests with the State Department of Education"）. As to the sixth paragraph, he contended that since arrests are ordinarily made by the police, the statement "They have arrested [Dr. King] seven times" would be read as referring to him; he further contended that the "They" who did the arresting would be equated with the "They" who committed the other described acts and with the "Southern violators." Thus, he argued, the paragraph would be read as accusing the Montgomery police, and hence him, of answering Dr. King's protests with "intimidation and violence," bombing his home, assaulting his person, and charging him with perjury. Respondent and six other Montgomery residents testified that they read some or all of the statements as referring to him in his capacity as Commissioner.

虽然这些陈述并没有提及本案被申请人沙利文的名字，但他认为在第三段中的"警察"指的就是他这个负责监管警察局的蒙哥马利县市政专员，所以他被指责和警察一起包围校园。他还认为这一段读起来是将封锁食堂以逼迫学生就范的事情归咎于警察，也归咎于他（在他看来，逼迫学生的事情应由政府教育部门承担责任）。就第六段，他认为既然逮捕通常是由警察执行的，那么"他们逮捕金博士 7 次"的叙述读起来就是指向他。他还认为从事逮捕的"他们"看起来和那些从事其他被描述的行为的"他们"以及"南方违宪者"所指向的是同一批人。由此，他认为这一段看起来就是在指控蒙哥马利警察，也是指控他，这些以"恐吓和暴力"应对金博士和平抗议、炸毁他家、殴打他、以伪证罪指控他的人。被申请人与另外 6 个蒙哥马利县居民做证说他们认为广告中的部分或全部陈述指向的就是作为市政专员的他。

It is uncontroverted that some of the statements contained in the two paragraphs were not accurate descriptions of events which occurred in Montgomery. Although Negro students staged a demonstration on the State Capitol steps, they sang the National Anthem and not "My Country, 'Tis of Thee." Although nine students were expelled by the State Board of Education, this was not for leading the demonstration at the Capitol, but for demanding service at a lunch counter in the Montgomery County Courthouse on another day. Not the entire student body, but most of it, had protested the expulsion, not by refusing to register, but by boycotting classes on a single day; virtually all the students did register for the ensuing semester. The campus dining hall was not padlocked on any occasion, and the only students who may have been barred from eating there were the few who had neither signed a preregistration application nor requested temporary meal tickets. Although the police were deployed near the campus in large numbers on three occasions, they did not at any time "ring" the campus, and they were not called to the campus in connection with the demonstration on the State Capitol steps, as the third paragraph implied. Dr. King had not been arrested seven times, but only four; and although he claimed to have been assaulted some years earlier in connection with his arrest for loitering outside a courtroom, one of the officers who made the arrest denied that there was such an assault.

无可置疑，这两段中的有些表述对发生在蒙哥马利的事件描述并不准确。虽然黑人学生确实在州议会厅前的台阶上集会，但他们唱的是国歌而非《我的国家，也是你的》。虽然有 9 个学生被州教育董事会开除，但并非因为学生领导在州议会的集会，而是因为另一天他们要求蒙哥马利县法院的午餐柜台为他们提供服务。不是所有学生，只是大部分学生通过抵制上课一天的方式抗议驱逐，而并非拒绝注册；几乎所有的学生都进行了下一学期的注册。校园食堂在任何时候都没有被封锁，可能被禁止在那里吃饭的学生只是极少数那些没有办理预先注册申请或者没有要求办理临时饭票的学生。虽然警方有 3 次在校园附近部署了大量警力，但他们在任何时候都没有"包围"校园，他们去校园并非像第三段所暗示的那样和在州议会大厦的示威有任何关系。金博士没有被逮捕过 7 次，只有 4 次。虽然他声称在很多年以前因为他在法庭前闲逛被逮捕时遭到殴打，但逮捕他的一个警察否认有殴打行为发生。

Respondent made no effort to prove that he suffered actual pecuniary loss as a result of the alleged libel. One of his witnesses, a former employer, testified that if he had believed the statements, he doubted whether he "would want to be associated with anybody who would be a party to such things that are stated in that ad," and that he would not re-employ respondent if he believed "that he allowed the Police Department to do the things that the paper say he did." But neither this witness nor any of the others testified that he had actually believed the statements in their supposed reference to respondent.

被申请人没有就他因起诉的诽谤所遭受的实际损失进行努力证实。被申请人的一个证人，前雇主，做证说如果他相信了报纸的陈述，他将怀疑是否还会有人跟做了广告中所陈述的那些事情的人保持联系；如果他相信了报纸上沙利文所做的那些他许可警察局做的事情，他就再也不会雇沙利文。但无论是这个证人还是其他证人都没有真正地认为报纸中的陈述指向的是被申请人。

The cost of the advertisement was approximately $ 4800, and it was published by the Times upon an order from a New York advertising agency acting for the signatory Committee. The agency submitted the advertisement with a letter from A. Philip Randolph, Chairman of the Committee, certifying that the persons whose names appeared on the advertisement had given their permission. Mr. Randolph was known to *The Times'* Advertising Acceptability Department as a responsible person, and in accepting the letter as sufficient proof of authorization it followed its established practice. There was testimony that the copy of the advertisement which accompanied the letter listed only the 64 names appearing under the text, and that the statement, "We in the south...warmly endorse this appeal," and the list of names thereunder, which included those of the individual petitioners, were subsequently added when the first proof of the advertisement was received. Each of the individual petitioners testified that he had not authorized the use of his name, and that he had been unaware of its use until receipt of respondent's demand for a retraction. The manager of the Advertising Acceptability Department testified that he had approved the advertisement for publication because he knew nothing to cause him to believe that anything in it was false, and because it bore the endorsement of "a number of people who are well known and whose reputation" he "had no reason to question." Neither he nor anyone else at *The Times* made an effort to confirm the accuracy of the advertisement, either by checking it against recent Times news stories relating to some of the described events or by any other means.

广告的费用大约 4800 美元。这份广告是由《纽约时报》根据纽约的一家广告代理机构受署名的委员会委托而发布的订单来印发的。代理机构随同广告还提交一封来自委员会主席拉尔夫·阿伯内斯的信，证实其名字出现在广告中的人认可，阿伯内斯对于《纽约时报》广告受理部来说是个负责任的人，这封信本身是表明确有此事的充分证据。但与这封信一起送来的广告文本中只有 64 个名字，并且"我们在南方……热烈赞同这一呼吁"以及包括本案申请人在内的人名，是在收到第一份广告文本之后加上的。每个独立申请人都称他们没有授权使用他的名字，直到他们收到了被申请人的诉请才意识到他们的名字被使用了。广告受理部经理做证说他之所以同意印发这一广告，是因为不知道这里面有虚假，因为有一大批知名人士的署名，这些人的名誉他无法质疑。他和《纽约时报》的其他人都没有人做出努力去核查最近《纽约时报》与广告中描述的事件有关的新闻报道，或用其他方式来核实广告的准确性。

【裁决过程与结果】（Procedure and Disposition）

The present action for libel was brought in the Cir-cuit Court of Montgomery County, Alabama, by a city commissioner of public affairs whose duties included the supervision of the police department; the action was brought against *The New York Times* for publication of a paid advertisement describing the maltreatment in the city of Negro students protesting segregation, and against four individuals whose names, among others, appeared in the advertisement. The jury awarded plaintiff damages of $ 500,000 against all defendants, and the judgment on the verdict was affirmed by the Supreme Court of Alabama in August, 1962 on the grounds that the statements in the advertisement were libelous per se, false, and not privileged, and that the evidence showed malice on the part of the newspaper; the defendants' constitutional objections were rejected on the ground that the First Amendment does not protect libelous publications.

The Newspaper as Petitioner sought review of the decision. On writs of certiorari, the Supreme Court of the United States reversed the judgment and remanded the case to the Alabama Supreme Court.

【裁判理由】（Reasons for Judicial Decision）

【原审意见】

In affirming the judgment, the Supreme Court of Alabama sustained the trial judge's rulings and instructions in all respects. It held that "where the words published tend to injure a person libeled by them in his reputation, profession, trade or business, or charge him with an indictable offense, or tend to bring the individual into public contempt," they are "libelous per se"; that "the matter complained of is, under the above doctrine, libelous per se, if it was published of and concerning the plaintiff"; and that it was actionable without "proof of pecuniary injury ..., such injury being implied."... It rejected petitioners' constitutional contentions with the brief statements that "The First Amendment of the U.S. Constitution does not protect libelous publications" and "The Fourteenth Amendment is directed against State action and not private action."

亚拉巴马州最高法院在维持原判过程中认可了初审法官的全部推论和观点，并给诽谤罪下了一个很宽的定义："任何刊出的文字只要有损被诽谤者的声誉、职业、贸易或生意，或是指责其犯有可被起诉的罪行，或是使其受到公众的蔑视，这些文字便构成了诽谤。"按照这一原则，上述被公开发布并与原告相关的指责已构成了诽谤，并且无须证明直接伤害的存在就可以起诉，因为伤害是当然存在的。这一判决还拒绝了本案申诉人在宪法有关内容方面的争辩，简要地称"美国宪法第一修正案并不保护诽谤性出版物"和"第十四修正案是针对州的行为，不针对个人行为。"

【生效判决意见】（Opinion by Brennan）

Under Alabama law as applied in this case, a publication is "libelous per se" if the words "tend to injure a person...in his reputation" or to "bring [him] into public contempt"; the trial court stated that the standard was met if the words are such as to "injure him in his public office, or impute misconduct to him in his office, or want of official integrity, or want of fidelity to a public trust..." The jury must find that the words were published "of and concerning" the plaintiff, but where the plaintiff is a public official his place in the governmental hierarchy is sufficient evidence to support a finding that his reputation has been affected by statements that reflect upon the agency of which he is in charge. Once "libel per se" has been established, the defendant has no defense as to stated facts unless he can persuade the jury that they were true in all their particulars. His privilege of "fair comment" for expressions of opinion depends on the truth of the facts upon which the comment is based. Unless he can discharge the burden of proving truth, general damages are presumed, and may be awarded without proof of pecuniary injury. A showing of actual malice is apparently a prerequisite to recovery of punitive damages, and the defendant may in any event forestall a punitive award by a retraction meeting the statutory requirements. Good motives and belief in truth do not negate an inference of malice, but are relevant only in mitigation of punitive damages if the jury chooses to accord them weight.

The question before us is whether this rule of liability, as applied to an action brought by a public official against critics of his official conduct, abridges the freedom of speech and of the press that is guaranteed by the First and Fourteenth Amendments.

按照本案适用的亚拉巴马州法律，一个出版物只要其措辞"意图伤害一个人的名誉或使其受公众蔑视"就将构成"诽谤"。初审法院认为如果有类似"伤害其公职、导致对其公职的误解、丧失官员的正直性或丧失公众信任"的措辞，就构成诽谤的标准。陪审团必须认定印发的措辞与原告有关，但原告在政府部门担任公众官员本身就足可证明其名誉会受到反映他所任职的机构的表述的影响。一旦诽谤成立，被告将无法就事实问题抗辩，除非他能说服陪审团这些表述都是真实的。他通过表达观点而所享有的公正评论的权益，将依赖于这一评论所基于的事实的真实性。除非他能够免除自己的举证责任，普通损害将被推定存在，无须证明就可被认定金钱赔偿。很明显，真实恶意的存在是要求惩罚性赔偿的前提，按照法律要求，被告可以通过撤回报道而防止收到惩罚性赔偿判决。动机善良和相信是真的并不能否定对恶意的认定，但如果陪审团愿意对此加以衡量的话，只会与减少惩罚性赔偿相关。

我们的问题是本案中有关批评一个政府官员的官方行为的责任认定规则，是否剥夺了宪法第一修正案和第十四修正案所保护的言论和表达的自由。

The constitutional guarantees require, we think, a federal rule that prohibits a public official from recovering damages for a defamatory falsehood relating to his official conduct unless he proves that the statement was made with "actual malice"—that is, with knowledge that it was false or with reckless disregard of whether it was false or not.

我们认为，宪法对于言论和表达自由的保护要求这样一个联邦规则，即当政府公职官员因处理公众事务遭受批评和指责使个人的名誉可能受到损害时，不能动辄以诽谤罪起诉和要求金钱赔偿，除非公职官员能拿出证据，证明这种指责是出于"真正的恶意"，即明知陈述虚假，或贸然不顾其是否虚假。

We hold today that the Constitution delimits a State's power to award damages for libel in actions brought by public officials against critics of their official conduct. Since this is such an action, the rule requiring proof of actual malice is applicable. While Alabama law apparently requires proof of actual malice for an award of punitive damages, where general damages are concerned malice is "presumed." Such a presumption is inconsistent with the federal rule. "The power to create presumptions is not a means of escape from constitutional restrictions," Bailey v. Alabama, 219 U.S. 219, 239; "the showing of malice required for the forfeiture of the privilege is not presumed but is a matter for proof by the plaintiff ..." Since the trial judge did not instruct the jury to differentiate between general and punitive damages, it may be that the verdict was wholly an award of one or the other. But it is impossible to know, in view of the general verdict returned. Because of this uncertainty, the judgment must be reversed and the case remanded.

我们现在持此观点：当政府公职官员提起诉讼要求获得针对其公职行为的批评言论的诽谤赔偿时，宪法给州划定了做出这一认定的权力界限。在本案中适用了需证明真实恶意存在的原则。亚拉巴马州对于给予惩罚性赔偿要求需以证明真实恶意存在为前提，但与普通损害赔偿相关的恶意是推定的。这一推定规则是与联邦规则不符的。创设推定的权利应受制于宪法，造成利益丧失的恶意不能推定而应由原告加以证明。原审法官没有告知陪审团有关普通赔偿和惩罚性赔偿的区别，这可能造成判决的赔偿全部是一个方面或另一个方面的。但我们不知道这个判决是指向于哪个方面。由于此不确定性，原审判决应当被推翻并发回重审。

【附合意见】（Concur by Black）

I concur in reversing this half-million-dollar judgment against *The New York Times* Company and the four individual defendants. In reversing the Court holds that "the Constitution delimits a State's power to award damages for libel in actions brought by public officials against critics of their official conduct."I base my vote to reverse on the belief that the First and Fourteenth Amendments not merely "delimit" a State's power to award damages to "public officials against critics of their official conduct" but completely prohibit a State from exercising such a power. Unlike the Court, therefore, I vote to reverse exclusively on the ground that *The Times* and the individual defendants had an absolute, unconditional constitutional right to publish in *The Times* advertisement their criticisms of the Montgomery agencies and officials.

我对撤销此要求纽约时报公司及其他四个被告赔偿 50 万美元的判决表示赞同。在撤销判决中法庭认为"宪法给州处理政府公职官员提起诉讼要求获得针对其公职行为的批评言论的诽谤赔偿案件划定权力界限"。我投票同意撤销是基于这样一种认识，即第一和第十四修正案并不仅仅是为州"给遭受与其公共职务行为相关的批评的公职人员"判决赔偿时设定了"权力界限"，而是完全禁止州行使这样的权力。与法庭不同，我投票推翻原判的唯一理由是几位被告有绝对和无条件的宪法权利在《纽约时报》的广告中批评蒙哥马利市各级政府机构及其官员。

【案件影响】（Impact of the Case）

纽约时报公司诉沙利文案是一项具有划时代意义的重要判决，为美国新闻媒体"敢把总统拉下马"式的新闻调查和报道自由提供了前所未有的法律保障。本判决公布后几个小时内，《纽约时报》发表声明，称"法庭的意见使得新闻自由比以往任何时候都更有保证"。通过本案，美国最高法院重申了第一修正案的重要性，并且实际上把通常由各州用普通法管辖的诽谤案件也纳入到宪法的保护范围，"真正的恶意"几乎成为以后衡量所有类似诽谤案的一个标准。纽约时报公司诉沙利文案确立的这一原则起初只适用于担任公职的政府官员，但最高法院后来又通过其他几个判决，将"真正的恶意"原则的适用范围从执行公务的政府官员，扩大到为公众所知的人物，即公众人物（public figure），但并不适用于非官员和非公众人物寻求赔偿的诽谤案，即使被指控为诽谤的陈述涉及"公共关注"的事情。

【思考问题】（Questions）

1. 美国宪法所保护的公民权利的内容有哪些？与我国有何不同？
2. 对公共事务进行随心所欲的言说是一项无条件的宪法权利吗？

二、行政法案例

马伯里诉麦迪逊案
Marbury v. Madison（1803）

【选读理由】（Selected Reason）

　　行政、立法、司法三权分立是美国的立国根基之一，但在美利坚合众国成立之初，司法的权威与行政、立法相比却比较薄弱。1803 年美国最高法院审理的马伯里诉麦迪逊案（William Marbury v. James Madison, Secretary of States of the United States）是一起原本被任命为治安法官的当事人起诉国务卿不履行职责发放委任状的行政诉讼案例，在当时环境下让最高法院下达执行令状，责令总统直接任命的负责掌管国玺的国务卿发放委任状并不现实，极有可能会被置之不理。时任最高法院首席大法官马歇尔巧妙地利用这桩原本很棘手的行政诉讼案件，提出了最高法院解释宪法及司法机关有权对国家立法行为、行政行为是否违宪做最终审查的观点，并使本案成为美国宪法的司法审查制度的开端。他不仅巧妙地解决了最高法院当时面临的重大危机，同时也维护了最高法院作为最高司法机关的权威和地位，巩固了美国三权分立的政治体制。

【案件事实】（Facts）

　　On his last day in office, President John Adams named forty-two justices of the peace and sixteen new circuit court justices for the District of Columbia under the *Organic Act*. The *Organic Act* was an attempt by the Federalists to take control of the federal judiciary before Thomas Jefferson took office.

　　约翰·亚当斯总统在其任期的最后一天根据《哥伦比亚特区组织法》任命了 42 位治安法官（或称太平绅士）以及哥伦比亚特区的 16 名新的巡回法庭法官。联邦党人制定《组织法》的目的是在托马斯·杰斐逊总统就职之前控制联邦司法系统。

　　The commissions were signed by President Adams and sealed by acting Secretary of State John Marshall (who later became Chief Justice of the Supreme Court and author of this opinion), but they were not delivered before the expiration of Adams's term as president. Thomas Jefferson refused to honor the commissions, claiming that they were invalid because they had not been delivered by the end of Adams's term.

　　委任状由亚当斯总统签署并由当时的国务卿约翰·马歇尔（之后成为最高法院的首席大法官以及本判决意见的作者）加盖国印，但是由于亚当斯总统的任期结束而未能及时送达至相关人员。杰斐逊总统拒绝颁发委任状，认为这些委任状由于在亚当斯总统任期结束之前未能送达而不具有任何法律效果。

　　William Marbury was an intended recipient of an appointment as justice of the peace. Marbury applied directly to the Supreme Court of the United States for a writ of mandamus to compel Jefferson's Secretary of State, James Madison, to deliver the commissions. The *Judiciary Act of*

1789 had granted the Supreme Court original jurisdiction to issue writs of mandamus "…to any courts appointed, or persons holding office, under the authority of the United States."

威廉·马伯里是委任状所任命的治安法官之一。马伯里直接向美国最高法院申请执行令状，请求最高法院命令杰斐逊政府的国务卿詹姆斯·麦迪逊颁发之前的委任状。《1789 年司法条例》授予了最高法院向美国行政区域内的所有法院或行政首长发布执行令状的初审管辖权。

At the last term, viz. December term, 1801, William Marbury, Dennis Ramsay, Robert Townsend Hooe, and William Harper, by their counsel, Charles Lee, esq. late attorney general of the United States, severally moved the court for a rule to James Madison, secretary of state of the United States, to show cause why a mandamus should not issue commanding him to cause to be delivered to them respectively their several commissions as justices of the peace in the district of Columbia. This motion was supported by affidavits of the following facts: that notice of this motion had been given to Mr. Madison; that Mr. Adams, the late president of the United States, nominated the applicants to the senate for their advice and consent to be appointed justices of the peace of the district of Columbia; that the senate advised and consented to the appointments; that commissions in the due form were signed by the said president appointing them justices, and that the seal of the United States was in due form affixed to the said commissions by the secretary of state; that the applicants have requested Mr. Madison to deliver them their said commissions, who has not complied with that request; and that their said commissions are withheld from them; that the applicants have made application to Mr. Madison as secretary of state of the United States at his office, for information whether the commissions were signed and sealed as aforesaid; that explicit and satisfactory information has not been given to that enquiry, either by the secretary of state or by any officer of the department of state; that application has been made to the secretary of the Senate for a certificate of the nomination of the applicants, and of the advice and consent of the senate, who has declined giving such a certificate; whereupon a rule was laid to show cause on the 4th day of this term.

在 1801 年 12 月开庭中，威廉·马伯里、丹尼斯·拉姆齐、罗伯特·汤森·胡以及威廉·哈珀，在他们的律师的帮助下，郑重请求法庭做出一项决定，要求国务卿詹姆斯·麦迪逊做出解释，为什么法庭不能颁发一项执行令，向他们送达神圣的哥伦比亚特区治安法官的委任状。这个请求得到如下事实支持：这个请求的通知已经送达了麦迪逊先生；亚当斯先生，美国前任总统，向参议院提名原告担任哥伦比亚特区的治安法官，以征求参议院的意见和同意；参议院接受和同意了该项任命；前任总统以正确的格式签署了该项任命法官的委任状，前任国务卿也以正确的形式在委任状上加盖了国印；原告曾经请求麦迪逊先生送达他们的上述委任状，但是被他拒绝了；上述委任状确实为他们所拥有；原告曾经在他的官邸，请求现任国务卿麦迪逊先生解释上述委任状是否被签署和封印；无论是国务卿还是国务院的其他官员都没有对上述质询给出清楚且令人满意的回答；原告曾经要求国务卿出示一份证书，证明总统曾经提名原告，以及参议院对此的意见和同意，但是他拒绝给出这样一份证书；因此，法庭做出一项决定要求他在该期限的第四天说明原因。

【裁判过程与结果】（Procedure and Disposition）

At a prior term, the Court granted an applicant a rule directing the Secretary of State of the

United States to show cause why a mandamus should not issue commanding him to deliver to the applicant his commission as a justice of the peace. No cause was shown, so the applicant moved for a mandamus.

The Court held that 13 of the *Act of 1789*, giving the Court authority to issue writs of mandamus to an officer, was contrary to the Constitution as an act of original jurisdiction, and therefore void.

【裁判理由】（Reason for Judicial Decision）

【生效判决意见】（OPINION BY: MARSHALL）

The first object of enquiry is,

Firstly, has the applicant a right to the commission he demands?

His right originates in an act of congress passed in February, 1801, concerning the Distriet of Columbia.

After dividing the district into two counties, the 11th section of this law enacts, "that there shall be appointed in and for each of the said counties, such number of discreet persons to be justices of the peace as the president of the United States shall, from time to time, think expedient, to continue in office for five years."

法院考察的第一个问题是：

一、申请人是否有权利得到他所要求的委任状？

他的权利来源于国会于 1801 年 4 月所通过的一项关于哥伦比亚特区的法令。

在把特区分成两个巡回区后，该法的第 11 条规定，将任命数量相等的合格的人来担任上述每一个巡回区的治安法官，总统会随时给出权宜之计，这些官员的任职期限是 5 年。

The Second section of the 2d article of the constitution declares, that "the president shall nominate, and, by and with the advice and consent of the senate, shall appoint ambassadors, other public ministers and consuls, and all other officers of the United States, whose appointments are not otherwise provided for."

The third section declares, that "he shall commission all the officers of the United States."

An act of congress directs the secretary of state to keep the seal of the United States, "to make out and record, and affix the said seal to all civil commissions to officers of the United States, to be appointed by the President, by and with the consent of the senate, or by the President alone; provided that the said seal shall not be affixed to any commission before the same shall have been signed by the President of the United States."

These are the clauses of the constitution and laws of the United States, which affect this part of the case. They seem to contemplate three distinct operations:

1st. The nomination. This is the sole act of the President, and is completely voluntary. 2nd. The appointment. This is also the act of the President, and is also a voluntary act, though it can only be performed by and with the advice and consent of the senate. 3rd. The commission. To grant a commission to a person appointed, might perhaps be deemed a duty enjoined by the constitution. "He shall," says that instrument, "commission all the officers of the United States."

宪法第 2 条第 2 款规定，总统将提名，并且在参议院的建议和同意下，任命大使、其他公共部长和顾问，以及所有的其他官员。

第 3 款规定，他有权委任所有的美利坚合众国官员。

国会的一项法令规定，国务卿保存合众国的印章，负责制作和登记，并且把上述封印加盖到所有的由总统任命、由国会同意，或者由总统单独任命的国内官员的委任状上去。如果在美国总统签署之前，上述封印将不能被加盖到任何委任状上。

这些是宪法和美国法律中的条款，它们将对本案产生影响。它们看起来是由三个独立的运作过程构成的：（1）提名。这是总统的独立行为，并且是完全自愿的。（2）任命。这也是总统的行为，它也是自愿的，尽管它需要在参议院的建议和同意下进行。（3）委任。授予一个被任命的人委任状，可能被认为是一项宪法规定的职责。宪法规定，他将任命所有美利坚合众国的官员。

The discretion of the executive is to be exercised until the appointment has been made. But having once made the appointment, his power over the office is terminated in all cases, where, by law, the officer is not removable by him. The right to the office is then in the person appointed, and he has the absolute, unconditional, power of accepting or rejecting it.

Mr. Marbury, then, since his commission was signed by the President, and sealed by the secretary of state, was appointed; and as the law creating the office, gave the officer a right to hold for five years, independent of the executive, the appointment was not revocable; but vested in the officer legal rights, which are protected by the laws of his country.

To withhold his commission, therefore, is an act deemed by the court not warranted by law, but violative of a vested legal right.

行政上的考量只能在任命做出的时候进行。但是一旦做出这项任命，他对该官员的权力将在任何情况下被停止，根据法律规定，对这个官员的任命是不能再随他的意志而转移的。是否就职的权利转移到被任命的人，他有绝对、无条件接受或者放弃它的权利。

马伯里已经被任命了，而且他的委任状已由总统签署，并且由国务卿封印。法律赋予他作为地方治安法官五年的任期，该法律独立于行政命令；这项任命是不可废止的；且赋予该法官受国家法律保护的合法权利。

因此，法院认为拒不发布委任状的行为不受法律保护，是对既得的合法权利的侵犯。

This brings us to the second enquiry; which is,

Secondly, if he has a right, and that right has been violated, do the laws of his country afford him a remedy?

The very essence of civil liberty certainly consists in the right of every individual to claim the protection of the laws, whenever he receives an injury. One of the first duties of government is to afford that protection. In Great Britain the king himself is sued in the respectful form of a petition, and he never fails to comply with the judgment of his court.

这将我们带入了第二个问题，那就是：

二、如果他有一项权利，并且这项权利被侵犯，国家的法律会为他提供一项补救措施吗？

公民自由权的本质就在于每个人都受法律的保护，无论他在何时受到了损害。政府的首要责任是去提供这种保护。在英国，国王也会以令人尊敬的形式被起诉，他永远不会不遵守法庭的判决。

But when the legislature proceeds to impose on that officer other duties; when he is directed peremptorily to perform certain acts; when the rights of individuals are dependent on the performance of those acts; he is so far the officer of the law; is amenable to the laws for his conduct; and cannot at his discretion sport away the vested rights of others.

但是，当立法机关赋予该官员其他责任时，当该官员有义务做出任何行为时，当个人的权利依赖于这些特定行为的履行时，他就是一个法律的执行官，他的行为就要服从法律，其裁量权也不能无视他人被授予的既得权利。

The conclusion from this reasoning is, that where the heads of departments are the political or confidential agents of the executive, merely to execute the will of the President, or rather to act in cases in which the executive possesses a constitutional or legal discretion, nothing can be more perfectly clear than that their acts are only politically examinable. But where a specific duty is assigned by law, and individual rights depend upon the performance of that duty, it seems equally clear that the individual who considers himself injured, has a right to resort to the laws of his country for a remedy.

这种论证的结论是：当部门首脑作为行政机构的政治代表或者秘密代表时，他们仅仅是执行总统的意愿，或者更确切地说，是行使行政机构所拥有的宪法或者法律赋予的自由裁量权。再明显不过的是，对这些行为只能进行政治性的审查。但是，只要法律赋予其特定的职责，而且个人权利的实现有赖于这些行为的实施，显然认为自己受到损害的个人有权要求得到国家法律的救助。

It is then the opinion of the court, 1st. That by signing the commission of Mr. Marbury, the president of the United States appointed him a justice of peace, for the county of Washington in the district of Columbia; and that the seal of the United States, affixed thereto by the secretary of state, is conclusive testimony of the verity of the signature, and of the completion of the appointment; and that the appointment conferred on him a legal right to the office for the space of five years. 2nd. That, having this legal title to the office, he has a consequent right to the commission; a refusal to deliver which, is a plain violation of that right, for which the laws of his country afford him a remedy.

这是法庭的意见：首先，通过签署马伯里的委任状，当时的美国总统已经任命其为哥伦比亚特区华盛顿郡的治安法官；由国务卿加盖其上的美国国印是总统已签署该委任状的绝对证据，并就此完成了任命；该任命赋予他法律上合法的五年任期。其次，由于其具有合法的任期，马伯里对委任状享有后续权利；拒绝发布委任状是对该权利的侵犯，对此其所在国家的法律为其提供了救济途径。

It remains to be enquired whether,

Thirdly, he is entitled to the remedy for which he applies. This depends on, 1st. The nature of the writ applied for, and, 2nd. The power of this court.

接下来要解决的问题是：

三、马伯里是否有权利获得他主张的救济。这取决于：（1）他申请的执行令状的性质；（2）本法院的职权。

The act to establish the judicial courts of the United States authorizes the Supreme Court "to issue writs of mandamus, in cases warranted by the principles and usages of law, to any courts appointed, or persons holding office, under the authority of the United States."

The constitution vests the whole judicial power of the United States in one Supreme Court, and such inferior courts as congress shall, from time to time, ordain and establish. This power is expressly extended to all cases arising under the laws of the United States; and consequently, in some form, may be exercised over the present case; because the right claimed is given by a law of the United States.

In the distribution of this power it is declared that "the supreme court shall have original jurisdiction in all cases affecting ambassadors, other public ministers and consuls, and those in which a state shall be a party. In all other cases, the supreme court shall have appellate jurisdiction."

It has been insisted, at the bar, that as the original grant of jurisdiction, to the supreme and inferior courts, is general, and the clause, assigning original jurisdiction to the supreme court, contains no negative or restrictive words; the power remains to the legislature, to assign original jurisdiction to that court in other cases than those specified in the article which has been recited; provided those cases belong to the judicial power of the United States.

设立合众国各级法院的司法条例，授权最高法院"有权在法律原则和法律惯例准许的情况下，根据美国法律的规定向任何合法设立的法院，或公职人员发出强制执行令"。

宪法把合众国的全部司法权授予最高法院，以及由国会随时命令和建立的各种下级法院。这项权力显然可以适用于合众国法律项下所有的情形；因此也可以适用于本案之中；因为主张的权利是由合众国法律赋予的。

在分配这项权力时，宪法宣布："最高法院对涉及大使、其他公使和领事，以及以州为一方当事人的案件有初审管辖权；在所有其他案件中，最高法院有上诉管辖权。"

在法庭上有人坚决主张，由于宪法中关于最高法院和下级法院的管辖权的授权是一般性的，而且授予最高法院初审管辖权的条款没有包含任何否定的或限制性的词语，所以，只要法律条文没有具体列举在司法管辖权范围里的案件，这些案件的初审管辖权是否分配给联邦最高法院就由国会来决定。

When an instrument organizing fundamentally a judicial system, divides it into one supreme, and so many inferior courts as the legislature may ordain and establish; then enumerates its powers, and proceeds so far to distribute them, as to define the jurisdiction of the supreme court by declaring the cases in which it shall take original jurisdiction, and that in others it shall take appellate jurisdiction; the plain import of the words seems to be, that in one class of cases its jurisdiction is original, and not appellate; in the other it is appellate, and not original.

To enable this court then to issue a mandamus, it must be shown to be an exercise of appellate jurisdiction, or to be necessary to enable them to exercise appellate jurisdiction.

It has been stated at the bar that the appellate jurisdiction may be exercised in a variety of forms, and that if it be the will of the legislature that a mandamus should be used for that purpose, that will must be obeyed. This is true, yet the jurisdiction must be appellate, not original.

It is the essential criterion of appellate jurisdiction, that it revises and corrects the proceedings in a cause already instituted, and does not create that cause. Although, therefore, a mandamus may be directed to courts, yet to issue such a writ to an officer for the delivery of a paper, is in effect the same as to sustain an original action for that paper, and therefore seems not to belong to appellate, but to original jurisdiction. Neither is it necessary in such a case as this, to enable the court to exercise its appellate jurisdiction.

The authority, therefore, given to the supreme court, by the act establishing the judicial courts of the United States, to issue writs of mandamus to public officers, appears not to be warranted by the constitution; and it becomes necessary to enquire whether a jurisdiction, so conferred, can be exercised.

建立基本司法体系的法律把司法体系分为一个最高法院和诸多由立法机关命令和建立的下级法院，然后列举其各自的权力，并进而对其权力加以分配。对于最高法院，该法律规定它对一些案件有初审管辖权，而对其他案件则有上诉管辖权；宪法上的词语似乎在一类案件中强调其初审管辖权，而在另一类案件中则强调其上诉管辖权。

那么，为使本院能够发出强制执行令，就必须表明是行使上诉管辖权，或者有必要使其行使上诉管辖权。

在法庭上已经表明，上诉管辖权可以以各种形式行使，假如为上述目的发出强制执行令是立法机关的意志，则该意志必须予以服从。事实是，该管辖权是上诉管辖权，而不是初审管辖权。

上诉管辖权的基本特点是，在已经提起的案件中它可以修订和改正程序，而不是立案。因此，虽然可以向法院发出强制执行令，但为送达文件而向官员发出这类强制执行令，在效力上与确认为该文件而提起的原始诉讼相同，因而必须先经过初审管辖之后，才能上诉到本院。本院只能对上诉管辖的案件行使强制执行令。

建立了合众国法院体系的法律——《司法条例》赋予最高法院向一切政府官员发出强制执行令的权力，显然没有得到宪法的授权，这就有必要查明：如此赋予的管辖权能否被行使？

Between these alternatives there is no middle ground. The constitution is either a superior, paramount law, unchangeable by ordinary means, or it is on a level with ordinary legislative acts, and like other acts, is alterable when the legislature shall please to alter it.

Certainly all those who have framed written constitutions contemplate them as forming the fundamental and para-mount law of the nation, and consequently the theory of every such government must be, that an act of the legislature, repugnant to the constitution, is void.

This theory is essentially attached to a written constitution, and is consequently to be considered, by this court, as one of the fundamental principles of our society. It is not therefore to be lost sight of in the further consideration of this subject.

在这两种选择之间没有中间道路。宪法要么是优先的、至高无上的法律，不得以普通方式改变；要么与一般法律处于同等的地位，像其他法律一样，立法机关可随意加以修改。

当然，所有那些制定成文宪法的人们都是想要制定国家根本的和最高的法律。因此一切这种政府的理论必定是：与宪法相抵触的立法机关的法案是无效的。

这种理论实质上是成文宪法的理论，理所当然地被本法院视为我们社会的基本原则之一。因此，在进一步考虑这一问题时必须铭记这一点。

It is emphatically the province and duty of the judicial department to say what the law is. Those who apply the rule to particular cases, must of necessity expound and interpret that rule. If two laws conflict with each other, the courts must decide on the operation of each.

So if a law be in opposition to the constitution; if both the law and the constitution apply to a particular case, so that the court must either decide that case conformably to the law, disregarding the constitution; or conformably to the constitution, disregarding the law; the court must determine which of these conflicting rules governs the case. This is of the very essence of judicial duty.

If then the courts are to regard the constitution; and the constitution is superior to any ordinary act of the legislature; the constitution, and not such ordinary act, must govern the case to which they both apply.

必须强调的是，确定法律是什么，是司法部门的权限和职责。那些把规则适用于具体案件的人们，有必要对规则进行阐释和解释。假如两个法律相互冲突，法院必须决定适用哪一个。

所以，假如一部法律与宪法相抵触，假如法律和宪法都适用某一具体案件，法院必须确定，要么该案件适用法律，而不顾宪法；要么适用宪法，而不管法律。法院必须决定这些相互冲突的规则中哪一个管辖该案。这就是司法职责的本质。

假如法院认为应适用宪法，认为宪法高于任何立法机关的一般法律，那么，对于宪法和一般法律都可以适用的案件，应适用宪法。

Thus, the particular phraseology of the constitution of the United States confirms and strengthens the principle, supposed to be essential to all written constitutions, that a law repugnant to the constitution is void; and that courts, as well as other departments, are bound by that instrument.

The rule must be discharged.

所以，美国宪法的具体措辞确认和强调了理应成为所有成文宪法所必备的原则，即，与宪法相抵触的法律无效，法院和其他政府部门都受这一规则的约束。

训令必须予以撤销。

【案件影响】（Impact of the Case）

一个要求行政机关人员做出某行政行为的行政诉讼案件，审理时适用了宪法，败在了管辖权问题上，马伯里诉麦迪逊案注定是一个经典案例。按照这一判决意见，马伯里若要从基层法院一级一级地上诉到最高法院，耗时太久，他只好撤回了起诉。马歇尔大法官借由此案，成为美国最高法院院史博物馆中唯一获得全身铜像待遇的大法官。一百多年之后，美国最高法院大法官卡多佐（Benjamin N. Cardozo）赞叹道："马歇尔在美国宪法上深深地烙下了他的思想印记。我们的宪法性法律之所以具有今天的形式，就是因为马歇尔在它尚有弹性和可塑性之时以自己强烈的信念之烈焰锻炼了它。"马歇尔传记的作者史密斯（Jean E. Smith）赞扬说："如果说乔治·华盛顿创建了美国，约翰·马歇尔则确定了美国的制度。"

【思考问题】（Questions）

1. 西方国家司法审查（亦称"违宪审查"）制度的理论依据和审查范围是什么？
2. 我国在司法中适用宪法作为法律依据的司法实践状况是怎样的？

三、合同法案例

哈德利诉巴克森德尔案

Hadley v. Baxendale（1854）

【选读理由】（Selected Reason）

　　按照英美合同法，当合同一方违约时，不论该合同是否已解除，另一方均有权起诉索取损害赔偿。但在 1854 年以前，英美合同法在违约的损害赔偿方面几乎无规则可循，赔偿额多半由陪审团估定，这种方式逐渐不能适应工商业发展的需要。1854 年英国财政法院对于哈德利诉巴克森德尔（Hadley and another v. Baxendale and others）一案的判决首次确定了损害赔偿的两项规则，这两项规则在实行普通法的国家里得到了普遍的赞同。直到现在，仍然为沿用英美法系的各国法院所遵循。

【案件事实】（Facts）

　　The first count of the declaration stated that, before and at the time of the making by the defendants of the promises hereinafter mentioned, the plaintiffs, Mr. Hadley and another, carried on the business of millers and mealmen in partnership, and were proprietors and occupiers of the City Steam Mills, Gloucester. They were possessed of a steamengine by means of which they worked the mills, and therein cleaned corn, ground the same into meal, and dressed the same into flour, sharps, and bran. The crank shaft of the steam-engine was broken, with the result that the engine was prevented from working, and the plaintiffs were desirous of having a new crank shaft made. They had ordered the shaft of Messrs Joyce & Co, of Greenwich, Kent, who had contracted to make it, but before Messrs Joyce & Co could complete the new shaft it was necessary that the broken shaft should be forwarded to their works at Greenwich in order that the new shaft might be made so as to fit the other parts of the engine which were not injured and so that it might be substituted for the broken shaft. The defendants were common carriers of goods and chattels for hire from Gloucester to Greenwich, carrying on business under the name of "Pickford & Co," and the plaintiffs, at the request of the defendants, delivered to them as such carriers the broken shaft to be conveyed by the defendants from Gloucester to Messrs Joyce & Co, at Greenwich for reward to the defendants. The plaintiff, alleged that in consideration thereof the defendants promised to convey the shaft from Gloucester to Greenwich and on the second day after the delivery of the shaft by the plaintiffs to the defendants to deliver it to Messrs Joyce & Co, but that the defendants did not deliver the shaft to Messrs Joyce & Co on the second day, but neglected to do so for the apace of seven days after the shaft had been delivered to them. In the second count the plaintiffs alleged that the defendants undertook to deliver the abaft to Messrs Joyce & Co within a reasonable time, but had failed to do so. The plaintiffs further said that by reason of the premises, the completing of the new shaft was delayed for five days, with the result that the plaintiffs were prevented from working their steam-mills, and from cleaning corn, and grinding the same into meal, and were unable to supply many of their customers with flour, sharps, and bran during that period, were obliged to buy flour to supply some of their other customers, were deprived of gains and profits which otherwise would have accrued to them, and were unable to employ their workmen to whom they were compelled to pay wages during that period. They claimed 300 pounds damages. The defendants denied liability on the first count, and with regard to the second they paid 25 pounds into court in satisfaction of the plaintiffs' claim under that count.

原告宣称的第一项论点是，在被告承诺订立本合同以前，原告哈德利和其他人，合伙经营着磨面粉和加工谷物生意，是格洛斯特城市蒸汽磨面厂的财产所有人和使用者。他们拥有一台蒸汽磨面机来进行磨面工作，清理谷物，把谷物磨成粗粉，把谷物加工成面粉、麸皮和糠。蒸汽磨面机的曲柄轴断了，这使得机器不能工作，原告们迫切希望制作一个新的曲柄轴。他们已经给肯特州格林尼治市的乔伊斯公司下了订单，对方已经签了合同同意制造。但在乔伊斯公司完成新曲轴之前，需要将断裂的曲轴送到他们在格林尼治的工厂以保证做出来的新曲轴能够适合蒸汽机没损坏的部分，这样就能够替代断轴。被告巴克森德尔和其他人，是接受雇佣从格洛斯特运送货物和动产去格林尼治的承运人，经营一家名为皮克福德的公司。原告在被告的要求下，将断轴交给他们以便由被告从格洛斯特运送给位于格林尼治的乔伊斯公司并支付酬金给被告。原告声称在此基础上被告承诺将断轴从格洛斯特运送至格林尼治，并在原告将断轴交给被告的第二天就运送给乔伊斯公司。但被告未在第二天将断轴运送给乔伊斯公司，由于疏忽直到断轴送给他们之后的七天后才送到。在原告宣称的第二项论点中，原告诉称被告承诺在合理的时间内将断轴送至乔伊斯公司，但未能做到。原告还称由于上述原因，新机轴制造完成的时间耽搁了五天，造成的后果是原告在此期间无法开动蒸汽磨面机，无法清理谷物并把谷物磨成面，从而不能向他们的顾客提供面粉、麸皮和糠，所以不得不买面粉供应给他们的顾客，也不能获得他们本应获得的收入和利润，在此期间也不能使用他们的工人却不得不支付工资。他们主张 300 英镑的赔偿。被告拒绝在第一项论点下承担责任，对第二项论点，他们向法庭支付了 25 英镑以满足原告在第二项主张下的索赔。

【裁决过程与结果】（Procedure and Disposition）

The jury at Gloucester Assizes found a verdict with 25 pounds damages beyond the amount paid into court. The defendants obtained a rule nisi for a new trial on the ground of misdirection in the Court of Exchequer.

【裁判理由】（Reasons for Judicial Decision）

【原审意见】（Opinion by Crompton J）

At the trial before CROMPTON, J, at Gloucester Assizes, it appeared that on May 13 a servant of the plaintiffs, whom they had sent to defendants' office, told the defendants' clerk, who was there, that the mill was stopped and the shaft must be sent immediately, and that, in answer to the inquiry when the shaft would be taken, the defendants' clerk said that if it was sent up by twelve o'clock any day it would be delivered at Greenwich on the following day. On May 14 the shaft was taken to the defendants' office, before noon, for the purpose of being conveyed to Greenwich, and the sum of 2 pounds 4s was paid for its carriage for the whole distance. At the same time the defendants' clerk was told that a special entry, if required, should be made to hasten its delivery. The delivery of the shaft at Greenwich was delayed by some neglect; and the consequence was, that the plaintiffs did not receive the new shaft for several days after they would otherwise have done, and the working of their mill was delayed and they lost the profits they would otherwise have received. The defendants objected that the damage alleged was too remote, and that the defendants were not liable with respect to it. The learned judge left the case generally to the jury, who found a verdict with 25 pounds damages beyond the amount paid into court.

克朗普顿法官在格洛斯特巡回法庭的审理表明，在 5 月 13 号原告的一个工人被派到被告办公室，告诉在那里的被告职员说，磨面厂停工了，机轴必须立即运送走。在被问到机轴什么时候被送走时，被告职工回答说如果它在某天 12 点以前送出，它会在第二天送到格林尼治。5 月 14 号机轴被带到被告办公室，在中午以前，以便送到格林尼治，对运输全程支付了 2 英镑 4 先令的运费。同时，被告的职员被告知，如果需要，应当就需要加快运输的情况做一个特殊的登记。由于某些疏忽机轴送到格林尼治延迟了，结果原告比预定的时间晚了几天才收到新机轴，磨面厂的工作被耽误了，造成了本应获取利润的损失。被告拒绝赔偿，因为原先所称的损失太离谱了，被告对其不应承担责任。法官将案子交给陪审团，陪审团做出裁决要求被告在已经支付给法庭的数额之外再付 25 英镑作为赔偿。

【生效判决意见】（Opinion by Alderson B）

Where two parties have made a contract, which one of them has broken the damages, which the other party ought to receive in respect of such breach of contract should be such as may fairly and reasonably be considered as either arising naturally, ie, according to the usual course of things, from such breach of contract itself, or such as may reasonably be supposed to have been in the contemplation of both parties at the time they made the contract as the probable result of the breach of it. If special circumstances under which the contract was actually made were communicated by the plaintiffs to the defendants, and thus known to both parties, the damages resulting from the breach of such a contract which they would reasonably contemplate would be the amount of injury which would ordinarily follow from a breach of contract under the special circumstances so known and communicated. But, on the other hand, if these special circumstances were wholly unknown to the party breaking the contract, he, at the most, could only be supposed to have had in his contemplation the amount of injury which would arise generally, and in the real multitude of cases not affected by any special circumstances, from such a breach of contract. For, had the special circumstances been known, the parties might have specially provided for the breach of contract by special terms as to the damages in that case; and of this advantage it would be very unjust to deprive them.

双方订立一个合同，有一方违反合同的规定，合同另一方应该获得由于这一违约行为而造成的损害赔偿。这一损害赔偿应是对违约所形成的后果进行公正与合理的考虑，也就是说，损害赔偿的认定应符合违约本身所造成的事情发展的通常结果，或者符合合同双方在订立合同时可以合理预见的违约的可能结果。如果原告与被告就订立合同所依据的特殊情况进行了充分的沟通，从而双方均已知道这种情况，那么违反一个合同所造成的损害赔偿就应该是他们能够合理预见到的、在双方所知道并已沟通的特殊情况下因违约行为而通常会造成的损失的数额。但是另一方面，如果该特殊情况对违约一方而言毫不知情，他最多只能被认定对在其可预见范围内的违约所造成的通常的损失数量负责。在大多数案件中违约所造成的损害后果并不会受到任何特殊情况的影响。在已经知道特殊情况的前提下，合同各方就可以对该特殊情况下违约可能造成的损失以特殊的条款做出特殊的约定，因此剥夺合同方所应享有的此项利益是非常不公平的。

The above principles are those by which we think the jury ought to be guided in estimating the damages arising out of any breach of contract. It is said that other cases, such as breaches of contract in the non-payment of money, or in the not making a good title to land, are to be treated as exceptions from this, and as governed by a conventional rule. But as, in such cases, both parties must be supposed to be cognizant of that well-known rule, these cases may, we think, be more properly classed under the rule above enunciated as to cases under known special circumstances, because there both parties may reasonably be presumed to contemplate the estimation of the amount of damages according to the conventional rule.

我们认为上述原则是陪审团在估算任何违约行为所造成的损失时所应接受的指导原则。其他的案例中，如没有金钱给付的违约行为，或者错误主张对土地的权利时，将被视为这种情况的例外，将适用传统的规则。在这些案例中，合同各方均应被认为已经认识到了这一众所周知的规则。我们认为这些案例更应当被归类于上述适用已知特殊情况规则的案例。因为合同双方均被合理地认定按照传统规则可以预见到损失的数量。

In the present case, if we are to apply the principles above laid down, we find that the only circumstances here communicated by the plaintiffs to the defendants at the time the contract was made were that the article to be carried was the broken shaft of a mill and that the plaintiffs were the millers of that mill. But how do these circumstances show reasonably that the profits of the mill must be stopped by an unreasonable delay in the delivery of the broken shaft by the carrier to the third person? Suppose the plaintiffs had another shaft in their possession put up or putting up at the time, and that they only wished to send back the broken shaft to the engineer who made it; it is clear that this would be quite consistent with the above circumstances, and yet the unreasonable delay in the delivery would have no effect upon the intermediate profits of the mill. Or, again, suppose that, at the time of the delivery to the carrier, the machinery of the mill had been in other respects defective, then, also, the same results would follow.

在现在这个案件中，如果适用上述规则，我们发现在合同订立时原告告知被告的唯一情况就是需要运送的货物是磨面机的一根断轴，原告是磨面厂主。这些情况如何合理地表明磨面厂的利润会因为承运人不合理地延迟将断轴送给第三方而受损？假设原告在手里有另外一个机轴及时更换上，那他们只是希望把断轴送回制造工厂。很显然这种情况极有可能存在，这样不合理的延迟对磨面厂当期利润就没有影响。又或者，假如在机轴送给承运人同时，磨面机同时发生了其他的故障，这也会产生同样的后果。

Here it is true that the shaft was actually sent back to serve as a model for a new one, that the want of a new one was the only cause of the stoppage of the mill, and that the loss of profit really arose from not sending down the new shaft in proper time, and that this arose from the delay in delivering the broken one to serve as a model. But it is obvious that, in the great multitude of cases of millers sending off broken shafts to third persons by a carrier under ordinary circumstances, such consequences would not, in all probability, have occurred, and these special circumstances were here never communicated by the plaintiffs to the defendants.

在本案中，这个机轴的确只是被送回去当作制作新机轴的模型，缺少一个新机轴是造成磨面厂停工的唯一原因。利润的损失真的是由于没有在适当的时间送回来新的机轴所造成的，而没有新机轴是由于延迟把当模型的断轴送到所造成的。但这很明显，在大多数案件中，磨面厂主在通常情况下将断轴交由承运人运送给第三方时，这样的结果几乎不可能发生。这一特殊情况原告从来没有告知被告。

It follows, therefore, that the loss of profits here cannot reasonably be considered such a consequence of the breach of contract as could have been fairly and reasonably contemplated by both the parties when they made this contract. For such loss would neither have flowed naturally from the breach of this contract in the great multitude of such cases occurring under ordinary circumstances, nor were the special circumstances, which, perhaps, would have made it a reasonable and natural consequence of such breach of contract, communicated to or known by the defendants. The judge ought, therefore, to have told the jury that, upon the facts then before them, they ought not to take the loss of profits into consideration at all in estimating the damages. There must, therefore, be a new trial in this case.

因此，这导致本案中利润的损失不能被合理地认定为双方在订立合同时所能够公正合理地预见到的违反合同所造成的后果。这样的损失既不会是发生于通常情况下的大多数案件中的违约行为所造成的自然的结果，也不属于特殊情况，即这种情况已经告知被告或为被告所知，会由于违约行为而合理并自然地发生。因此，法官应该告诉陪审团，基于上述事实，他们不应该在估算损失时将利润考虑在内。因此必须就本案进行重新审理。

【案件影响】（Impact of the Case）

本案确立了损害赔偿范围的两项规则：其一，这种损失在一般情况下必须是因违约而自然发生的；其二，这种因违约而产生的损失必须是在订立合同时就可以合理预见到的。此项规则，一是用来处理通常情况下的损害赔偿问题，二是用来处理特殊情况下的损害赔偿问题。在第一项规则中未特别提出合理预见规则，因为一般情况下因违约而自然造成的损失，是任何人都应当预见到的；而第二项规则中所涉及的是特殊情况下的额外损失赔偿，如果违约的一方对此特殊情况全然不知，自不应负赔偿之责，所以第二项规则特别强调了合理预见的问题。

可预见规则是合同法中违约损害赔偿制度的重要内容之一。美国学者格兰特·吉尔莫提及本案时写道："自1854年起，契约的损害赔偿理论获得了全面的讨论，其起点是哈德利诉巴克森德尔案。"

【思考问题】（Questions）

1. 在何种情况下应限制或排除可预见规则的适用？
2. 《中华人民共和国合同法》对合同违约损害赔偿的可预见规则是怎样规定的？

四、侵权法案例

帕斯格拉芙诉长岛火车站案
Palsgraf v. Long Island Railroad Co.（1928）

【选读理由】（Selected Reason）

纽约上诉法院在1928年5月28日做出判决的帕斯格拉芙一案（Helen Palsgraf, Respondent, v. The Long Island Railroad Company, Appellant），是美国侵权法历史上最重要、最具有传奇色彩的案例之一。本杰明·卡多佐（Benjamin Cardozo）法官在本案判决书中确立了分析疏忽大意的过失侵权行为的新标准，即被告只对可预见的原告承担责任，由此奠定了该案在美国侵权法史上里程碑式的地位。

【案件事实】（Fact）

Plaintiff was standing on a platform of defendant's railroad after buying a ticket to go to Rockaway Beach. A train stopped at the station, bound for another place. Two men ran forward to catch it. One of the men reached the platform of the car without mishap, though the train was already moving. The other man, carrying a package, jumped aboard the car, but seemed unsteady as if about to fall. A guard on the car, who had held the door open, reached forward to help him in, and another guard on the platform pushed him from behind. In this act, the package was dislodged, and fell upon the rails. It was a package of small size, about fifteen inches long, and was covered by a newspaper. In fact it contained fireworks, but there was nothing in its appearance to give notice of its contents. The fireworks when they fell exploded. The shock of the explosion threw down some scales at the other end of the platform, many feet away. The scales struck the plaintiff, causing injuries for which she sues.

帕斯格拉芙太太和她的女儿正在纽约长岛火车站的站台上等待一辆从纽约东去洛克威海滩的火车。当火车站的两个工作人员帮一位旅客登上一辆已开动的火车时，不小心碰掉这位旅客携带的一个包裹。事实上，包裹内竟是烟花爆竹，掉在铁轨上发生爆炸。爆炸的冲击力将数英尺之外的一杆秤击倒，砸在了帕斯格拉芙太太的头上。受到伤害和惊吓，几天之后，帕斯格拉芙得了严重的口吃症，虽经治疗，但她的身体从未得到完全恢复。那位携带烟花爆竹的旅客登上火车后去向不明，于是，帕斯格拉芙诉长岛火车站要求赔偿。

【裁决过程与结果】（Procedure and Disposition）

A judgment of the Supreme Court in favor of the plaintiff, upon the verdict of a jury for $6,000, was entered in the office of the clerk of the county of Kings on the 31st day of May, 1927. The defendant, the Long Island Railroad Company, appealed in the Appellate Division of the Supreme Court in the second judicial department. The judgment was affirmed in favor of plaintiff entered upon the verdict. The judgment of the Appellate Division and that of the Trial Term was reversed, and the complaint dismissed, with costs in all courts.

【裁判理由】(Reasons for Judicial Decision)

【生效判决意见】(Opinion by Cardozo)

The conduct of the defendant's guard, if a wrong in its relation to the holder of the package, was not a wrong in its relation to the plaintiff, standing far away. Relatively to her it was not negligence at all. Nothing in the situation gave notice that the falling package had in it the potency of peril to persons thus removed. Negligence is not actionable unless it involves the invasion of a legally protected interest, the violation of a right. "Proof of negligence in the air, so to speak, will not do". "Negligence is the absence of care, according to the circumstances". The plaintiff as she stood upon the platform of the station might claim to be protected against intentional invasion of her bodily security. Such invasion is not charged. She might claim to be protected against unintentional invasion by conduct involving in the thought of reasonable men an unreasonable hazard that such invasion would ensue. These, from the point of view of the law, were the bounds of her immunity, with perhaps some rare exceptions, survivals for the most part of ancient forms of liability, where conduct is held to be at the peril of the actor. If no hazard was apparent to the eye of ordinary vigilance, an act innocent and harmless, at least to outward seeming, with reference to her, did not take to itself the quality of a tort because it happened to be a wrong, though apparently not one involving the risk of bodily insecurity, with reference to some one else. "In every instance, before negligence can be predicated of a given act, back of the act must be sought and found a duty to the individual complaining, the observance of which would have averted or avoided the injury." "The ideas of negligence and duty are strictly correlative." The plaintiff sues in her own right for a wrong personnel to her, and not as the vicarious beneficiary of a breach of duty to another.

被告守卫的行为，即使对于包裹持有人来说是一个错误，对于站在很远地方的原告来说也并不是一个错误。相对她来说，这不是疏忽。没有任何迹象表明这个正在掉落的包裹存在危及远处人们安全的潜在危险。过失是不可诉的，除非它侵害了法律所保护的利益或侵害了权利。"没有证据证明的过失不是过失"，"过失是指在特定情形下的注意义务的缺失"。原告站在火车站站台上有权主张其身体安全不受故意侵害，但原告并未指就被故意侵害提出指控。她也有权主张免受非故意的侵害，这一非故意的侵害须是由于理性人能够意识到的、会造成侵害后果的不合理危险所造成的。从法律角度来看，这些是她获得免受侵害之法律救济的界限。除此之外可能还有极少的案例，大多是法律责任的古老形式，可以就行为人本身的行为存在的危险性认定构成侵权行为。对于保持日常生活中一般警觉性的人而言，并没有发现明显的危险，这个至少看起来无可非议和无害的行为，对她而言并不足以构成侵权，因为它的发生只是一个意外的错误。因为很明显没有迹象表明会有人因此卷入到身体受伤的情形中，无论对原告还是对于其他人。"在任何情形下，一个行为被认定为疏忽之前，索赔的人需要发现并证实存在这一行为背后的义务，这一义务如果得到了履行，就能避免伤害发生。""疏忽和义务是严格并存的。"原告的起诉要针对她个人的错误行为而造成的权利受损，不能是针对其他人的义务的违背所造成的间接的利益受损。

A different conclusion will involve us, and swiftly too, in a maze of contradictions. A guard stumbles over a package which has been left upon a platform. It seems to be a bundle of newspapers. It turns out to be a can of dynamite. To the eye of ordinary vigilance, the bundle is abandoned waste, which may be kicked or trod on with impunity. Is a passenger at the other end of the platform protected by the law against the unsuspected hazard concealed beneath the waste? If not, is the result to be any different, so far as the distant passenger is concerned, when the guard stumbles over a valise which a truckman or a porter has left upon the walk? The passenger far away, if the victim of a wrong at all, has a cause of action, not derivative, but original and primary. His claim to be protected against invasion of his bodily security is neither greater nor less because the act resulting in the invasion is a wrong to another far removed. In this case, the rights that are said to have been violated, the interests said to have been invaded, are not even of the same order. The man was not injured in his person nor even put in danger. The purpose of the act, as well as its effect, was to make his person safe. If there was a wrong to him at all, which may very well be doubted, it was a wrong to a property interest only, the safety of his package. Out of this wrong to property, which threatened injury to nothing else, there has passed, we are told, to the plaintiff by derivation or succession a right of action for the invasion of an interest of another order, the right to bodily security. The diversity of interests emphasizes the futility of the effort to build the plaintiff's right upon the basis of a wrong to some one else. The gain is one of emphasis, for a like result would follow if the interests were the same. Even then, the orbit of the danger as disclosed to the eye of reasonable vigilance would be the orbit of the duty. One who jostles one's neighbor in a crowd does not invade the rights of others standing at the outer fringe when the unintended contact casts a bomb upon the ground. The wrongdoer as to them is the man who carries the bomb, not the one who explodes it without suspicion of the danger.

如果我们得出不同的结论，将很快陷入矛盾之中。一个守卫撞倒了一个留在站台上的包裹，这看起来似乎是一捆报纸。但它却是一罐炸药。对保持普通警觉的眼睛，这捆东西就是被废弃的垃圾，随意踢一脚或踩一下都不会有事。法律会对站在站台另一端的乘客所受到的隐藏在垃圾里的根本未被意识到的危险提供保护吗？如果不，这和守卫被一个卡车司机或搬运工留在便道上的包裹绊倒了给远距离的乘客造成伤害有什么不同的结果吗？乘车远去的乘客，如果的确是不法行为的受害者，会拥有原始、直截了当的诉由。他如果提出有关要求保护其身体安全不受侵害的主张将恰如其分，因为造成侵害的行为是对他这个正在远去的人所犯的错误。但在这种情况下，所谓被侵害的权利或利益与本案的情况完全是两种情况。这名乘车而去的乘客自己本身并未受到损害，甚至没有陷入被损害的危险境地中。诉讼的意图和效果是为了保障他的人身安全。如果对于他来说有不法行为存在，这一点本身被极大地质疑，也只是对财产利益的错误行为，即他的行李安全。除了对财产产生的损害之外，这一行为对其他任何人或物都没有构成威胁，然而这一行为在原审法院看来，却使得原告派生性地获得了或者说继承了一项诉讼权利，即保护其另一法律范畴下的利益不受损害和人身安全不被侵害的权利。然而为了强调利益的多样性而试图在对他人实施的不法行为这一基础上构建起原告受保护的权利的努力是毫无价值的。需要强调的是，相同的利益认定应当给出类似的裁判结果。尽管如此，一个正常的小心谨慎的人所感知的危险的范围决定应承担责任的范围。假如一个人在拥挤的人群中不小心碰了他旁边的人，使得该人携带的炸弹落地爆炸，他并没有侵犯站在周围的其他人的权利。对于他们来说，不法行为人是携带炸弹的人，而不是对危险毫不知情的引爆炸弹的人。

The risk reasonably to be perceived defines the duty to be obeyed, and risk imports relation; it is risk to another or to others within the range of apprehension. Even today, and much oftener in earlier stages of the law, one acts sometimes at one's peril. Under this head, it may be, fall certain cases of what is known as transferred intent, an act willfully dangerous to A resulting by misadventure in injury to B. These cases aside, wrong is defined in terms of the natural or probable, at least when unintentional. The range of reasonable apprehension is at times a question for the court, and at times, if varying inferences are possible, a question for the jury. Here, by concession, there was nothing in the situation to suggest to the most cautious mind that the parcel wrapped in newspaper would spread wreckage through the station....The law of causation, remote or proximate, is thus foreign to the case before us. The question of liability is always anterior to the question of the measure of the consequences that go with liability. If there is no tort to be redressed, there is no occasion to consider what damage might be recovered if there were a finding of a tort. We may assume, without deciding, that negligence, not at large or in the abstract, but in relation to the plaintiff, would entail liability for any and all consequences, however novel or extraordinary. There is room for argument that a distinction is to be drawn according to the diversity of interests invaded by the act, as where conduct negligent in that it threatens an insignificant invasion of an interest in property results in an unforseeable invasion of an interest of another order, as, e. g., one of bodily security. Perhaps other distinctions may be necessary. We do not go into the question now. The consequences to be followed must first be rooted in a wrong.

The judgment of the Appellate Division and that of the Trial Term should be reversed, and the complaint dismissed, with costs in all courts.

被合理察觉的危险决定了需要遵守的责任，危险表明了法律关系；只有在被意识到的范围内才构成对其他个人或其他人们的危险。即便是今天，或在法律发展的早期我们经常会看到，一个人的行为本身有时就构成了危险。在这种情况下，会出现一些被称为故意转移的案例，一个意图对 A 产生危害的行为却不幸意外地伤害了 B。这些案例之外，错误被界定为一个具有自然或可能性的术语，至少包括非故意的因素。合理意识的范围常常是法庭上的焦点问题，如果可能存在不同的结论，常常是损害的焦点问题。在本案中，即使做出让步，在最谨慎的人看来，也没有任何迹象表明报纸覆盖的包裹将会在火车站内造成坠毁物。……因果关系法律观点，无论是远因或近因，均不适合我们面前的案例。责任的问题总是在考虑对责任所产生的后果所应采取的补救措施之前进行考虑。如果没有需要救济的侵权行为，也没有必要考虑假设存在侵权的情况下应赔偿什么损失。我们有理由认为，仅对于原告来说，一旦在本案中认定过失存在，将产生对任何可能造成的结果的法律责任，无论这个结果多么新奇或不同寻常。对行为所侵害利益做多样性的区分仍然有争辩的空间，在这种情况下仅对财产利益产生了无关紧要的侵害的行为，造成了对其他法律权益的不可预见的侵害，比如某种人身安全。然而可能还需要做其他必要的区分，我们现在不讨论这些问题。造成的结果必须首先根源于某个不法行为。

上诉部门和初审法院的判决均应被撤销，起诉被驳回，诉讼费用由原告承担。

【不同意见】（Dissent by Andrews）

Mrs. Palsgraf was standing some distance away. How far cannot be told from the record—

apparently twenty-five or thirty feet. Perhaps less. Except for the explosion, she would not have been injured. We are told by the appellant in his brief "it cannot be denied that the explosion was the direct cause of the plaintiff's injuries." So it was a substantial factor in producing the result — there was here a natural and continuous sequence—direct connection. The only intervening cause was that instead of blowing her to the ground the concussion smashed the weighing machine which in turn fell upon her. There was no remoteness in time, little in space. And surely, given such an explosion as here it needed no great foresight to predict that the natural result would be to injure one on the platform at no greater distance from its scene than was the plaintiff. Just how no one might be able to predict. Whether by flying fragments, by broken glass, by wreckage of machines or structures no one could say. But injury in some form was most probable.

Under these circumstances I cannot say as a matter of law that the plaintiff's injuries were not the proximate result of the negligence. That is all we have before us. The court refused to so charge. No request was made to submit the matter to the jury as a question of fact, even would that have been proper upon the record before us. The judgment appealed from should be affirmed, with costs.

帕斯格拉芙当时站在一定距离之外，究竟多远没有记录，大约 7.62 到 9.144 米（25 到 30 英尺）。如果不是这次爆炸，她不会受伤。上诉人告诉我们："不可否认的是，爆炸直接造成了原告的伤害。"因此，爆炸是导致伤害的关键因素，在爆炸和伤害之间存在自然和连续的序列——一种直接联系。唯一的干扰原因是，不是爆炸直接击倒了原告，而是气浪掀翻磅秤，磅秤击倒了原告。原因和结果在时间上并不遥远，在空间上只是有一点点距离而已。像这么严重的爆炸，不需要什么了不起的前瞻性，就可以预见到它将会给距离事故中心近于原告的任何人造成损害。无论是被横飞的碎片，还是被破碎的玻璃，或者是被机器或设备的残骸，谁也说不好。但造成某种形式的伤害是极有可能的。

在此情况下，我不能说作为一个法律问题原告所受的伤害不是过失的最直接后果。这是摆在我们面前的全部。法庭拒绝这一起诉。也没有要求向陪审团将这一问题作为事实问题提出来，尽管他们在我们之前可能得出正确的结论。上诉的判决应当被维持。

【案件影响】（Impact of the Case）

这是一个令人不可思议的案子。帕斯格拉芙无辜地被伤害，却没有得到任何赔偿。可以说，美国律师和法学院学生无人不知这一案件，但普通民众知之者寥寥。在 65 年后的 1989 年 6 月 16 日的《纽约时报》上仍提到：可怜的帕斯格拉芙由于在错误的时间站在了错误的地方而在美国法学院的教科书中赢得了有限的不朽的名声，但她所受的伤害将永远被遗忘。按照帕斯格拉芙一案对分析疏忽大意的过失侵权行为确立的标准，如果一个正常的人（reasonable person），处在被告的位置，按当时的情形，能够预见到对原告造成伤害的危险，这时，原告就是可预见的，被告就对原告负有谨慎从事的义务（duty of care）。如果由于被告的疏忽违反对原告的这一义务，从而造成对原告的伤害，被告就应当对原告承担责任。一个人不可能对其引起的所有伤害都承担法律责任，也并不是所有的伤害都能获得法律补偿。这似乎不合情理，但世界万事万物都处在普遍联系之中，法律必须在某处划一条界线。

【思考问题】（Questions）

1. 原审法院是如何认定被告火车站工作人员存在着"过失"的？
2. 怎样理解我国《侵权责任法》规定的安全保障义务的"合理限度"？

五、知识产权法案例

尼科尔诉环球电影公司案

Nichols v. Universal Pictures Co. （1930）

【选读理由】（Selected Reason）

　　司法实践中如何判断文学作品的相似问题始终是法院需要回答的问题。美国法院也不例外。根据思想与表达二分法原则，版权不保护思想，只保护表达。但是在文学作品中（如戏剧作品），哪些是不受保护的思想，哪些是受保护的表达，哪些是不受保护的表达，有时是一个很复杂的问题。"字面相似"比较直观，易于判断。"非字面相似"如果属于受保护的表达的相似，即构成侵权；如果"非字面相似"属于思想的相似或者不受保护的表达的相似则不构成侵权。由联邦第二巡回法庭在 1930 年 11 月 10 日做出判决的尼科尔诉环球电影公司案（Nichols v. Universal Pictures Corporation et al.）即属于第二种情形。汉德法官正是在此案中首创了著名的"抽象鉴定法"，以阐述该问题的答案。

【案件事实】（Facts）

　　Abie's Irish Rose presents a Jewish family living in prosperous circumstances in New York. The father, a widower, is in business as a merchant, in which his son and only child helps him. The boy has philandered with young women, who to his father's great disgust have always been Gentiles, for he is obsessed with a passion that his daughter-in-law shall be an orthodox Jewess. When the play opens, the son, who has been courting a young Irish Catholic girl, has already married her secretly before a Protestant minister, and is concerned to soften the blow for his father, by securing a favorable impression of his bride, while concealing her faith and race. To accomplish this he introduces her to his father at his home as a Jewess, and lets it appear that he is interested in her, though he conceals the marriage. The girl somewhat reluctantly falls in with the plan; the father takes the bait, becomes infatuated with the girl, concludes that they must marry, and assumes that of course they will, if he so decides. He calls in a rabbi, and prepares for the wedding according to the Jewish rite.

　　上诉人的《阿比的爱尔兰玫瑰》描写了一个生活在纽约富人区的只有父子俩的犹太家庭。父亲是个商人，并固执地坚持他的儿子必须娶正统的犹太女子为妻。儿子违背了父亲的意志，与一个爱尔兰的天主教女子秘密结婚。为了减轻此事对父亲的打击，儿子向父亲隐瞒了新娘的信仰和种族以及他们的婚姻，并告诉父亲对方是一位犹太姑娘。父亲请来了拉比（犹太教的牧师），按照犹太人的仪式准备婚礼。

　　Meanwhile the girl's father, also a widower, who lives in California, and is as intense in his own religious antagonism as the Jew, has been called to New York, supposing that his daughter is to marry an Irishman and a Catholic. Accompanied by a priest, he arrives at the house at the moment when the marriage is being celebrated, but too late to prevent it, and the two fathers, each infuriated by the proposed union of his child to a heretic, fall into unseemly and grotesque antics. The priest and the rabbi become friendly, exchange trite sentiments about religion, and agree that the match is good. Apparently out of abundant caution, the priest celebrates the marriage for a third time, while the girl's father is inveigled away. The second act closes with each father, still outraged, seeking to find some way by which the union, thus trebly insured, may be dissolved.

与此同时，这位姑娘的父亲也被请到了纽约。与犹太人父亲一样，这位父亲也固守其宗教信仰，拒斥其他教派。他认为自己女儿将要嫁的是一位爱尔兰天主教男子。在牧师的陪伴下，他到达正在举行婚礼的地方。于是，真相大白，两位父亲都因其孩子与异教徒结合而怒不可遏。而牧师与拉比则友好地交换了对于宗教的感想，都认为这一结合很好。姑娘的父亲被骗走以后，牧师为这个婚姻主持了第三次仪式。之后，两位父亲仍旧极为愤怒，都在寻求解除他们孩子的婚姻的办法。

The last act takes place about a year later, the young couple having meanwhile been abjured by each father, and left to their own resources. They have had twins, a boy and a girl, but their fathers know no more than that a child has been born. At Christmas each, led by his craving to see his grandchild, goes separately to the young folks' home, where they encounter each other, each laden with gifts, one for a boy, the other for a girl. After some slapstick comedy, depending upon the insistence of each that he is right about the sex of the grandchild, they become reconciled when they learn the truth, and that each child is to bear the given name of a grandparent. The curtain falls as the fathers are exchanging amenities, and the Jew giving evidence of an abatement in the strictness of his orthodoxy.

一年以后，两位父亲都宣布放弃这一努力。这时年轻夫妇有了一对一男一女双胞胎。他们的父亲都只知道有一个孩子出生了。圣诞节时，急于见到外孙的两位老人各自来到这对年轻人的家并在那里相遇，两人都带来了礼物，一人给男孩，一人给女孩。当他们得知事实，并且各有一个孩子用了自己的教名时，两人和解了。

The Cohens and The Kellys presents two families, Jewish and Irish, living side by side in the poorer quarters of New York in a state of perpetual enmity. The wives in both cases are still living, and share in the mutual animosity, as do two small sons, and even the respective dogs. The Jews have a daughter, the Irish a son; the Jewish father is in the clothing business; the Irishman is a policeman. The children are in love with each other, and secretly marry, apparently after the play opens. The Jew, being in great financial straits, learns from a lawyer that he has fallen heir to a large fortune from a great-aunt, and moves into a great house, fitted luxuriously. Here he and his family live in vulgar ostentation, and here the Irish boy seeks out his Jewish bride, and is chased away by the angry father. The Jew then abuses the Irishman over the telephone, and both become hysterically excited. The extremity of his feelings makes the Jew sick, so that he must go to Florida for a rest, just before which the daughter discloses her marriage to her mother.

环球电影公司的《科恩家和凯利家》描写了生活于纽约穷人区，长期以来互相憎恨的犹太人家庭和爱尔兰人家庭。犹太家庭有一个女儿，爱尔兰家庭有一个儿子。两个孩子相爱并秘密结婚。一位想娶犹太人女儿的律师告诉犹太人，他将继承一大笔财产。此后，犹太人搬进了一幢富丽堂皇的大房子里，并粗俗地炫耀其财富。爱尔兰男子来寻找他的犹太新娘，被愤怒的犹太人父亲赶走。随后，犹太人父亲打电话辱骂爱尔兰人父亲，两人都变得极度激动。犹太人父亲因此病倒，到佛罗里达休养。

On his return the Jew finds that his daughter has borne a child; at first he suspects the lawyer, but eventually learns the truth and is overcome with anger at such a low alliance. Meanwhile, the Irish family who have been forbidden to see the grandchild, go to the Jew's house, and after a violent scene between the two fathers in which the Jew disowns his daughter, who decides to go back with her husband, the Irishman takes her back with her baby to his own poor lodgings. The lawyer, who had hoped to marry the Jew's daughter, seeing his plan foiled, tells the Jew that his fortune really belongs to the Irishman, who was also related to the dead woman, but offers to conceal his knowledge, if the Jew will share the loot. This the Jew repudiates, and, leaving the astonished lawyer, walks through the rain to his enemy's house to surrender the property. He arrives in great dejection, tells the truth, and abjectly turns to leave. A reconciliation ensues, the Irishman agreeing to share with him equally. The Jew shows some interest in his grandchild, though this is at most a minor motive in the reconciliation, and the curtain falls while the two are in their cups, the Jew insisting that in the firm name for the business, which they are to carry on jointly, his name shall stand first.

他回来后，发现女儿生了一个小孩，对女儿竟下嫁给仇人的儿子无比愤怒。一直被禁止去看望新生儿的爱尔兰人一家到了犹太人家中，两位父亲发生了剧烈冲突。女儿被父亲赶走，她带着孩子回到了她丈夫那贫寒的家。此时，那位实现不了目的的律师向犹太人父亲披露，其所继承的财产实际上属于爱尔兰人。如果犹太人父亲愿意与之分享，该律师将保守秘密，但被犹太人父亲拒绝。他冒雨去仇敌的家中告知真相，归还财产。当犹太人父亲即将离去时，爱尔兰父亲同意与他平等地分享这些财产。至此，双方和解。

【裁决过程与结果】（Procedure and Disposition）

Appellant Nichols is the author of a play, *Abie's Irish Rose*, which it may be assumed was properly copyrighted under section five, subdivision (d), of the *Copyright Act*,17 USCA & 5(d). Appellee produced publicly a motion picture play, *The Cohens and the Kellys*, which the appellant alleges was taken from it. Appellant alleged that Appellee's production of the film infringed his copyright to the play work and brought a legal action against the Appellee to the court. Subsequent the decision by the United States Districts Court for the Southern District of New York, which concluded that producer's motion picture did not infringe upon appellant's copyright in the play, Appellant author appealed to Circuit Court of Appeals, Second Circuit.

The Appellate court affirmed the judgment for Appellee, finding the two stories were different as to incident and character, and thus there was no infringement. The Appellee, "the prevailing party," was entitled to a reasonable attorney's fee (section 40 of the Copyright: 17 USCA & 40).

【裁决理由】（Reasons for Judicial Decision）

【生效判决意见】（Opinion by Hand）

It is of course essential that any protection of literary property, whether at common-law or under statute, that the right cannot be limited literally to the text, else a plagiarist would escape by immaterial variations. Then the question is whether the part so taken is "substantial," and therefore not a "fair use" of the copyrighted work; it is the same question as arises in the case of any other copyrighted work. But when the plagiarist does not take out a block in situ, but an abstract of the whole, decision is more troublesome. Upon any work, and especially upon a play, a great number of patterns of increasingly generality will fit equally well, as more and more of the incident is left out. The last may perhaps be no more than the most general statement of what the play is about, and at times might consist only of its title, but there is a point in this series of abstractions where they are no longer protected, since otherwise the playwright could prevent the use of his "ideas," to which, apart from their expression, his property is never extended. Nobody has ever been able to fix that boundary, and nobody ever can. In some cases the question has been treated as though it were analogous to lifting a portion out of the copyrighted work, but the analogy is not a good one, because, though the skeleton is a part of the body, it pervaded and supports the whole. In such cases we are rather concerned with the line between expression and what is expressed. As respects plays, the controversy chiefly centers upon the characters and sequence of incident, these being the substance.

重要的是，无论是在普通法还是在制定法中对文学作品版权的保护不能仅仅局限于作品的原文上，否则抄袭者可通过对其作品中一些非实质性意义的变化来逃脱制裁。因此需要判断被指控抄袭的部分是实质性的，还是合理使用的。抄袭者不是逐字不动抄袭而是模仿作品的抽象部分时，判断是否构成侵权就非常困难。对任何作品，尤其是戏剧作品来说，当越来越多的枝节被剔除出去以后，剩下的可能就只是有关作品内容的最一般讲述，有时唯有作品的标题。这些都不受保护。没有人能够，并且永远不会有人能够划出那个界限。这就类似于将人身上的骨骼抽去，但正是骨骼支撑着整个身体（作品）。在此种情形下我们更关注表达和已经表达之间的界限。对戏剧作品来说，争议主要集中于人物和情节，这些是作品的实质。

We found the plot of the second play was too different to infringe; because the most detailed pattern, common to both, eliminated so much from each that its content went into the public domain; and for this reason we said, "this mere subsection of a plot was not susceptible of copyright." But we do not doubt that two plays may correspond in plot closely enough for infringement. How far that correspondence must go is another matter. Nor need we hold that the same may not be true as the characters, quite independently of the "plot" proper, though, as far as we know, such a case has never arisen. These would be no more than Shakespeare's "ideas" in the play, as little capable of monopoly as Einstein's Doctrine of Relativity, or Darwin's theory of the origin of Species. It follows that the less developed the character, the less they can be copyrighted; that is the penalty an author must bear for marking them indistinctly.

我们认定被上诉人作品与上诉人作品截然不同。因为两部作品中最一般化的情节内容已经进入了公共领域，基于此理由我们认为它不受版权保护。此类角色和情节如同莎士比亚戏剧中的思想，因而认为它们同爱因斯坦的相对论理论和达尔文的物种进化理论一样不能被垄断。角色越一般化，越不受版权保护。

In the two plays at bar we think both as to incident and character, the defendant took no more—assuming that it took anything at all—than the law allowed. The stories are quite different. One is of a religious zealot who insists upon his child's marrying no one outside his faith; opposed by another who is in this respect just like him, and is his foil. Their difference in race is merely an obbligato to the main theme, religion. They sink their differences through grandparental pride and affection. In the other, zealotry is wholly absent; religion does not even appear. It is true that parents are hostile to each other in part because they differ in race; but the marriage of their son to a Jew does not apparently offend the Irish family at all, and it exacerbates the existing animosity of the Jew, principally because he has become rich, when he learns it. They are reconciled through the honesty of the Jew and the generosity of the Irishman; the grandchild has nothing whatever to do with it. The only matter common to the two is a quarrel between a Jewish and an Irish father, the marriage of their children, the birth of grandchildren and a reconciliation.

　　此案中两部作品并不相同。第一部作品中父亲都是自己所信仰宗教的虔诚教友，他们种族的差异只是宗教主题的陪衬而已。他们都通过对孙子的爱而缓解了宗教和种族差异。在被上诉人作品中，狂热的宗教行为完全不存在，宗教甚至就没有出现。的确，双方父亲相互憎恨一部分是因为种族。但是，爱尔兰人儿子跟犹太人女儿的婚姻根本没有使爱尔兰人愤怒，只是在犹太人变得富有之后加剧了他对爱尔兰人的敌意。他们之间最终由于犹太人的诚实和爱尔兰人的宽容大方而和解了。两部作品中的共同点仅仅是犹太父亲和爱尔兰父亲间的争吵，他们子女的婚姻，孙子的出生和最终和解。

If the defendant took so much from the plaintiff, it may well have been because her amazing success seemed to prove that this was a subject of enduring popularity. Even so, granting that plaintiff's play was wholly original, and assuming that novelty is not essential to a copyright, there is no monopoly in such a background. Though the plaintiff discovered the vein, she could not keep it to herself; so defined, the theme was too generalized an abstraction from what she wrote.   It was only a part of her "ideas".

　　如果被上诉人抄袭了大量的上诉人作品，那完全是因为上诉人作品的成功恰恰证明了这是一个经久不衰的主题。即使假设上诉人作品完全是原创的，在此类背景下也不能形成垄断。尽管上诉人发现了脉络，但是她不能独占；因为此类主题太一般化，是作者所写内容的抽象，只是她的思想的一部分。

The plaintiff's Jew is quite unlike the defendant's. His obsession is his religion, on which depends such racial animosity as he has. He is affectionate, warm and patriarchal. None of these fit the defendant's Jew, who shows affection for his daughter only once, and who has none but the most superficial interest in his grandchild. He is tricky, ostentatious and vulgar, only by misfortune redeemed into honesty. Both are grotesque, extravagant and quarrelsome; both are fond of display; but these common qualities make up only a small part of their simple pictures, no more than any one might lift if he chose. The Irish fathers are even more unlike; the plaintiff's a mere symbol for religious fanaticism and patriarchal pride, scarcely a character at all. Neither quality appears in the defendant's, for while he goes to get his grandchild, it is rather out of a truculent determination not to be forbidden, than from pride in his progeny. For the rest he is only a grotesque hobbledehoy, used for low comedy of the most conventional sort, which any one might borrow, if he chanced not to know the exemplar.

　　上诉人作品中犹太人跟被上诉人作品中的不同。他极度忠于其所信宗教，以及基于其上的种族仇恨。但同时他又是一个慈爱的，温情的父亲。这些与被上诉人作品中只有一次表现出爱自己女儿和只对自己孙子表面感兴趣的犹太人不吻合。他狡猾，粗俗。两部作品中父亲都性格古怪，爱炫耀，动辄争吵，都喜欢显摆。但是这些共同之处每个人在创作时都可以借用。两部作品中的爱尔兰父亲更加不同：上诉人作品中的爱尔兰人是一个宗教狂热分子，有极严重的家长制作风；这两点在被上诉人作品中都没有出现，并且他充其量只是一个略富有喜剧色彩的角色，这是任何人在创作此类作品时都会使用的。

Still, as we already said, her copyright did not cover everything that might be drawn from her play; its content went some extent into the public domain. We have to decide how much, and while we are as aware as anyone that the line, wherever it is drawn, will seem arbitrary, that is no excuse for not drawing it; it is a question such as courts must answer in nearly all cases.

我们认为上诉人作品中这些人物和情节一定程度上已经进入了公共领域。我们必须要决定版权保护中思想和表达之间的界线在哪里。这是法院在几乎所有案件中要回答的问题。

The plaintiff has prepared an elaborate analysis of the two plays, showing a "quadrangle" of the common characters, in which each is represented by the emotions which he discovers. She presents the resulting parallelism as proof of infringement, but the adjectives employed are so general as to be quite useless. Take for example the attribute of "love" ascribed to both Jews. The plaintiff has depicted her farther as deeply attached to his son, who is his hope and joy; not so, the defendant.

上诉人在提起诉讼时对两部剧本进行了细致的分析，她按照其所塑造的人物的不同情感与被上诉人作品中相应人物做出列示，结果两剧中角色一一对应，呈现一种相互平行的正方形，据此证明被上诉人侵权。但是她使用的形容词过于宽泛。以"爱"这个词为例，上诉人将作品中父亲描写为深爱其儿子，儿子是他唯一的希望和快乐源泉。而被上诉人作品中不是，其并未强调这点。

We hope that in this class of cases such evidence may in the future be entirely excluded, and the case confined to the actual issues: that is, whether the copyrighted work was original, and whether the defendant copied it, so far as the supposed infringement is identical.

我们希望在此类案件中，此类证据可以全部被排除掉，案件仅仅限于真正的争议，即是否作品是原创的，被上诉人是否有抄袭行为。

【案件影响】（Impact of the Case）

此案判决回答了在文学作品中哪些是受保护的，哪些是不受保护的，并确立了著名的抽象鉴定法。汉德法官认为文学作品中的角色和情节是否受保护并没有一条非常清晰的界限，它是否受保护取决于其复杂性以及在具体作品中的发展演进。"角色越一般化，就越难获得保护。"这对中国法院处理此类案件不无裨益。

【思考问题】（Questions）

1. 多年来，对于思想与表达二分法的含义，美国法院至少发展起两种不同的理论。其一为"清晰区别鉴定"（Clear distinction test）；其二为"抽象鉴定"（Abstractions test）。这两种理论的适用范围是怎样的？

2. 当思想与表达不可分时，如何保护知识产权？

六、公司法案例

沃尔克沃斯基诉卡尔顿案

Walkovszky v. Carlton（1966）

【选读理由】（Selected Reason）

英国于 1855 年颁布了《有限责任法》，明确规定具备法定条件的公司一经注册完毕，股东即只负有限责任，责任的限度为股东所持股份的名义价值。这条定律又称"公司面纱"规则，就是说真正的债务人股东可以隐身于公司这条"面纱"之后；公司是"法人"，可以自行承担债务和风险，债权人追债时也只能追到公司为止。有限责任制度对鼓励投资、发展生产发挥了重要作用，曾被誉为现代社会最伟大的发现之一。法律总是在平衡两难。在"公司面纱"规则下，常有胆大妄为之徒假公司之名损人利己。因而，按照美国的案例法，在某些情况下又可以"揭去公司的面纱"，即不承认公司的"有限责任"的保护，而要求公司的主要持股人、母公司或控股公司对公司的债务负无限责任。这就是美国纽约州上诉法院 1966年审理的沃尔克沃斯基诉卡尔顿案（John Walkovszky, Respondent, v. William Carlton, Appellant, et al., Defendants）中所肯定的规则。

【案件事实】（Facts）

The plaintiff was severely injured four years ago in New York City when he was run down by a taxicab owned by the defendant Seon Cab Corporation and negligently operated at the time by the defendant Marchese. The individual defendant, Carlton, is claimed to be a stockholder of 10 corporations, including Seon, each of which has but two cabs registered in its name, and it is implied that only the minimum automobile liability insurance required by law (in the amount of $ 10,000) is carried on any one cab. Although seemingly independent of one another, these corporations are alleged to be "operated...as a single entity, unit and enterprise" with regard to financing, supplies, repairs, employees and garaging, and all are named as defendants. The plaintiff asserts that he is also entitled to hold their stockholders personally liable for the damages sought because the multiple corporate structure constitutes an unlawful attempt "to defraud members of the general public" who might be injured by the cabs.

4 年前原告沃尔克沃斯基在纽约市被一辆出租车撞成重伤。出租车属于被告方赛昂出租车公司，当时开车的是被告马彻斯。另一自然人被告卡尔顿，据称是包括赛昂出租公司在内的共 10 家出租车公司的股东，每家公司有且仅有两辆出租车登记在公司名下，而每家公司仅为每辆出租车投保了法律所要求的最低限额的汽车责任保险（保险金额 1 万美元）。原告称，这些公司表面看似互相独立，但其实在财务、供货、修理、雇员和车库等方面"均以一个实体、单位或企业运作"。这些公司均被原告作为被告。原告称，他有权要求这些公司的股东对其起诉的索赔承担个人责任，因为这种多元公司结构实际上是非法的，其目的是要"欺骗公众"，而公众有可能被出租车伤害。

The action is not only against that defendant and the driver of the taxicab, but also: (a) against nine other corporations in whose names other taxicabs were registered (the Seon Cab Corp. and each of said nine corporations having the registration for respective sets of two taxicabs); and (b) against two additional corporations and three individuals. The complaint further alleges that, despite these registrations, all the defendants own all the taxicabs and maintain and operate them "as a single network and enterprise." Liability is sought to be imposed upon all the defendants on the theory that all of them owned the taxicab which was involved in the accident, i.e., that the corporate veil of Seon Cab Corp. should be pierced.

此次诉讼不仅针对被告和出租车司机，还包括：（1）其他9个出租车公司，这些出租车公司名下登记着其他出租车（塞昂出租车公司和其他9个出租车公司各自在其名下登记两辆出租车）；（2）另外两个公司和三个个人。该诉讼还称，尽管有这些注册，所有的被告"以一个单一的网络和企业"拥有所有这些出租车并维护和运营它们。基于所有的被告共同拥有这些涉及事故的出租车，所有的被告都应该承担责任，这一理论即为塞昂出租车公司的"公司面纱"应当被刺穿。

In support of this claim, the complaint further alleges: (1) that Seon Cab Corp. and the said group of nine corporations were "organized, managed, dominated and controlled as the alter egos and creatures" of the three individual defendants, "who were the stockholders, directors and officers" of all the corporate defendants; (2) that all the employees of the corporations, including the one who was driving the taxicab in question at the time of the accident, "were the employees of all the defendants"; (3) that all these employees "were assigned interchangeably" to the corporations "by the defendants" and were centrally supervised; (4) that "the receipts, disbursements, assets and properties of the said corporations were interchanged and intermingled by the defendants as their own"; (5) that all the corporations "purchased centrally all supplies, automobile parts, oil, gas and tires"; (6) that all the taxicabs were garaged centrally; (7) that "all other operations and properties of all the said corporations were operated, controlled, managed and maintained as a single entity, unit and enterprise by the defendants"; and (8) that funds borrowed by the corporations (on notes which were personally indorsed by the individual defendants) "were used centrally to purchase taxicabs and otherwise maintain and operate the taxicab fleet as an entity and economic unit." The complaint also asserts claims to the effect that the creation of the corporations and the use of the corporations in the manner above outlined constituted a fraud on the public, including plaintiff, in that injured persons would not be able to recover the full amount of damages sustained by them; that the corporations were "mere shams and fictions, the instruments and agents of the defendants"; and that Seon Cab Corp. and the said group of nine corporations did not have sufficient capital to act as the registered owners of the taxicabs. There are still further allegations that the registration of the respective sets of two taxicabs in the names of each of 10 corporations constituted a breach of Regulations of the Police Department of the City of New York.

为了支持这一主张，原告还称：（1）塞昂出租车公司和其他9个公司团伙是由3个被告"作为一个变装的个体而组建、管理、支配和控制"的，"他们是所有被告公司的股东、董事和高级管理人员"；（2）公司的所有员工，包括在事故发生时驾驶出租车的那名员工"是所有被告的员工”；（3）所有这些员工由被告交替分派到这些公司并受到集中管理；（4）"所有公司的收入、支出、资产和财产均由被告们自己进行互换和混合"；（5）所有企业"集中采购所有用品、汽车配件、石油、天然气和轮胎"；（6）所有的出租车都集中停放；（7）"所有公司的其他运营和财产被做为一个实体、单位或企业由被告予以运作、控制、管理和维护"；（8）公司借来的资金（支票是由个别被告做的个人背书）"被集中用来采购出租车和其他维护设备以使整个出租车队得以作为一个实体经济单位运作"。原告还宣称，上述这些公司的组建方式和使用方式，对原告在内的大众构成欺诈，因为受伤的人将无法得到他们所受损害的全额赔偿。公司将"仅仅是掩饰和表象，是被告的工具和代理"；而塞昂出租车公司和另外 9 个公司均没有充足的资金成为出租车的注册业主。还有更进一步的指控认为，10 个出租车公司名下分别登记 2 辆出租车，在手续上违反了纽约市警察部门的规定。

【裁决过程与结果】（Procedure and Disposition）

In an action to recover damages for personal injury, the plaintiff appeals from an order of the Supreme Court, Richmond County, entered March 13, 1964, which granted the defendant Carlton's motion to dismiss the complaint as to him on the ground that it fails to state a cause of action (CPLR 3211, subd. [a], par. 7). Order reversed, with $ 10 costs and disbursements, and motion denied. The time of the defendant Carlton to serve his answer is extended until 20 days after service of a copy of the order entered hereon.

On July 6, 1965, the Appellate Division of the Supreme Court in the Second Judicial Department gave their opinion which held that "despite the existence of the separate corporations and the division of the registration of the 20 taxicabs among the 10 corporations, the complaint sufficiently alleges that the entire business in question was in reality a single enterprise operated by a single entity, and that any acts of any of the corporations were committed by the actor as an agent for all the other defendants. Accordingly, the complaint is valid as against the individual defendant Carlton."

John Walkovszky appealed. The Court of Appeals of New York reversed the lower court's decision and held that plaintiff's complaint failed to allege that defendant was doing business in his individual capacity on November 29, 1966.

【裁判理由】（Reasons for Judicial Decision）

【生效判决意见】（OPINION BY: FULD）

The law permits the incorporation of a business for the very purpose of enabling its proprietors to escape personal liability (see, e.g., Bartle v. Home Owners Co-op., 309 N. Y. 103, 106), but manifestly, the privilege is not without its limits. Broadly speaking, the courts will disregard the corporate form, or, to use accepted terminology, "pierce the corporate veil," whenever necessary "to prevent fraud or to achieve equity." (International Aircraft Trading Co. v. Manufacturers Trust Co., 297 N. Y. 285, 292.) In determining whether liability should be extended to reach assets beyond those belonging to the corporation, we are guided, as Judge Cardozo noted, by "general rules of agency." (Berkey v. Third Ave. Ry. Co., 244 N. Y. 84, 95.) In other words, whenever anyone uses control of the corporation to further his own rather than the corporation's business, he will be liable for the corporation's acts "upon the principle of *respondeat superior* applicable even where the agent is a natural person". Such liability, moreover, extends not only to the corporation's commercial dealings but to its negligent acts as well.

　　法律允许设立公司，以便公司的所有者逃避个人责任(见巴尔特尔诉住房所有者合作社案)，但很明显，此特权并非没有限制。从广义上说，为了防止欺诈或出于公平原因，只要有必要，可以不考虑公司形式，用行话说，就是"揭去公司面纱"(见国际飞机交易公司诉制造商信托公司案)。在确定赔偿责任是否可涉及公司之外资产时，我们遵循卡尔多索法官所提到的"代理关系规则"(伯基诉第三大道·雷公司案)。换言之，只要有人控制公司，背离公司业务，使公司为其个人所用，则他必须基于"雇主责任规则"对公司行为负个人责任，即便代理人是一个自然人。这种责任不仅适用于商业交易，而且适用于公司的疏忽行为。

In the Mangan case (247 App. Div. 853, mot. for lv. to app. den. 272 N. Y. 676, supra), the plaintiff was injured as a result of the negligent operation of a cab owned and operated by one of four corporations affiliated with the defendant Terminal. Although the defendant was not a stockholder of any of the operating companies, both the defendant and the operating companies were owned, for the most part, by the same parties. The defendant's name (Terminal) was conspicuously displayed on the sides of all of the taxis used in the enterprise and, in point of fact, the defendant actually serviced, inspected, repaired and dispatched them. These facts were deemed to provide sufficient cause for piercing the corporate veil of the operating company—the nominal owner of the cab which injured the plaintiff—and holding the defendant liable. The operating companies were simply instrumentalities for carrying on the business of the defendant without imposing upon it financial and other liabilities incident to the actual ownership and operation of the cabs.

　　在纽约州上诉法院审理的曼根案中，一辆出租车司机因其疏忽而撞伤原告，出租车属于与被告"终点站公司"有关的4家公司中的一家公司所有。尽管被告并非其中任何一家公司的股东，但由几位股东同时拥有被告和这几家运营公司。这些公司所有的出租车车身上都明显地印有被告的名称(终点站公司)，而且被告也曾检查修理和调度出租车，并且提供相关服务。基于这些事实，完全有理由揭开运营公司的"公司面纱"，将其作为应该负责的被告，尽管运营公司仅仅是出租车的名义拥有者。运营公司仅仅是被告开展业务的工具，并未承担与实际控制和运营出租车相关的财务问题和其他责任。

In the case before us, the plaintiff has explicitly alleged that none of the corporations "had a separate existence of their own", and, as indicated above, all are named as defendants. However, it is one thing to assert that a corporation is a fragment of a larger corporate combine which actually conducts the business. (See Berle, The Theory of Enterprise Entity, 47 Col. L. Rev. 343, 348-350.) It is quite another to claim that the corporation is a "dummy" for its individual stockholders who are in reality carrying on the business in their personal capacities for purely personal rather than corporate ends. (See African Metals Corp. v. Bullowa, 288 N. Y. 78, 85.) Either circumstance would justify treating the corporation as an agent and piercing the corporate veil to reach the principal but a different result would follow in each case. In the first, only a larger corporate entity would be held financially responsible while, in the other, the stockholder would be personally liable, either the stockholder is conducting the business in his individual capacity or he is not. If he is, he will be liable; if he is not, then, it does not matter—insofar as his personal liability is concerned—that the enterprise is actually being carried on by a larger "enterprise entity". (See Berle, The Theory of Enterprise Entity, 47 Col. L. Rev. 343.)

本案的情况是，原告指称，任何一家公司都没有以其自身单独存在。如上文所示，原告将所有公司都作为被告。但指称一家公司是某家集团公司的一部分是一回事（见伯尔莱所撰《企业实体理论》一文，载于《哥伦比亚法学院法学研究》第47期），而指责公司"形同虚设"则是另一回事。"形同虚设"在此处是指公司为个别股东所用，沦为完全服务于其个人目的的工具，根本没有任何公司本身的目的（见非洲金属公司诉布卢瓦一案）。上述两种情况下都有理由将公司视为代理，揭开"公司面纱"，要求主体负责，但两种情况的结果自然不同。在第一种情况下，只会让一家更大的大公司负资金方面的责任；而在第二种情况下，股东个人必须承担责任。股东要么是以其个人身份经营业务，要么不是。如果是前者，他必须承担个人责任；如果是后者，则企业是否由一家更大的"企业实体"经营与个人责任无关（见伯尔莱所撰《企业实体理论》，《哥伦比亚法学院法学研究》第47期）。

At this stage in the present litigation, we are concerned only with the pleadings and, since CPLR 3014 permits causes of action to be stated "alternatively or hypothetically", it is possible for the plaintiff to allege both theories as the basis for his demand for judgment. In ascertaining whether he has done so, we must consider the entire pleading, educing therefrom "whatever can be implied from its statements by fair and reasonable intendment." Reading the complaint in this case most favorably and liberally, we do not believe that there can be gathered from its averments the allegations required to spell out a valid cause of action against the defendant Carlton.

在本案现阶段，我们仅考虑诉讼请求。既然《民事诉讼法》第3014条允许在阐述诉讼理由时使用"此外或假设"等词，原告可以用两种理论作为其诉讼要求的根据。在确定原告是否做到这点时，我们应该考虑整个诉讼请求，"从公平、合理的角度去推断所用言辞"。从最有利、最自由的角度看本案的诉讼请求，我们认为，诉讼请求并未提出针对被告卡尔顿的有效诉由。

The individual defendant is charged with having "organized, managed, dominated and controlled" a fragmented corporate entity but there are no allegations that he was conducting business in his individual capacity. Had the taxicab fleet been owned by a single corporation, it would be readily apparent that the plaintiff would face formidable barriers in attempting to establish personal liability on the part of the corporation's stockholders. The fact that the fleet ownership has been deliberately split up among many corporations does not ease the plaintiff's burden in that respect. The corporate form may not be disregarded merely because the assets of the corporation, together with the mandatory insurance coverage of the vehicle which struck the plaintiff, are insufficient to assure him the recovery sought. If Carlton were to be held individually liable on those facts alone, the decision would apply equally to the thousands of cabs which are owned by their individual drivers who conduct their businesses through corporations organized pursuant to section 401 of the *Business Corporation Law* and carry the minimum insurance required by subdivision 1 (par. [a]) of section 370 of the *Vehicle and Traffic Law*. These taxi owner-operators are entitled to form such corporations (cf. Elenkrieg v. Siebrecht, 238 N. Y. 254), and we agree with the court at Special Term that, if the insurance coverage required by statute "is inadequate for the protection of the public, the remedy lies not with the courts but with the

Legislature." It may very well be sound policy to require that certain corporations must take out liability insurance which will afford adequate compensation to their potential tort victims. However, the responsibility for imposing conditions on the privilege of incorporation has been committed by the Constitution to the Legislature (N. Y. Const., art. X,1) and it may not be fairly implied, from any statute, that the Legislature intended, without the slightest discussion or debate, to require of taxi corporations that they carry automobile liability insurance over and above that mandated by the *Vehicle and Traffic Law*.

卡尔顿作为个人被告被指责"设立、管理、主导并控制了"一个支离破碎的公司实体，但原告并未指控被告在以个人目的从事业务活动。如果出租车仅由一家公司独家占有，则原告显然难以表明公司股东应承担个人责任。诚然，出租车由许多家公司分别拥有，但这并不能完成举证责任。本案涉及公司的资产以及撞伤原告的汽车的必备保险不足于支付原告所要求的赔偿金，但不能仅仅因此而否认公司形式的存在。如果本院认定，仅依据本案事实卡尔顿即承担个人责任，则该决定也将适用于成千上万的出租车，而这些出租车也是个人根据《商业公司法》第 401 节通过有组织的公司开展业务，并根据《车辆交通法》第 370 节第一段保了最低险。这些出租车车主与运营者有权设立这些公司（见艾兰克里格诉塞布拉彻特案）。一审法院认为，如果法定保险额"不足于保护公众，则应该通过立法机构，而不是法院寻求补救办法"。不妨要求某些公司投保足够的责任保险金，以使其潜在侵权受害者可以得到足够补偿。但《宪法》已规定由立法机构负责制定有关设立公司特权的规定（《纽约州规章》第 10 条第 1 节）。根据现有的任何法规，无法看出立法机构默许，不经任何讨论或辩论即可要求出租车公司的汽车责任保险额高出《车辆交通法》所规定的要求。

This is not to say that it is impossible for the plaintiff to state a valid cause of action against the defendant Carlton. However, the simple fact is that the plaintiff has just not done so here. While the complaint alleges that the separate corporations were undercapitalized and that their assets have been intermingled, it is barren of any "sufficiently [particularized] statements" (CPLR 3013; see 3 Weinstein-Korn-Miller, N. Y. Civ. Prac., par. 3013.01 et seq., p. 30-142 et seq.) that the defendant Carlton and his associates are actually doing business in their individual capacities, shuttling their personal funds in and out of the corporations "without regard to formality and to suit their immediate convenience." (Weisser v. Mursam Shoe Corp., 127 F. 2d 344, 345, supra.) Such a "perversion of the privilege to do business in a corporate form" (Berkey v. Third Ave. Ry. Co., 244 N. Y. 84, 95, supra) would justify imposing personal liability on the individual stockholders. (See African Metals Corp. v. Bullowa, 288 N. Y. 78, supra.) Nothing of the sort has in fact been charged, and it cannot reasonably or logically be inferred from the happenstance that the business of Seon Cab Corporation may actually be carried on by a larger corporate entity composed of many corporations which, under general principles of agency, would be liable to each other's creditors in contract and in tort.

但这不是说原告无法针对被告找出可以成立的诉讼理由，事实是原告并未这样做。起诉书指称多家公司的资本不足，资产混乱，但根本没有任何"足够详细的说明"（见《民事诉讼法》，温斯坦、科恩和米勒著）指称卡尔顿与其助手以个人身份从事业务，将自己的资金与公司资金混为一体，"只顾眼前需要，根本不顾公司的形式"（见威赛尔诉莫尔山姆制鞋公司案）。倘若如此滥用以公司这种形式从事业务的特权（见伯基诉第三大道·雷公司案），则有理由要求个人股东承担个人责任(见非洲金属公司诉布洛瓦案)。但本案中并未提出任何类似的事实，而且就本案的情况而言，没有理由认为或按逻辑推断赛昂出租车公司的业务实际上由一家更大的公司实体进行，而这家公司实体又由许多公司组成。根据代理的一般原则，这些公司相互之间对其他公司的合同与侵权方面的债权人承担责任。

In point of fact, the principle relied upon in the complaint to sustain the imposition of personal liability is not agency but fraud. Such a cause of action cannot withstand analysis. If it is not fraudulent for the owner-operator of a single cab corporation to take out only the minimum required liability insurance, the enterprise does not become either illicit or fraudulent merely because it consists of many such corporations. The plaintiff's injuries are the same regardless of whether the cab which strikes him is owned by a single corporation or part of a fleet with ownership fragmented among many corporations. Whatever rights he may be able to assert against parties other than the registered owner of the vehicle come into being not because he has been defrauded but because, under the principle of respondeat superior, he is entitled to hold the whole enterprise responsible for the acts of its agents.

In sum, then, the complaint falls short of adequately stating a cause of action against the defendant Carlton in his individual capacity.

The order of the Appellate Division should be reversed, with costs in this court and in the Appellate Division, the certified question answered in the negative and the order of the Supreme Court, Richmond County, reinstated, with leave to serve an amended complaint.

但是，起诉书中要求被告承担个人责任的依据并非代理原则，而是欺诈。这一诉讼理由经不起推敲。如果一家出租车公司的所有者或经营者只投保法定最低风险保险金额并不是欺诈行为，那么一家企业也不仅仅因为它由许多这样的出租车公司组成而成为非法或欺诈性的公司。不管撞伤原告的出租车是一家公司所拥有的，还是多家分支公司拥有的车队中的一部分，原告的受伤情况不会改变。除车辆的注册车主外，原告对其他人还有何种权利并不取决于是否有欺诈行为，而是取决于根据雇主责任规则，原告是否有权让整个企业为其代理的行为负责。

简言之，起诉书并未阐明将卡尔顿作为个人被告的理由。

撤销纽约最高法院上诉部门的决定，本院及最高法院上诉部门的诉讼费用由被上诉人承担。本院对调卷审理的本案给予否定回答，恢复纽约州最高法院里士满县法庭的一审判决，允许原告提交修改后的起诉书。

【反对意见】(DISSENT BY: KEATING)

The issue presented by this action is whether the policy of this State, which affords those desiring to engage in a business enterprise the privilege of limited liability through the use of the corporate device, is so strong that it will permit that privilege to continue no matter how much it is abused, no matter how irresponsibly the corporation is operated, no matter what the cost to the public. I do not believe that it is.

Under the circumstances of this case the shareholders should all be held individually liable to this plaintiff for the injuries he suffered. At least, the matter should not be disposed of on the pleadings by a dismissal of the complaint.

本案的争议焦点是，本州给予那些渴望从事企业经营的人通过运用公司制度以获得有限责任的特权的公共政策，是否足够强大到允许这些特权继续存在，无论这一特权如何被滥用，无论公司的运营多么不负责任，也无论公众付出怎样的代价。我不相信这点。

在本案的情况下，对本案原告所受的伤害，股东们都应该承担个人责任。至少，这件事不应该在要求驳回起诉的动议请求环节就被处理掉了。

In Minton v. Cavaney (56 Cal. 2d 576) the Supreme Court of California had occasion to discuss this problem in a negligence case. The corporation of which the defendant was an organizer, director and officer operated a public swimming pool. One afternoon the plaintiffs' daughter drowned in the pool as a result of the alleged negligence of the corporation.

Justice Roger Traynor, speaking for the court, outlined the applicable law in this area. "The figurative terminology 'alter ego' and 'disregard of the corporate entity'", he wrote, "is generally used to refer to the various situations that are an abuse of the corporate privilege...The equitable owners of a corporation, for example, are personally liable when they treat the assets of the corporation as their own and add or withdraw capital from the corporation at will...; when they hold themselves out as being personally liable for the debts of the corporation...; or when they provide inadequate capitalization and actively participate in the conduct of corporate affairs". (56 Cal. 2d, p. 579; italics supplied.)

Examining the facts of the case in light of the legal principles just enumerated, he found that "[it was] undisputed that there was no attempt to provide adequate capitalization. [The corporation] never had any substantial assets. It leased the pool that it operated, and the lease was forfeited for failure to pay the rent. Its capital was 'trifling compared with the business to be done and the risks of loss'". (56 Cal. 2d, p. 580.) It seems obvious that one of "the risks of loss" referred to was the possibility of drownings due to the negligence of the corporation. And the defendant's failure to provide such assets or any fund for recovery resulted in his being held personally liable.

在明顿诉卡瓦尼案中，加利福尼亚最高法院有机会在一个疏忽过失案件中讨论这个问题。该案涉及的公司经营一处公共游泳池，被告则设立了这家公司，并身兼公司的董事和高级管理。一天下午，原告的女儿因为公司涉嫌过失而在游泳池里淹死了。

法院的主审法官罗杰·特雷纳概括了这个领域所适用的法律。他写道："比较形象的专用术语'变装'和'否认法人人格'，通常用来指滥用公司特权的各种情况……例如，当公司的股权持有者在他们将公司的资产视同为他们自己的财产并随意对公司增加或取回资本金时，他们应承担个人责任……还有就是当他们一直对公司的债务承担个人责任时……或当他们没有提供与公司业务成合理比例的足够的资本金并积极参与公司事务时。"

基于上述法律原则审查该案的事实，他认为："毫无疑问，被告没有尝试过提供足够的资本。[公司]从未有过任何实质性的资产。它运营的游泳池是租赁的，租约因为没付租金而解除了。它的资本金与公司要做的事和面临的风险损失相比是微不足道的。"很明显，其中一个面临的风险损失指的是发生溺水事故而要求公司承担过失责任的可能性。被告未能提供该等资产或赔偿基金，因此应该承担个人责任。

What I would merely hold is that a participating shareholder of a corporation vested with a public interest, organized with capital insufficient to meet liabilities which are certain to arise in the ordinary course of the corporation's business, may be held personally responsible for such liabilities. Where corporate income is not sufficient to cover the cost of insurance premiums above the statutory minimum or where initially adequate finances dwindle under the pressure of competition, bad times or extraordinary and unexpected liability, obviously the shareholder will not be held liable (Henn, Corporations, p. 208, n.7).

The only types of corporate enterprises that will be discouraged as a result of a decision allowing the individual shareholder to be sued will be those such as the one in question, designed solely to abuse the corporate privilege at the expense of the public interest.

For these reasons I would vote to affirm the order of the Appellate Division.

我仅认为，一个公司的参与股东应被赋予关注公众利益的责任，当其组建的公司的资本不足以满足在公司日常经营中所出现的负债时，股东可能会亲自负责这类负债。而当公司的收入并不足以支付法定最低限额的保险基金的投保费用时，或最初充分的资本因为竞争压力、时机不好或超出预料的意外责任而变得捉襟见肘时，很明显股东就不应承担责任。

如果按照本判决结果，由于股东个人会被起诉而常被打击的一类公司，将只是那些设计完全用来牺牲公共利益而滥用公司特权的公司。

为了这些理由，我投票维持最高法院上诉部门的决定。

【案件影响】（Impact of the Case）

"揭开公司面纱"是为阻止公司独立人格的滥用和保护公司债权人利益及社会公共利益，就具体法律关系中的特定事实，否认公司与其背后的股东各自独立的人格及股东的有限责任，责令公司的股东（包括自然人股东和法人股东）对公司债权人或公共利益直接负责，以实现公平、正义目标之要求而设置的一种法律措施。其最终目的是为了防止欺诈和实现公平。

美国历史上的不少判例规则经过时间的验证后又被立法机构纳入成文法律，但"揭开公司面纱"规则仍然只是判例法，并不见于各州公司法之中。该规则虽然极负盛名，但在实践中法院却很少使用。事实上，纽约州最高法院虽然在卡尔顿案中确定了"揭开公司面纱"规则，但仍判该规则并不适用于本案。法院在使用该规则时慎之又慎，其原因是判该规则适用就直接否定了公司存在的必要。

【思考问题】（Questions）

1. 本案中有的法官认为交足法定最低保险金额后被告不再有责任，而有的法官认为交足法定保险金额也并不能完全摆脱责任，你怎么看？

2. 我国公司法律实践中对于"揭开公司法人面纱"原则是如何规定和适用的？

七、商法案例

雷兰德船运公司诉诺维奇联合火灾保险公司案

Leyland Shipping Co. v. Norwich Union Fire Insurance Society Ltd.（1918）

【选读理由】（Selected Reason）

近因原则，是英国海上保险法最早确立的用以认定因果关系的基本原则，目前被公认为保险法的基本原则之一。所谓"近因原则"，是指保险人承担赔偿责任的范围应限于以承保风险为近因造成的损失。明确近因概念的重要案例是 1918 年 1 月 31 日英国上议院做出判决的雷兰德船运公司诉诺维奇联合火灾保险公司一案。

【案件事实】（Facts）

The Ikaria was on a voyage from South America to Havre and London. When stopped, on 30 January 1915 (Saturday) about twenty-five miles north-west of Havre for the purpose of taking up a pilot, she was struck abreast of No. 1 hatch by a torpedo fired by a German submarine. Two large holes were made in the vessel and No. 1 hold filled with water. The crew went on board a tug, fearing that the Ikaria might sink at once, but as she kept afloat they returned to her and brought bar into the outer harbour of Havre. She was moored alongside the Quai d'Escale, where she was always afloat, and would have been saved if she had been allowed to remain there. A gale sprung up on 31 January (Sunday) causing the vessel to range and bump against the quay. The port authorities were apprehensive that she might sink, blocking the quay, which was urgently required for purposes connected with the war, and ordered that she should leave the quay and either be beached outside the harbour altogether or anchored in the outer harbour near the breakwater spoken of in the evidence as the Batardeau. The latter position was chosen, and the vessel was anchored with her head towards the Batardeau. There was a good deal of wind and sea. As the vessel was very much by the head in consequence of the damage done by the torpedo, at each low tide she took the ground forward, while the rest of bar structure was water-borne. She was thereby subjected to considerable strain, and the bulkhead between No. 1 and No. 2 holds having been weakened by the explosion of the torpedo, the forward and crumpledup, and she became a total loss on Tuesday, February 2. The appellants (plaintiffs) contended that her loss was due to the perils of the seas at her anchorage in the outer harbour. The respondents (defendants) contended that it was caused by hostilities. Both courts below have held that it was so caused by the torpedo, and that, as the warranty applied, the respondents were not liable.

"艾卡丽亚号"轮船正在从南美开往阿弗尔和伦敦。1915 年 1 月 30 日（星期六）它停在离阿弗尔港西北 25 英里的地方，以便于登载领航员，它的 1 号舱口被德国潜艇发射的鱼雷击中了。甲板上有两个大洞，1 号船舱进满了水。因为担心"艾卡丽亚号"会立即沉没，船员们登上了一艘拖轮。但它继续浮着，船员返回船上航行，并把它拖到阿弗尔的外港。它停泊在码头边上，一直浮在水面上，本来如果它被允许留在那里，它就会得到救援。31 日（星期日），狂风突起，该船频频撞击码头，港口当局担心船沉没港内堵塞码头，而码头在战争中是至关重要的，于是勒令其离开码头，要么搁浅在港口外，要么停泊在以附近的防波堤作为围堰的外港。该船选择停在后一个地方，抛锚并使其船头正对防波堤。该处风和海水很大。由于船头部受鱼雷爆炸造成的损害非常严重，在每一个低潮时它都会搁浅，造成其他船体进水。它被大力扭动，1 号和 2 号船舱之间的隔离壁已经因鱼雷爆炸而损坏，于是就破碎了，这艘船在 2 月 2 日（星期二）就全部损毁了。上诉人（原告）认为它损失的原因是它在外港锚泊遭遇的海上危险。被上诉人（被告）认为这是由于战争造成的。两个法院都认为这是由鱼雷造成的，因此，按照保单，被上诉人不承担责任。

【裁决过程与结果】（Procedure and Disposition）

This is an appeal from a judgment of the Court of Appeal affirming the judgment of ROWLATT, J, in favour of the respondents, the do defendants in the action. The action was brought by thc appellants on a policy of marine insurance upon the steamship Ikaria. The appeal was dismissed with costs.

【裁判理由】（Reasons for Judicial Decision）

【生效判决意见 1】（Judgment by Lord Finlay Lc）

In my opinion, ROWLATT, J, and the Court of Appeal were right in holding that the loss of this vessel was a consequence of hostilities, and, therefore, not covered by the policy sued on. The only chance of saving the vessel after she had been struck by the torpedo was to take her into port, and Havre was obviously the proper port to take her to. The decision of the harbour authorities that the vessel could not be permitted to remain at the Quai d'Escale was final. That decision was given for very intelligible and weighty reasons, and there is no ground for thinking that the port authorities committed any error of judgment in ordering the removal, but those in charge of the ship had to obey the order, right or wrong. The Quai d'Escale consequently was no longer available for the vessel. The case must be dealt with just as if the episode of the vessel's being taken to that quay had not occurred, and she had been taken in the first instance straight to the anchorage near the Batardeau. What was the cause of her becoming a total wreck there? In my opinion, in substance, it was the injury by the torpedo. The injuries received from the torpedo made it impossible for the vessel to keep the sea. She was taken into port. At the anchorage to which she was ordered she took the ground forward at low tides as her draught forward was 82 feet (owing to the injury caused by the torpedo) as against 16 ft aft, and she was greatly strained by the seas in this position. No. 1 bulkhead, which had been seriously weakened by the explosion of the torpedo, gave way, the vessel breaking her back, crumpling up forward and becoming a total wreck. She was not lost by any new peril, but by the natural consequences of the explosion of the torpedo.

在我看来，罗拉特法官和上诉法院都认为造成该船损失的是战争，这是正确的，因此不在被诉的保险范围内。在它被鱼雷击中后唯一挽救的机会是带它到港口，阿弗尔显然是它应该去的港口。该港口当局最终决定是该船不能留在码头。这一决定是基于可理解的重大原因，并没有理由认为港口当局做出的要求移泊决定犯了错误，但涉及的船舶必须服从命令，无论是对还是错。停靠码头对这艘船来说是不能实现的。这个案件应从这艘船从未被带到码头的角度来处理，如果它在第一时间直接到靠近围堰的位置锚泊。它在那里变成残骸的原因是什么？在我看来，实质上，它是被鱼雷损坏的。鱼雷造成的伤害使船不能保持在海上。它曾被带进了港口，在后来被命令锚泊的位置，它在低潮时搁浅。因为相对于 16 英尺的船尾来说，它的吃水线是 82 英尺（由鱼雷造成的伤害），它在这个位置的海面上受到了极大的压力。鱼雷的爆炸严重削弱 1 号舱，使它失去控制，船尾部折断，向前揉成一团，成了残骸。它并没有因任何新的危险受到损失，这都是鱼雷爆炸造成的自然后果。

【生效判决意见 2】（Judgment by Shaw L）

In this way the discussion of the scope of proxima cause is very relevant and its ascertainment vital. In my opinion, too much is made of refinements upon this subject. The doctrine of cause has been since the time of Aristotle, and the famous category of material, formal, efficient and final causes, one involving the subtlest of distinctions. The doctrine applied in these to existences rather than to occurrences. But the idea of the cause of an occurrence or the production of an event or the bringing about of a result is an idea perfectly familiar to the mind and to the law, and it is in connection with that that the notion of proxima cause is introduced. Of this, I will venture to remark that one must be careful not to lay the accent upon the word "proximate" in such a sense as to lose sight of or destroy altogether the idea of cause itself. The true and overruling principle is to look at a contract as a whole, and to ascertain what the parties to it really meant. What was it which brought about the loss, the event, the calamity, the accident? And this not in an artificial sense, but in that real sense which part to a contract must have had in their minds when they spoke of cause at all. To treat proxima cause as the cause which is nearest in time is out of the question. Causes are spoken of as if they were as distinct from one another as beads in a row or links in a chain, but—if this metaphysical topic has to be referred to—it is not wholly so. The chain of causation is a handy expression, but the figure is inadequate. Causation is not a chain but a net. At each point influences, forces, events, precedent and simultaneous, meet, and the radiation from each point extends infinitely. At the point where these various influences meet it is for the judgment as upon a matter of fact to declare which of the causes thus joined at the point of effect was the proximate and which was the remote cause.

这样对近因的范围的讨论很有意义且十分重要。在我看来，这一问题已经发生了很大的改变。关于原因的学说自亚里士多德时代以来就有探讨，知名的范畴包括实质的、正式的、有效的和最终的原因，涉及微妙的区别。这中间适用的原则是存在而不是导致发生。但是将原因作为发生或造成事件或带来结果的想法是更符合思维和法律的，与此相关就引出了近因的概念。对此，我说的是，一定要小心不要把重点放在"近"上从而忽略或破坏对原因本身的认识。真正的、应优先适用的原则是将合同视为一个整体来弄清合同当事方的真实意思。是什么造成了损失、事件、灾难或事故？这不能是人为的印象，而应是在他们谈到原因时在思想意识中的认识，是真正意义上作为合同的一部分。将近因视为在时间上最接近的原因是不值得讨论的。我们所说的原因与一排中的一个珠子或链子中的一节是不同的，从抽象的角度来说，它与此完全不同。因果关系不是一条链，而是一张网。在每一个点上的影响、力量、事件、在先出现或同时出现、巧合以及辐射，从每个点无限延展。根据多种影响因素交合的这个点对事实发生的影响力可以进行判断并表明产生综合影响的近因或远因。

What does "proximate" here mean? To treat proximate cause as if it was the cause which is proximate in time is, as I have said, out of the question. The cause which is truly proximate is that which is proximate in efficiency. That efficiency may have been preserved although other causes may meantime have sprung up, which have yet not destroyed it, or truly impaired it, and it may culminate in a result of which it still remains the real efficient cause to which the event can be ascribed. I illustrate that by the present case. Did the vessel perish because she was torpedoed or by a peril of the sea apart from that? It is replied: "She perished by a peril of the sea because sea water entered the gash in her side which the torpedo made." Certainly the entry of sea water was a peril of the sea, and certainly that entry of sea water was proximate in time to the sinking. But how could there be any exception in the case of a vessel lost in harbour or at sea to a loss by perils of the sea, if the proximate cause in the sense of nearness in time to the result were the thing to be looked to? It is hardly possible for the mind to figure anything which would interfere with or be an exception to a cause so proximate as the entry of sea water into or over the hull as the vessel sinks in the waves. The result of this is that the consideration of the exception of the consequences of hostilities, or indeed any other exception so far as I can at present figure, if that consideration be limited to a cause proximate in time, destroys the exception altogether. It might as well never have been written. In my opinion, accordingly, proximate cause is an expression referring to the efficiency as an operating factor upon the result. Where various factors or causes are concurrent, and one has to be selected, the matter is determined as one of fact, and the choice falls upon the one to which may be variously ascribed the qualities of reality, predominance, efficiency. Fortunately, this much would appear to be in accordance with the principles of a plain business transaction and it is not at all foreign to the law.

这里的"近"是什么意思？正如我所说，把近因作为在时间上接近的原因是不对的。真正的近因，应当是效力上最接近的那个原因。尽管可能还会有其他原因出现，但这并不能使近因的原因效力消失或对其产生真正的破坏作用，其效力将依然存续，并对结果有着真实的效力影响。以本案为例来说，轮船的毁灭是因为鱼雷击中还是因为海难？答案是"它毁于海难，因为海水从鱼雷造成的裂缝里灌进来"。当然，海水进来是海上危险，海水的进入在时间上是最接近沉没的。如果近因被视为在时间上最接近后果的原因，那么一艘损失在海港或海洋里的船怎么可能还会有海上危险之外的原因呢？很难想象，沉入海中的船除了进水或船体被淹没之外，还有其他情况成为所谓"近因"。这样做的结果就是，将战争作为例外情况加以考虑，或者任何我现在能想到的真正的例外情况，如果近因被限制为时间上最近的原因，将会完全破坏这种例外情况。这也可能从未被论述过。因此在我看来，近因是对造成结果的影响力的表达，如果多种因素或原因同时发生，需要确定一个原因作为近因，这种选择取决于这一原因从多个方面造成后果的现实能力、支配地位和影响力。幸运的是，这些看起来与简单的商业交易中所适用的原则是一致的，对法律而言也并不陌生。

【案件影响】（Impact of the Case）

本案判决否定了判定近因的时间标准，并进而提出了判定近因的效力标准，被视为近因规则的起源。这一规则要求法院在同时存在的多个原因中选择一个作为主力原因，如果该原因属于承保事项，则保险人对全部损失承担保险责任；如果该原因属于除外责任，甚至属于非承保事项，则保险人的责任免除。近因被认为是对造成损失产生最大效力的原因，而并不必然是因果链中的最后一环。它应当是对损害结果的发生最应承担责任的原因。这一规则是英美国家目前最为流行的因果关系判定规则，使得法院可以选择自己认为的对造成损害结果负有最大过错的主体来承担责任，从而满足了法院做出符合其理想标准的公平判决的意愿，因而它对法院颇有吸引力。但同时，该规则也被批评为是最为随意且不具有可预测性的方法。克拉克教授认为："这种利用'普通常识'去选择一个原因的方法的不可预测性导致了随意的结果和为数众多的判断标准。"原因很简单，在因果关联中选择一个原因作为主力原因将把法官对正义的关注引入此过程之中，而这种认识在不同法官中、甚至同一个法官在不同案件情境中都有不同的考量，因而极大地增加了判决结果的不可预知性。因此，它的适用在系统层面上难以实现公平。对主力原因的选择甚至将取决于当事人讲述损失是如何发生的"艺术"。

【思考问题】（Questions）

1. 在艾思宁顿诉意外保险公司案中，被保险人打猎时从树上掉下来受伤，爬到公路边等待救援时因夜间天冷又感染肺炎死亡，保险范围仅包含意外事故不包括疾病，应怎样认定保险公司的赔偿责任？

2. 《中华人民共和国保险法》对近因原则是如何规定的？近因可以有多个吗？

八、经济法案例

美国诉微软公司案

United States v. Microsoft Corp.（2000）

【选读理由】（Selected Reason）

　　一般认为，美国 1890 年颁布的《抵制非法限制与垄断保护贸易及商业法》是世界上最早的反垄断立法。因最初是由参议院议员约翰·谢尔曼提出的议案，故又称《谢尔曼法》，由于当时企业兼并多是通过"托拉斯"的形式进行，所以这部法律也叫《反托拉斯法》。100 多年来，美国出现了不少反垄断裁决的重大经典案例，比如洛克菲勒家族的"石油帝国"因垄断市场在 1911 年被肢解为 30 多个独立石油公司；曾垄断美国电话市场的美国电报电话公司在 1984 年被分离成一个继承母公司名称的电报电话公司（专营长途电话业务）和 7 个地区性电话公司。20 世纪 90 年代以后，随着国际上技术创新竞争日趋激烈，美国政府反垄断的目标不再是简单防止市场独占、操纵价格等，而是着眼于如何阻止专利保护以外的技术垄断，以保障美国继续占领科技创新的前沿。1998 年 5 月 18 日，美国司法部联合 20 个州（有一个州后来退出了）对微软公司起诉，指控它通过视窗操作系统"捆绑"销售其他软件从而构成了市场垄断，美国联邦哥伦比亚地区法院于 1999 年 11 月 5 日做出裁决，后该案由美国司法部联合 19 个州再次起诉，美国联邦哥伦比亚地区法院基于前述裁决确认的事实于 2000 年 6 月 7 日对该案做出裁决，要求微软拆分，该案成为 20 世纪最大的反垄断案。

【案件事实】（Facts）

　　Defendant Microsoft Corporation is organized under the laws of the State of Washington, and its headquarters are situated in Redmond, Washington. Since its inception, Microsoft has focused primarily on developing software and licensing it to various purchasers. In 1981, Microsoft released the first version of its Microsoft Disk Operating System, commonly known as "MS-DOS." When the International Business Machines Corporation ("IBM") selected MS-DOS for pre-installation on its first generation of PCs, Microsoft's product became the predominant operating system sold for Intel-compatible PCs. In 1985, Microsoft began shipping a software package called Windows. In 1995, Microsoft introduced a software package called Windows 95, which enjoyed unprecedented popularity with consumers, and in June 1998, Microsoft released its successor, Windows 98.

　　被告微软公司是根据华盛顿州的法律设立的，总部位于该州的雷蒙德。微软公司从设立之初就主要从事软件开发活动，同时授权各种购买者使用该公司开发的软件。1981 年，微软发布了首版"微软磁盘操作系统"，即人们所熟知的 MS-DOS。国际商用机器公司（IBM）选择 MS-DOS 作为第一代个人电脑的预装系统，微软的产品成为个人手提电脑中最主要的操作系统。1985 年，微软公司发布了一种名为"视窗"（Windows）的套装软件。1995 年，微软公司又发布了一个名为"视窗95"的套装软件，该软件获得空前成功。1998 年 6 月，微软趁势发布了"视窗 98"操作系统。

Microsoft is the leading supplier of operating systems for PCs. The company transacts business in all fifty of the United States and in most countries around the world. Microsoft licenses copies of its software programs directly to consumers. The largest part of its MS-DOS and Windows sales, however, consists of licensing the products to manufacturers of PCs (known as "original equipment manufacturers" or "OEMs"), such as the IBM PC Company and the Compaq Computer Corporation ("Compaq"). An OEM typically installs a copy of Windows onto one of its PCs before selling the package to a consumer under a single price.

微软公司是个人电脑操作系统的领先的供应商，在全美 50 个州和全世界大多数国家开展业务。微软直接授权用户使用软件程序副本。然而，授权个人电脑制造商（称为"初始设备制造商"或 OEMs）——例如 IBM 个人电脑公司和康柏电脑公司——使用其产品构成 MS-DOC 和视窗系统销量的最大份额。初始设备制造商的典型做法是将"视窗"系统预装在每一台个人电脑上，然后再按照单一价格将个人电脑出售给消费者。

Currently there are no products, nor are there likely to be any in the near future, that a significant percentage of consumers world-wide could substitute for Intel-compatible PC operating systems without incurring substantial costs. Therefore, in determining the level of Microsoft's market power, the relevant market is the licensing of all Intel-compatible PC operating systems world-wide. Microsoft enjoys so much power in the market for Intel-compatible PC operating systems that if it wished to exercise this power solely in terms of price, it could charge a price for Windows substantially above that which could be charged in a competitive market. Moreover, it could do so for a significant period of time without losing an unacceptable amount of business to competitors. In other words, Microsoft enjoys monopoly power in the relevant market.

目前以及短期内，没有能够占据主要市场消费份额的产品可以以不太大的成本替代英特尔兼容的个人电脑操作系统。因此，在确定微软的市场影响力的水平方面，相关市场是指全球范围内英特尔兼容的个人电脑操作系统被授权使用的范围。微软在英特尔兼容的个人电脑操作系统中享有如此之大的权力，如果它希望能在价格方面行使这一权力，那么它对视窗系统收取实际上高于充分竞争市场价格的价格。即便它这样做，在一段时间内也不会把重要的市场份额输给竞争对手。换句话说，微软在相关市场享有垄断权力。

Viewed together, three main facts indicate that Microsoft enjoys monopoly power. First, Microsoft's share of the market for Intel-compatible PC operating systems is extremely large and stable. Second, Microsoft's dominant market share is protected by a high barrier to entry. Third, and largely as a result of that barrier, Microsoft's customers lack a commercially viable alternative to Windows.

综合来看，三个主要的事实表明，微软享有垄断权力。首先，微软在英特尔兼容的个人电脑操作系统的市场份额是非常巨大的和稳定的。其次，微软的主要市场份额受到很高的准入壁垒保护。最后，主要是由于这一准入壁垒，微软的客户缺乏商业上可行的替代视窗系统的方案。

Many of the tactics that Microsoft has employed have also harmed consumers indirectly by unjustifiably distorting competition. The actions that Microsoft took against Navigator hobbled a form of innovation that had shown the potential to depress the applications barrier to entry sufficiently to enable other firms to compete effectively against Microsoft in the market for Intel-compatible PC operating systems. That competition would have conduced to consumer choice and nurtured innovation. The campaign against Navigator also retarded widespread acceptance of Sun's Java implementation. This campaign, together with actions that Microsoft took with the sole purpose of making it difficult for developers to write Java applications with technologies that would allow them to be ported between Windows and other platforms, impeded another form of innovation that bore the potential to diminish the applications barrier to entry. There is insufficient evidence to find that, absent Microsoft's actions, Navigator and Java already would have ignited genuine competition in the market for Intel-compatible PC operating systems. It is clear, however, that Microsoft has retarded, and perhaps altogether extinguished, the process by which these two middleware technologies could have facilitated the introduction of competition into an important market.

微软所采取的策略不公平地扭曲了竞争，对消费者构成间接损害。微软公司针对领航者浏览器所采取的行动，扼杀了一种创新的形式，这种创新看起来有潜力越过市场壁垒以使其他公司能够进入与英特尔兼容的个人电脑操作系统市场，从而开展与微软公司的有效竞争。这种竞争会给消费者提供更多的选择并推动创新。针对领航者浏览器的行动阻止了用户对太阳公司 Java 语言应用程序的普遍接受。这一行动之外，微软公司还采取了一些措施，这些措施的唯一目标，是使开发员很难用 Java 语言开发出在技术上同时适用于视窗系统和其他平台的应用程序。微软的这些做法阻碍了另一种形式的创新，而这种创新原本有可能消除应用程序市场进入方面的障碍。没有足够的证据可以证明，如果微软公司不如此行动，领航者和 Java 会实现在与英特尔兼容的个人电脑操作系统市场上的充分竞争。但很明显，微软阻止了，并且可能是完全消除了这两个中间件技术可能会做到的，在一个重要的市场上引入竞争的路径。

Most harmful of all is the message that Microsoft's actions have conveyed to every enterprise with the potential to innovate in the computer industry. Through its conduct toward Netscape, IBM, Compaq, Intel, and others, Microsoft has demonstrated that it will use its prodigious market power and immense profits to harm any firm that insists on pursuing initiatives that could intensify competition against one of Microsoft's core products. Microsoft's past success in hurting such companies and stifling innovation deters investment in technologies and businesses that exhibit the potential to threaten Microsoft. The ultimate result is that some innovations that would truly benefit consumers never occur for the sole reason that they do not coincide with Microsoft's self-interest.

最重要的伤害是微软的行动所传达给每个有潜力革新计算机工业的企业的信息。虽然它的行动是针对网景、IBM、康柏、英特尔和其他公司，但微软公司会用自己巨大的市场影响力，牺牲足够的利润以打击任何坚持创新的公司，因为这种创新对微软的核心产品构成强烈的威胁。微软过去曾成功地打击了那些公司并扼杀了创新，有效阻止了看起来有潜力威胁微软的技术和经营方面的投资。这样造成的最终后果是，真正有益于消费者的创新不再出现，只有一个原因，那就是不符合微软的利益。

【裁判过程与结果】（Procedure and Disposition）

Plaintiff, United States of America, having filed its complaint herein on May 18, 1998;

Plaintiff States, having filed their complaint herein on the same day; Defendant Microsoft Corporation ("Microsoft") having appeared and filed its answer to such complaints; The Court having jurisdiction of the parties hereto and of the subject matter hereof and having conducted a trial thereon and entered Findings of Fact on November 5, 1999, and Conclusions of Law on April 3, 2000;The Court having entered judgment in accordance with the Findings of Fact and the Conclusions of Law on April 3, 2000, that Microsoft has violated §§ 1 and 2 of the *Sherman Act*, 15 U.S.C. §§ 1, 2, as well as the following state law provisions: Cal Bus. & Prof. Code §§ 16720, 16726, 16727, 17200; Conn. Gen. Stat. §§ 35-26, 35-27, 35-29; D.C. Code §§ 28-4502, 28-4503; Fla. Stat. chs. 501.204(1), 542.18, 542.19; 740 Ill. Comp. Stat. ch. 10/3; Iowa Code §§ 553.4, 553.5; Kan. Stat. §§ 50-101 et seq.; Ky. Rev. Stat. §§ 367.170, 367.175; La. Rev. Stat. §§ 51:122, 51:123, 51:1405; Md. Com. Law II Code Ann. § 11-204; Mass. Gen. Laws ch. 93A, § 2; Mich. Comp. Laws §§ 445.772, 445.773; Minn. Stat. § 325D.52; N.M. Stat. §§ 57-1-1, 57-1-2; N.Y. Gen. Bus. Law § 340; N.C. Gen. Stat. §§ 75-1.1, 75-2.1; Ohio Rev. Code §§ 1331.01, 1331.02; Utah Code § 76-10-914; W.Va. Code §§ 47-18-3, 47-18-4; Wis. Stat. § 133.03(1)-(2).

Upon the record at trial and all prior and subsequent proceedings herein, it is this 7th day of June, 2000, The court ordered divestiture of defendant computer technology company's operating systems business from its applications business after finding defendant violated provisions of the *Sherman Antitrust Act.*

【裁判理由】（Reason for Judicial Decision）

The United States, nineteen individual states, and the District of Columbia ("the plaintiffs") bring these consolidated civil enforcement actions against defendant Microsoft Corporation ("Microsoft") under the *Sherman Antitrust Act*, 15 U.S.C. Ë 1 and 2. The plaintiffs charge, in essence, that Microsoft has waged an unlawful campaign in defense of its monopoly position in the market for operating systems designed to run on Intel-compatible personal computers ("PCs"). Specifically, the plaintiffs contend that Microsoft violated 2 of the *Sherman Act* by engaging in a series of exclusionary, anticompetitive, and predatory acts to maintain its monopoly power. They also assert that Microsoft attempted, albeit unsuccessfully to date, to monopolize the Web browser market, likewise in violation of 2. Finally, they contend that certain steps taken by Microsoft as part of its campaign to protect its monopoly power, namely tying its browser to its operating system and entering into exclusive dealing arrangements, violated 1 of the Act.

美国联邦政府、19 个州以及哥伦比亚特区政府（原告）依据美国法典第 15 章第 1、2 部分的《谢尔曼法》对被告微软公司联合提起民事执法诉讼。原告指控，在本质上微软公司为了保障其在英特尔兼容的个人电脑操作系统市场上的垄断地位，从事了非法的行动。具体而言，原告认为微软通过一系列的排除竞争、限制竞争和掠夺性行为来维持其垄断力，违反了《谢尔曼法》第 2 条。他们还声称，微软试图垄断浏览器市场，虽然到现在尚未成功，垄断浏览器市场，同样违反了第 2 条。最后，他们认为微软为保护其垄断地位所采取的一些措施，即将浏览器捆绑进操作系统从而形成独占的交易，违反了第 1 条。

Upon consideration of the Court's Findings of Fact ("Findings"), filed herein on November 5, 1999, as amended on December 21, 1999, the proposed conclusions of law submitted by the parties, the briefs of amici curiae, and the argument of counsel thereon, the Court concludes that Microsoft maintained its monopoly power by anticompetitive means and attempted to monopolize the Web browser market, both in violation of 2. Microsoft also violated 1 of the Sherman Act by unlawfully tying its Web browser to its operating system. The facts found do not support the conclusion, however, that the effect of Microsoft's marketing arrangements with other companies constituted unlawful exclusive dealing under criteria established by leading decisions under 1.

基于法院 1999 年 11 月 5 日做出并于 1999 年 12 月 21 日修改的对所确认事实的裁决、当事各方提交的法律建议、法院顾问的法律意见及律师的辩论意见，法庭认为，微软通过排除竞争试图垄断浏览器市场而维持其垄断地位，违反了《谢尔曼法》的第 2 条。微软还通过非法地在操作系统上捆绑浏览器而违反了《谢尔曼法》第 1 条。然而审理查明的事实并不足以认定微软对其他公司进行营销方面上的安排所产生的影响构成了符合《谢尔曼法》第 1 条的判决先例所确定的标准下的非法排他经营。

The nineteen states and the District of Columbia ("the plaintiff states") seek to ground liability additionally under their respective antitrust laws. The Court is persuaded that the evidence in the record proving violations of the *Sherman Act* also satisfies the elements of analogous causes of action arising under the laws of each plaintiff state. For this reason, and for others stated below, the Court holds Microsoft liable under those particular state laws as well.

19 个州和哥伦比亚特区（原告）根据各自的反垄断法，想要让微软承担另外的责任。法庭被说服，认为记录在案证明微软违反《谢尔曼法》的证据同样满足每个原告州的法律所要求的提出类似的诉讼的要素。基于这一原因以及其他原因，法庭认为微软在特定的州的法律规定之下亦应承担责任。

Section 2 of the *Sherman Act* declares that it is unlawful for a person or firm to "monopolize... any part of the trade or commerce among the several States, or with foreign nations..." 15 U.S.C. 2. This language operates to limit the means by which a firm may lawfully either acquire or perpetuate monopoly power. Specifically, a firm violates 2 if it attains or preserves monopoly power through anticompetitive acts. See United States v. Grinnell Corp., 384 U.S. 563, 570-71, 16 L. Ed. 2d 778, 86 S. Ct. 1698 (1966) ("The offense of monopoly power under 2 of the *Sherman Act* has two elements: (1) the possession of monopoly power in the relevant market and (2) the willful acquisition or maintenance of that power as distinguished from growth or development as a consequence of a superior product, business acumen, or historic accident."); Eastman Kodak Co. v. Image Technical Services, Inc., 504 U.S. 451, 488, 119 L. Ed. 2d 265, 112 S. Ct. 2072 (1992) (Scalia, J., dissenting) ("Ourmonopolization doctrines are...directed to discrete situations in which a defendant's possession of substantial market power, combined with his exclusionary or anticompetitive behavior, threatens to defeat or forestall the corrective forces of competition and thereby sustain or extend the defendant's agglomeration of power").

《谢尔曼法》第 2 条宣布个人或公司"垄断州际间或与国际的商业和贸易的任何部分"是非法的。美国诉格林内尔公司案中提到违反《谢尔曼法》第 2 条有关垄断的行为有两个要素：（1）在相关市场上享有垄断力；（2）试图获得或保持的垄断力，不同于基于优质产品、灵活商业经营或历史机遇而自然形成的成长或发展。伊士曼柯达公司诉图像技术服务公司案也提道："我们认定垄断的原则是……导致一种离散状况，在此状况下，被告拥有实质的市场权利，结合自己排除或限制竞争行为，威胁消除竞争或形成一种调和竞争的力量，从而维持或扩展被告结成更大群体的权利。"

In this case, Microsoft early on recognized middleware as the Trojan horse that, once having, in effect, infiltrated the applications barrier, could enable rival operating systems to enter the market for Intel-compatible PC operating systems unimpeded. Simply put, middleware threatened to demolish Microsoft's coveted monopoly power. Alerted to the threat, Microsoft strove over a period of approximately four years to prevent middleware technologies from fostering the development of enough full-featured, cross-platform applications to erode the applications barrier. In pursuit of this goal, Microsoft sought to convince developers to concentrate on Windows-specific APIs and ignore interfaces exposed by the two incarnations of middleware that posed the greatest threat, namely, Netscape's Navigator Web browser and Sun's implementation of the Java technology. Microsoft's campaign succeeded in preventing—for several years, and perhaps permanently—Navigator and Java from fulfilling their potential to open the market for Intel-compatible PC operating systems to competition on the merits. Findings PP 133, 378. Because Microsoft achieved this result through exclusionary acts that lacked procompetitive justification, the Court deems Microsoft's conduct the maintenance of monopoly power by anticompetitive means.

在本案中，微软一开始将中间件识别为木马，因为它曾经渗透过应用壁垒。这一中间件能够使富有竞争力的操作程序在与英特尔兼容的个人电脑操作系统市场上畅通无阻地进行竞争。简单来说，中间件威胁微软公司，使其丧失巨大的市场垄断力。为防范威胁，微软用了四年的时间阻拦中间件技术，防止它发展特色明显的、能够跨平台运行的应用程序来弱化应用壁垒的作用。为达到这一目标，微软说服开发者专注于开发基于视窗系统的应用程序接口，放弃会给微软造成巨大威胁的以两种形式的中间件为接口的产品，即网景公司的领航者浏览器和太阳公司的 Java 技术应用。微软的行动会在几年的时间里，甚至将永远地阻止领航者和 Java 充分发挥自身潜力，打开与英特尔兼容的个人电脑操作系统市场，并与其展开业绩竞争。因为微软是通过排除竞争获得这样的结果，由此缺乏促进竞争的正当性，法院认定微软通过反竞争的方法来维持其垄断力。

In accordance with the Conclusions of Law filed herein this date, it is, this 3rd day of April, 2000,

ORDERED, ADJUDGED, and DECLARED, that Microsoft has violated Ë 1 and 2 of the *Sherman Act*, 15 U.S.C. Ë 1, 2, as well as the following state law provisions: Cal Bus. & Prof. Code Ë 16720, 16726, 17200; Coun. Gen. Stat. Ë 35-26, 35-27, 35-29; D.C. Code Ë 28-4502, 28-4503 ; Fla. Stat. chs. 501.204(1), 542.18, 542.19; 740 Ill. Comp. Stat. ch. 10/3; Iowa Code Ë 553.4, 553.5; Kan. Stat. Ë 50-101 et seq.; Ky. Rev. Stat. Ë 367.170, 367.175; La. Rev. Stat. Ë 51:122, 51:123, 51:1405; Md. Com. Law II Code Ann. 11-204; Mass. Gen. Laws ch. 93A, 2; Mich. Comp. Laws Ë 445.772, 445.773; Minn. Stat. 325D.52; N.M. Stat. Ë 57-1-1, 57-1-2; N.Y. Gen. Bus. Law Ë 340; N.C. Gen. Stat. Ë 75-1.1, 75-2.1; Ohio Rev. Code Ë 1331.01, 1331.02; Utah Code 76-10-914; W.Va. Code Ë 47-18-3, 47-18-4; Wis. Stat. 133.03(1)-(2); and it is

FURTHER ORDERED, that judgment is entered for the United States on its second, third, and fourth claims for relief in Civil Action No. 98-1232; and it is

FURTHER ORDERED, that the first claim for relief in Civil Action No. 98-1232 is dismissed with prejudice; and it is

FURTHER ORDERED, that judgment is entered for the plaintiff states on their first, second, fourth, sixth, seventh, eighth, ninth, tenth, eleventh, twelfth, thirteenth, fourteenth, fifteenth, sixteenth, seventeenth, eighteenth, nineteenth, twentieth, twenty-first, twenty-second, twenty-fourth, twenty-fifth, and twenty-sixth claims for relief in Civil Action No. 98-1233; and it is

FURTHER ORDERED, that the fifth claim for relief in Civil Action No. 98-1233 is dismissed with prejudice; and it is

FURTHER ORDERED, that Microsoft's first and second claims for relief in Civil Action No. 98-1233 are dismissed with prejudice;　and it is

FURTHER ORDERED, that the Court shall, in accordance with the Conclusions of Law filed herein, enter an Order with respect to appropriate relief, including an award of costs and fees, following proceedings to be established by further Order of the Court.

按照截至 2000 年 4 月 3 日提交的法律意见，做出如下裁定、判决：

微软违反了《谢尔曼法》第 1、2 条，美国法典第 15 卷第 1、2 条，以及下述诸州法律规定：加利福尼亚州《行业与职业法典》第 16720、16726、16727、17200 条，康涅狄格州《反托拉斯法》第 35～26 条、35～27 条、35～29 条；《特区法典》第 28～4502 条、28～4503 条……并进一步裁定判决支持美国政府第 2、3、4 项民事诉讼请求，驳回第 1 项诉讼请求；支持各州第 1、2、4、6、7、8、9、10、11、12、13、14、15、16、17、18、19、20、21、22、24、25、26 项诉讼请求；驳回第 5 项诉讼请求；驳回微软第 1、2 项索赔请求；裁定应按照法律意见在后续的诉讼程序中做出有关诉讼费用的裁定。

Upon the record at trial and all prior and subsequent proceedings herein, it is this 7th day of June, 2000, hereby:

ORDERED, ADJUDGED, AND DECREED as follows:

1. Divestiture

a. Not later than four months after entry of this Final Judgment, Microsoft shall submit to the Court and the Plaintiffs a proposed plan of divestiture. The Plaintiffs shall submit any objections to the proposed plan of divestiture to the Court within 60 days of receipt of the plan, and Microsoft shall submit its response within 30 days of receipt of the plaintiffs' objections.

b. Following approval of a final plan of divestiture by the Court (the "Plan") (and the expiration of the stay pending appeal set forth in section 6.a), Microsoft shall implement such Plan.

c. The Plan shall provide for the completion, within 12 months of the expiration of the stay pending appeal set forth in section 6.a., of the following steps:

i. The separation of the Operating Systems Business from the Applications Business, and the transfer of the assets of one of them (the "Separated Business") to a separate entity along with (a) all personnel, systems, and other tangible and intangible assets (including Intellectual Property) used to develop, produce, distribute, market, promote, sell, license and support the products and services of the Separated Business, and (b) such other assets as are necessary to operate the Separated Business as an independent and economically viable entity.

ii. Intellectual Property that is used both in a product developed, distributed, or sold by the Applications Business and in a product developed, distributed, or sold by the Operating Systems

Business as of April 27, 2000, shall be assigned to the Applications Business, and the Operating Systems Business shall be granted a perpetual, royalty-free license to license and distribute such Intellectual Property in its products, and, except with respect to such Intellectual Property related to the Internet browser, to develop, license and distribute modified or derivative versions of such Intellectual Property, provided that the Operating Systems Business does not grant rights to such versions to the Applications Business. In the case of such Intellectual Property that is related to the Internet browser, the license shall not grant the Operating Systems Business any right to develop, license, or distribute modified or derivative versions of the Internet browser.

iii. The transfer of ownership of the Separated Business by means of a distribution of stock of the Separated Business to Non-Covered Shareholders of Microsoft, or by other disposition that does not result in a Covered Shareholder owning stock in both the Separated Business and the Remaining Business.

d. Until Implementation of the Plan, Microsoft shall:

i. preserve, maintain, and operate the Operating Systems Business and the Applications Business as ongoing, economically viable businesses, with management, sales, products, and operations of each business held as separate, distinct and apart from one another as they were on April 27, 2000, except to provide the accounting, management, and information services or other necessary support functions provided by Microsoft prior to the entryof this Final Judgment;

ii. use all reasonable efforts to maintain and increase the sales and revenues of both the products produced or sold by the Operating Systems Business and those produced or sold by the Applications Business prior to the Implementation of the Plan and to support research and development and business development efforts of both the Operating Systems Business and the Applications Business;

iii. take no action that undermines, frustrates, interferes with, or makes more difficult the divestiture required by this Final Judgment without the prior approval of the Court;

and iv. file a report with the Court 90 days after entry of this Final Judgment on the steps Microsoft has taken to comply with the requirements of this section 1.d.

基于庭审记录及审判程序，在 2000 年 6 月 7 日裁定、判决并宣告如下：

1. 拆分

a. 在做出本判决后 4 个月内，微软应当向本院和诸原告递交拆分计划，诸原告应当自收到该计划起 60 日内将其对拆分计划的反对意见递交本院。微软应当于收到原告反对意见的 30 日内递交答复意见。

b. 本院批准最终拆分计划（以下简称"计划"）后，微软应当实施该计划。

c. 该计划应当规定（微软）在本判决第 6a 条规定的上诉的 12 个月的期限内，完成下列行为：

（ⅰ）将操作系统业务从应用软件业务中独立出来，并将操作系统业务的资产转移到一个独立的实体中去。这些资产包括(a)用于操作系统的开发、生产、分销、市场开拓、推广、销售、许可、产品与服务支持的全体员工、系统及其他有形资产和无形资产（包括知识产权）；(b)为保证操作系统作为一个独立的、有经济效益的实体运行所必需的其他资产。

（ⅱ）自 2000 年 4 月 27 日起，用于应用软件业务产品开发、分销或销售的知识产权和用于操作系统业务产品开发、分销或销售的知识产权应当属于应用软件业务。授予操作系统业务永久免费使用特许证，允许其许可并在其产品上使用上述知识产权。如果操作系统业务不将上述知识产权的改进或者派生版本授权给应用软件业务，则允许操作系统业务开发、许可和分销知识产权的上述版本，但是与互联网浏览器有关的知识产权除外。如果上述知识产权与互联网浏览器有关，则不得授予操作系统业务任何开发许可、分销互联网浏览器改进或者派生版本的权利。

(iii) 转移操作系统业务所有权的方式为：将该业务的股票分配给微软公司的非公司成员股东，或者用其他处理方式使微软的本公司成员股东不同时持有独立出来的业务和保留下来的业务的股票。

d. 直到实施拆分计划时，微软应当：

（i）通过经营、销售、生产和运行自 2000 年 4 月 27 日起各自独立的操作系统业务与应用软件业务，来保持、维护各业务连续有效运行，判决前由微软提供的财务、管理、信息服务或其他必要的支持功能除外。

（ii）尽力保持和增长在实施拆分计划之前由操作系统公司和应用软件公司各自生产或销售的产品的销售和收入，尽力支持操作系统公司和应用软件公司的科研、开发及各自业务开发的成果。

（iii）未经本院许可不得采取措施破坏、阻挠、干涉本判决规定的拆分，或者为拆分制造困难。

(iv) 微软在判决后的 90 日内向本院报告它为遵守第 1d 条要求所采取的措施。

【案件影响】（Impact of the Case）

本案因微软凭借其视窗软件操作系统优势在"视窗 98"系统内置入"探索者"浏览器，从而扼杀了对手在以浏览器为主的互联网市场上的竞争机会而引发。2000 年 6 月 7 日杰克逊法官做出拆分微软公司判决后，微软上诉主张杰克逊法官对其抱有成见。2001 年 6 月，哥伦比亚特区联邦上诉法院驳回地方法院的判决，并将案件发回地方法院，由一个新法官重新审理。在案件重新审理期间，微软公司与司法部谈判表示愿意放松对个人电脑制造商的许可限制，最终微软反垄断案在美国以达成和解协议而告终。

确定垄断的标准，是打击非法垄断、维护竞争秩序的先决条件。美国《谢尔曼法》对于大型企业的垄断一直给以重点防范和打击。尽管有人对此提出质疑，称对大型企业接二连三的垄断指控是对成功者的处罚，会挫伤这些公司进取的积极性，但不可否认，美国《谢尔曼法》的运用有效地遏制了非法垄断不断膨胀的势头，对于维护自由竞争和经济秩序起到了积极作用。

【思考问题】（Questions）

1. 依据美国《谢尔曼法》，应如何认定一个企业构成垄断？
2. 由检察机关作为反垄断法的原告，在我国是否有法律依据？

九、证券法案例

美国诉奥海根案

United States v. O'Hagan（1996）

【选读理由】（Selected Reason）

传统的依赖关系理论以内部人负有忠实或依赖义务作为构成内幕交易责任的前提条件，但这一理论在奥海根案中遇到了困局。在收购要约公布前已离职的奥海根，即交易相对人并不承担任何忠实或依赖义务。在本案中美国联邦最高法院基于管制内幕交易以维护证券市场安全、增强投资人信心的考虑，构建了"盗用"理论，对原有归责原则进行了发展性诠释。

【案件事实】（Facts）

Respondent James Herman O'Hagan was a partner in the law firm of Dorsey & Whitney in Minneapolis, Minnesota. In July 1988, Grand Metropolitan PLC (Grand Met), a company based in London, England, retained Dorsey & Whitney as local counsel to represent Grand Met regarding a potential tender offer for the common stock of the Pillsbury Company, headquartered in Minneapolis. Both Grand Met and Dorsey & Whitney took precautions to protect the confidentiality of Grand Met's tender offer plans. O'Hagan did no work on the Grand Met representation. Dorsey & Whitney withdrew from representing Grand Met on September 9, 1988. Less than a month later, on October 4, 1988, Grand Met publicly announced its tender offer for Pillsbury stock.

被告詹姆斯·赫曼·奥海根是位于明尼苏达州明尼波利斯市 Dorsey & Whitney 律师事务所的一名合伙人。1988 年 7 月，位于英国伦敦的 Grand Met 公司欲公开收购位于明尼波利斯市的公司 Pillsbury，委托 Dorsey & Whitney 律师事务所代理其法律事务。Grand Met 和 Dorsey & Whitney 均对收购计划采取了适当的保密措施。奥海根本人亦未参与收购事务。1988 年 9 月 9 日 Dorsey & Whitney 辞去委托。10 月 4 日，Grand Met 公开了其对 Pillsbury 公司的收购要约。

On August 18, 1988, while Dorsey & Whitney was still representing Grand Met, O'Hagan began purchasing call options for Pillsbury stock. Each option gave him the right to purchase 100 shares of Pillsbury stock by a specified date in September 1988. Later in August and in September, O'Hagan made additional purchases of Pillsbury call options. By the end of September, he owned 2,500 unexpired Pillsbury options, apparently more than any other individual investor. O'Hagan also purchased, in September 1988, some 5,000 shares of Pillsbury common stock, at a price just under $ 39 per share. When Grand Met announced its tender offer in October, the price of Pillsbury stock rose to nearly $ 60 per share. O'Hagan then sold his Pillsbury call options and common stock, making a profit of more than $ 4.3 million.

1988 年 8 月 18 日，委托合同持续期间，奥海根购买了 Pillsbury 公司的股票购买期权，每份期权赋予其于 1988 年 9 月特定日期前购买 100 股普通股的权利。其后 8、9 月间，奥海根购入了更多股票购买期权。到 9 月底，他持有 2500 份未到期期权，是同期个人投资者中持有数最多的。同时，奥海根以每股 39 美元买入了 5000 股普通股。当 Grand Met 于 10 月公开其收购要约时，股价涨至每股 60 美元。奥海根抛出所持股票与购买的期权，获利超过 430 万美元。

The Securities and Exchange Commission (SEC) subsequently commenced an investigation of O'Hagan and others who had heavily invested in Pillsbury securities shortly before its takeover by Grand Met. O'Hagan later was charged in a 57-count indictment for mail fraud, securities fraud, and money laundering. The indictment alleged that O'Hagan defrauded his law firm and its client, Grand Met, by using for his own trading purposes material, nonpublic information regarding Grand Met's planned tender offer. The case proceeded to trial, and a jury convicted O'Hagan on all 57 counts. The district court sentenced O'Hagan to 41 months of imprisonment.

证券交易委员会随后对奥海根以及其他在收购前大量购入股票的人展开了调查。奥海根因邮件欺诈、证券欺诈和洗钱共获 57 项指控。起诉书称奥海根利用其所在律师事务所与其客户间未公开的收购信息，谋取私利，构成欺诈。案件进入到审判阶段，陪审团裁决 57 项罪名成立。地方法院判了奥海根 41 个月有期徒刑。

This case concerns the interpretation and enforcement of §10(b) and §14(e) of the *Securities Exchange Act* of 1934, and rules made by the Securities and Exchange Commission pursuant to these provisions, Rule 10b-5 and Rule 14e-3(a). Two prime questions are presented. The first relates to the misappropriation of material, nonpublic information for securities trading; the second concerns fraudulent practices in the tender offer setting. In particular, we address and resolve these issues: (1) Is a person who trades in securities for personal profit, using confidential information misappropriated in breach of a fiduciary duty to the source of the information, guilty of violating §10(b) and Rule 10b-5? (2) Did the Commission exceed its rulemaking authority by adopting Rule 14e-3(a), which proscribes trading on undisclosed information in the tender offer setting, even in the absence of a duty to disclose?

该案涉及 1934 年《证券交易法》第 10（b）条及第 14（e）条，以及证券交易委员会据此制定规则 10b-5 和规则 14e-3（a）的解释及适用。两个问题由此提出，一是证券交易中实质性未公开信息的盗用；二是要约收购中的欺诈。本案争议点如下：第一，违反对信息来源所负忠实义务的人，盗用重要信息以谋私利买卖证券行为，是否构成《证券交易法》10（b）条款以及规则 10b-5 条之罪？第二，证券交易委员会规则 14e-3（a）条规定，公开收购时，禁止利用未经披露的信息进行交易，该规定并未以披露义务的存在为前提，是否超越证券交易法 14（e）条款的授权？

【裁决过程与结果】（Procedure and Disposition）

The case proceeded to trial, and a jury convicted O'Hagan on all 57 counts. The district court sentenced O'Hagan to 41 months of imprisonment. O'Hagan appealed. A divided panel of the Court of Appeals for the Eighth Circuit reversed all of O'Hagan's convictions. On certiorari, the United States Supreme Court reversed, in 7-2 majority, the Eighth Circuit's judgment and remanded the case to the Eighth Circuit.

【裁判理由】（Reasons for Judicial Decision）

【原审判决意见】（Opinion by HANSEN）

The touchstones of 10(b) liability then, are "manipulation" and "deception" "in connection with the purchase or sale of any security". Our focus in this case is on the deception element of 10(b). The first theory is what has been termed the "classical theory". The gravamen of the classical theory is that the "insider owes a fiduciary duty to the corporation's shareholders not to trade on inside information for his personal benefit". This theory, however, does not reach those individuals who trade securities based on material, nonpublic information and who owe no fiduciary duty to the shareholders of the company whose securities are traded; these persons are the so-called "outsiders."

10（b）条款下责任的标准是与买卖证券相关的"操纵"与"欺诈"。本案的焦点是 10（b）条款下的欺诈。第一种理论被称为"传统理论"。传统理论的核心在于内部人基于对公司股东的忠实义务不得以其内部信息谋取私利。这一理论并不涉及那些基于非公开信息进行证券交易以及对公司股东不负有忠实义务的交易者，这些人被称为"外部人"。

The misappropriation theory extends the reach to outsiders who would not ordinarily be deemed fiduciaries of the corporate entities in whose stock they trade. It focuses not on the insider's fiduciary duty to the issuing company or its shareholders but on whether the insider breached a fiduciary duty to any lawful possessor of material non-public information.

盗用理论将规则 10b-5 扩大适用于外部人。其关注点不在于内部人对公司或股东的忠实义务上，而在于内部人对任何未公开信息的知情者是否有忠实义务。

In the case, the government proceeded against O'Hagan on the 10(b) and Rule 10b-5 counts under the misappropriation theory. The government contended that O'Hagan breached a fiduciary duty to Dorsey & Whitney and Grand Met when, through his employment at Dorsey & Whitney, he obtained confidential, material, and nonpublic information concerning Grand Met's interest in acquiring Pillsbury, and subsequently used that information as a basis for trading in Pillsbury securities. O'Hagan contends that the misappropriation theory is an impermissible basis upon which to impose 10(b) liability. Specifically, he argues that the theory cannot be squared with either the plain text of 10(b) or the Supreme Court's teachings regarding the scope of conduct that may be regulated under that statute.

本案中，政府根据盗用理论起诉奥海根违反 10（b）条款以及规则 10b-5。政府诉称奥海根在受雇于 Dorsey & Whitney 期间获取了涉及 Grand Met 公司收购的未公开信息，并随后利用这些信息进行股票交易，违反了对 Dorsey & Whitney 律师事务所以及对 Grand Met 公司的忠实义务。奥海根主张盗用理论不能适用于 10（b）条款下的责任。

we hold that 10(b) liability cannot be based on the misappropriation theory. We reject the misappropriation theory, in part, because it permits the imposition of 10(b) liability based upon the mere breach of a fiduciary duty without a particularized showing of misrepresentation or nondisclosure. A careful reading of the Supreme Court's decisions in *Chiarella*, *Dirks*, and *Central Bank* reveals that only a breach of a duty to parties to the securities transaction or, at the most, to other market participants such as investors, will be sufficient to give rise to 10(b) liability.

我们认为 10（b）条款下的责任不能建立在盗用理论基础上。部分原因是盗用理论不以不实陈述或未披露信息为要件，不符合本法的规定。检视最高法院在 Chiarella 案、Dirks 案以及 Central Bank 案的判决后，我们认为 10（b）条款下的责任仅在违反针对证券交易当事人义务或至多对其他市场参与者诸如投资者的义务时承担。

Accordingly, we hold that the misappropriation theory is not a valid basis upon which to impose criminal liability under 10(b). Thus, because O'Hagan's convictions for securities fraud under 10(b) and Rule 10b-5 in Counts 21-37 were premised solely on the misappropriation theory, these convictions must be vacated.

因此，我们认为盗用理论不能构成 10（b）条款下的刑事责任的理论基础。由此，基于奥海根违反 10（b）条款及规则 10 b-5 的证券欺诈指控第 21 项至第 37 项的裁决必须被撤销。

The first sentence in 14(e) was enacted in 1968 as part of the Williams Act. The purpose of the Williams Act is to insure that public shareholders who are confronted by a cash tender offer for their stock will not be required to respond without adequate information. The legislative history thus shows that the sole purpose of the *Williams Act* was the protection of investors who are confronted with a tender offer. The second sentence of 14(e) is a rulemaking provision that was enacted in 1970, two years after the original *Williams act*. Rule 14e-3(a) is a disclosure provision. An individual violates the rule when "he trades on the basis of material nonpublic information concerning a pending tender offer that he knows or has reason to know has been acquired 'directly or indirectly' from an insider of the offeror or issuer, or someone working on their behalf." Thus, the rule creates a duty to disclose this information, or to abstain from trading, "regardless of whether such information was obtained through a breach of fiduciary duty." "creates a duty in those traders who fall within its ambit to abstain or disclose, without regard to whether the trader owes a pre-existing fiduciary duty to respect the confidentiality of the information."

14（e）条款第一句于 1968 年出现在《威廉姆斯法案》中。该法案旨在确保要约收购中股东有权获取足够信息。立法史表明了《威廉姆斯法案》保护投资者的宗旨。第二句制定于 1970 年，比《威廉姆斯法案》晚两年。规则 14e-3（a）是有关信息披露的规范。任何人只要持有有关要约收购的内幕信息，并且知道或应当知道此信息系源自收购方，那么无论其身份如何或以何种方式获得该信息，也无论其与收购方之间是否直接或间接地存在信任关系，均不得未经披露而利用该信息买卖目标公司的股票。

We thus turn our attention to the text of 14(e). The statute empowers the SEC to "define" and "prescribe means reasonably designed to prevent" "acts and practices" which are "fraudulent." Thus, by dissecting the language and structure of the statute, it becomes clear that the terms "define" and "prescribe" relate to "acts and practices" meeting the statutory definition of "fraudulent." A straightforward exercise in statutory construction then affords no basis for concluding that 14(e) authorizes the SEC to create its own definition of fraud in implementing the statute. Simply put, the enabling provision of 14(e) permits the SEC to identify and regulate those "acts and practices" which fall within the 14(e) legal definition of "fraudulent," but it does not grant the SEC a license to redefine the term.

对《证券交易法》第 14 条进行的文义分析表明，法规仅授权证券交易委员会对欺诈的具体行为或实践进行界定与描述。从法条的语言及结构上看，界定与描述须与法律对欺诈的定义相符。关于何为欺诈，法律早有界定，并未授权证券交易委员会重新界定。

In Schreiber, the Court explicitly held that 14(e) is modeled after the broad antifraud provisions of 10(b) and Rule 10(b)-5. Moreover, in the course of interpreting manipulation, the Court turned to the meaning that term had been given under 10(b), noting that "Congress used the phrase 'manipulative or deceptive' in 10(b) as well, and we have interpreted 'manipulative' in that context to require misrepresentation." We note that 10(b) and 14(e) are contained in the same statutory enactment, the Securities Exchange Act of 1934—strong evidence that the terms are to be given the same meaning. Chiarella held that fraudulent under 10(b) requires the breach of a fiduciary obligation. Accordingly, we hold that "fraudulent" under 14(e) must be interpreted to require the breach of a fiduciary obligation or similar trust relationship.

在 Schreiber 案中，法院明确表明证券交易法第 14 条之立法模式是仿照 10（b）条款以及规则 10（b）-5。此外，此案中对于操纵的定义是回溯到第 10 条中去看的，因此第 14 条的解释也要回到第 10 条。第 10 条与第 14 条共存于同一部法律规范中，其术语应有相同含义。在 Chiarella 案中，法院认为 10（b）条款下的欺诈要求违背忠实义务。因此，我们认为 14（e）条款下的欺诈必须被解释为以违背忠实义务或其他类似信任关系为前提。

We hold that the SEC exceeded its rulemaking authority under 14(e) when it promulgated Rule 14e-3(a) without including a requirement of a breach of a fiduciary obligation. Accordingly, we must vacate O'Hagan's securities fraud convictions under these provisions.

我们认为证券交易委员会规则 14e-3（a）中未规定忠实义务属越权立法，因此，奥海根据此构成的证据欺诈罪裁决须予以撤销。

【生效判决意见】（Opinion by GINSBERG）

A person who trades in securities for personal profit, using confidential information misappropriated in breach of a fiduciary duty to the source of the information, may be held liable for violating 10(b) and Rule 10(b)-5.

为谋取私利，利用违反对信息来源忠实义务获得的保密信息进行证券交易可能会承担违反 10（b）条款及规则 10（b）-5 项下的责任。

Section 10(b) proscribes (1) using any "deceptive device" (2) "in connection with the purchase or sale of any security," in contravention of SEC rules. The Commission adopted Rule 10(b)-5 pursuant to its 10(b) rulemaking authority; liability under Rule 10(b)-5 does not extend beyond conduct encompassed by 10(b)'s prohibition. Under the "traditional" or "classical theory" of insider trading liability, a violation of 10(b)and Rule 10(b)-5 occurs when a corporate insider trades in his corporation's securities on the basis of material, confidential information he has obtained by reason of his position. Such trading qualifies as a "deceptive device" because there is a relationship of trust and confidence between the corporation's shareholders and the insider that gives rise to a duty to disclose or abstain from trading. Under the complementary "misappropriation theory" urged by the Government here, a corporate "outsider" violates 10(b) and Rule 10(b)-5 when he misappropriates confidential information for securities trading purposes, in breach of a fiduciary duty owed to the source of the information, rather than to the persons with whom he trades.

10（b）条款包括下列两个要件：（1）欺骗行为；（2）与证券买卖有关。证券交易委员会根据 10（b）条款制定了规则 10（b）-5，两项规则下义务范围完全一致。依据内幕交易责任的传统理论，内部人基于其地位获取信息买入股票即违反 10（b）条款和规则 10（b）-5。此种交易被冠以欺诈是因为内部人和公司股东间存在一种信赖关系，这种关系导致对内幕信息要么披露，要么放弃。根据盗用理论，外部人盗用机密信息买卖证券谋取私利也违反了 10（b）条款和规则 10（b）-5，因其违反了作为信息来源人，而不仅仅是信息相对人的忠实义务。

Misappropriation, as just defined, is the proper subject of a 10(b) charge because it meets the statutory requirement that there be "deceptive" conduct "in connection with" a securities transaction. First, misappropriators deal in deception: A fiduciary who pretends loyalty to the principal while secretly converting the principal's information for personal gain dupes or defrauds the principal. A company's confidential information qualifies as property to which the company has a right of exclusive use; the undisclosed misappropriation of such information constitutes fraud akin to embezzlement. Deception through nondisclosure is central to liability under the misappropriation theory. Conversely, full disclosure forecloses liability: Because the deception essential to the theory involves feigning fidelity to the information's source, if the fiduciary discloses to the source that he plans to trade on the information, there is no "deceptive device" and thus no 10(b) violation. Second, 10(b)'s requirement that the misappropriator's deceptive use of information be "in connection with the purchase or sale of [a] security" is satisfied by the misappropriation theory because the fiduciary's fraud is consummated, not when he obtains the confidential information, but when, without disclosure to his principal, he uses the information in purchasing or selling securities. The transaction and the breach of duty coincide, even though the person or entity defrauded is not the other party to the trade, but is, instead, the source of the nonpublic information. Because undisclosed trading on the basis of misappropriated, nonpublic information both deceives the source of the information and harms members of the investing public, the misappropriation theory is tuned to an animating purpose of the Exchange Act: to ensure honest markets, thereby promoting investor confidence.

盗用，正如定义所述，与根据 10（b）条款进行控告要满足法定要求相吻合，即证券交易中有欺诈行为。其一，盗用者进行欺诈交易：受托人假意忠诚于委托人，欺骗委托人，利用委托人的信息谋取私利。公司的保密信息被视为公司财产，公司对此有专用权。秘密滥用此类信息等同于挪用公司财产。通过不披露信息进行欺诈是盗用理论承担责任的核心。相反的，全部披露排除了责任，因为本理论中的核心要素欺诈包含着对信息来源的假意忠诚。若受托人向交易信息的来源披露了其信息交易计划，欺诈就不复存在，进而也不会违反 10（b）条款。其二，10（b）条款中规定的盗用者的欺诈行为应与买卖证券相关的规定满足了盗用理论，因受托人的欺诈行为并非成就于其获取秘密信息时，而在于利用信息买卖证券而未将其披露给其委托人时。即使受欺诈者不是交易的相对方而是信息来源者，交易的同时也违反了义务。因为基于盗用的秘密交易以及非公开信息不但欺骗了信息来源者，同时也损害了公众投资者的利益，所以盗用理论和证券交易法的宗旨相吻合：确保市场安全从而增强投资者信心。

Vital to this Court's decision that criminal liability may be sustained under the misappropriation theory is the Exchange Act's requirement that the Government prove that a person "willfully" violated Rule 10(b)-5 in order to establish a criminal violation, and the Act's provision that a defendant may not be imprisoned for such a violation if he proves that he had no knowledge of the Rule.

法院判决的关键是盗用理论下刑事责任的承担符合证券法的规定，政府须证明被告有违法的故意，而且法律规定，若被告并不知晓规则 10（b）-5 的规定，则不能因此受到追究。

As relevant to this case, the SEC did not exceed its rulemaking authority under 14(e) by adopting Rule 14e-3(a) without requiring a showing that the trading at issue entailed a breach of fiduciary duty. Section 14(e) prohibits "fraudulent...acts...in connection with any tender offer," and authorizes the SEC to "define, and prescribe means reasonably designed to prevent, such acts." Adopted under that statutory authorization, Rule 14e-3(a) forbids any person to trade on the basis of material, nonpublic information that concerns a tender offer and that the person knows or should know has been acquired from an insider of the offeror or issuer, or someone working on their behalf, unless within a reasonable time before any purchase or sale such information and its source are publicly disclosed. Rule 14e-3(a) imposes a duty to disclose or abstain from trading whether or not the trader owes a fiduciary duty to respect the confidentiality of the information.

与此案件相关的是，证券交易委员会根据 14（e）条款制定的规则 14e-3（a）中未要求违反信托义务的规定并未超越其立法权限。14（e）条款规定了涉及收购要约的欺诈行为，而且授权证券交易委员会对此类行为进行界定。在法律授权下，规则 14e-3（a）禁止任何人在明知或应知该信息来源于内部人诸如要约人、发行人或其雇员的情况下，利用保密的要约收购信息进行交易，除非在买卖证券前的合理期限内该信息被披露。规则 14e-3（a）要求交易人对保密信息或选择披露或放弃交易，不论其是否负有信托义务。

【案件影响】（Impact of the Case）

出于打击证券欺诈的考虑，美国实务界一直在探索内幕交易的主体范围。最早的"平等享有信息理论"，秉承"非公开即禁止"将所有人不加区分地纳入内幕交易的责任主体，虽有利于打击，但法律层面上失于严谨。Chiarella 案后，法院以忠实与依赖义务作为承担责任的前提，虽界定清晰，但法网失之过宽。盗用理论的提出，正是在忠实与依赖义务的基础上，将内幕交易的主体范围扩展到外部人，体现了对证券市场以及投资者信心的保障。

【思考问题】（Questions）

1. 除"盗用理论"外，美国在内幕交易执法实践中用于追究内幕交易人员责任的理论还有哪些？

2. 如何加大我国对证券内幕交易行为的打击力度？

十、信托法案例

巴特利特诉巴克莱银行信托公司案
Bartlett v. Barclays Bank Trust co.（1980）

【选读理由】（Selected Reason）

信托因其特有的财产管理模式适合现代商业社会的财产状况与投资理财观念，被越来越广泛地应用于现代民商事活动中。作为调整信托法律关系的信托法在各国法律体系中的地位日益凸显。英国具有悠久的信托法历史与发达的信托法体系。受托人的信义义务是信托法律问题的重要内容，因为受托人作为信托财产的守护者和信托财产的法律上的所有权人，对信托财产处于绝对优势的控制地位，而受益人作为利益上的所有权人处于相对弱势地位。如果没有法律对受托人进行约束，就难免发生占有财产者滥用其地位的情形。实践中对受托人有没有尽到信义义务的判断标准很难把握。虽然英国于 1925 年制定了《受托人法》、1961 年制定了《受托人投资法》等，但在判决中起重要决定作用的还是一系列有约束力的判例。1980 年英国高等法院大法官庭审理的巴特利特诉巴克莱银行信托公司案（Bartlett v. Barclays Bank Trust Co.）是具有现代商事信托典型意义的重要案例。

【案件事实】（Facts）

This is an action against a trust corporation for breach of trust. It is claimed that the trust corporation, and its banking predecessor ("the bank"), failed to exercise proper supervision over the management of a family company which they controlled. As a result, it is said, the trust suffered an avoidable loss in excess of £1/2 million due to a disastrous property speculation by the company.

这是一个起诉信托公司违反信托义务的案件。原告诉称信托公司和它的作为银行的前身（简称银行）未能对它们所控制的一个家族公司行使正当的管理监督权，这导致委托人因为这家公司的损失惨重的财产投机行为而遭受了本可避免的超过 50 万英镑的损失。

On 23rd July 1920 Sir Herbert Bartlett Bt made a settlement for the benefit of his wife and issue. The trustee was Barclays Bank Ltd. The settled property consisted of debenture stock and 498 (later 499) out of 500 shares in Bartletts Trust Ltd ("BTL"). This company had been incorporated in the previous May to take over and manage properties belonging to Sir Herbert and his wife. By 1960, after both had died, there were seven settled shares in the trust fund. Five of the settled shares were held on trusts for the benefit of the settlor's five surviving children. Each child had a life interest and a power to appoint income to a surviving spouse. Subject thereto the capital was divisible between the issue of the life tenant living at the life tenant's death; failing issue, there was an accruer to the other shares.

1920 年 7 月 23 日，准男爵赫伯特·巴特利特先生将其妻子作为受益人进行了一项信托，受托人是巴克莱银行公司。移交的信托资产包括公司债券和巴特利特信托公司（简称 BTL）

500 份股份中的 498 份（后来变成 499 份）。巴特利特信托公司在之前的 5 月份已经注册成立，可以接受和管理属于赫伯特和他妻子的财产。到 1960 年，两人死亡后，信托基金有 7 份股份，其中 5 份处于信托中，受益人是委托人的 5 个仍在世的孩子。每个孩子都有终生的权益可以将信托收益交给其还在世的配偶。这样，资金可以由活着的人在其死亡前指定分配，如果未分配，累积下来的收益会留给其他人。

The property of BTL consisted at this time mainly of some 21 freehold properties with a book value of about £300,000 and ten leasehold properties with a book value of about £250,000. The leases had about 24 to 45 years to run. There were also a number of freehold properties, including reversions to two of the leaseholds, held in a sinking fund for amortising leaseholds, and some investments and a few other assets. The properties were mainly office blocks, shop properties and residential properties, with a rent roll of about £93,000. The company had an office in Victoria Street, London, and at one time a work force for maintenance of buildings.

巴特利特信托公司在这个时候的财产主要包括账面价值约 30 万英镑的 21 个永久业权不动产和账面价值约 25 万英镑的租赁物业，租赁期限大约为 24～45 年。另外还有一些永久业权的物业，包括两个返租的和为摊销土地使用资金而作为偿债基金计提但未表现在账面上的，另外还有一些投资和其他资产。这些资产主要是写字楼、商店和住宅，大约有 9.3 万英镑的租金。这家公司在伦敦维多利亚街有一间办公室，一度还有负责建筑维修的工人团队。

His Lordship, having reviewed the relevant evidence, found of following facts. At a meeting with the BTL board, in February 1961, Mr. Mahony was told that brokers had advised the board, in connection with the proposed public issue of BTL shares, that it would be better if BTL had investments in property development. Mr. Mahony promised to give favourable consideration to such investment by BTL on the footing that any investment was limited to the net proceeds from the sale of the Albany Buildings, ie to some £500,000 to £600,000. At BTL's 1961 annual general meeting the speech of Mr. Roberts, the chairman, included a statement that the BTL board intended to invest available moneys in property development and did not link such investment with the proposed public quotation of BTL shares. The statement disclosed a major change of direction for BTL (into property development) to be taken in the closing stages of the life of the trust. However, Mr. Mahony, though present at the meeting, did not remind Mr. Roberts that the bank had not yet taken advice on, or given further consideration to the policy of investment in property development, and his attendance note merely recorded that everything was under control. Moreover he gave evidence that he regarded the BTL board as a team of well-equipped professionals and was content to leave things to them. From 1961 onwards Mr. Roberts, at BTL's monthly board meetings, introduced various development schemes for consideration by the board but merely disclosed to the bank, at BTL's annual general meetings, such information relating to the schemes as it was considered appropriate to disclose. The board adopted a system of not consulting the bank, unless it was directly involved as a shareholder, and not providing it with a regular flow of information, and merely gave it information in advance of and at BTL's annual general meetings. The transition of BTL to a policy of speculative development did not provoke the bank to make any particular enquiries or alert it to the need for special vigilance. Two of the development projects put forward by Mr. Roberts were at Guildford, a scheme which was likely to cost some £1,250,000, and the redevelopment of a site at the Old Bailey in the City of London. The board embarked on those schemes without consulting the bank. However, throughout Mr. Roberts had acted in a way he thought was justified and calculated to bring benefit to the trust estate.

　　法官经审查相关证据确认了以下事实。在 1961 年 2 月与巴特利特信托公司董事会召开的会议上，马奥尼先生被告知，经纪人已经建议董事会，为了公开发行巴特利特信托公司的股票，最好让巴特利特信托公司先投资房地产开发。马奥尼答应对巴特利特开展此类投资予以优先考虑，但前提是投资资金限于使用出售奥尔巴尼大楼的净收益，即大约 50～60 万英镑。在巴特利特信托公司 1961 年度会议上，主席罗伯茨先生在演讲中声明巴特利特信托公司将投资房地产开发，但没有将这些投资事项与巴特利特信托公司股份被建议公开发行联系起来。这一声明披露了巴特利特信托公司在此后的信托期间内的房地产开发发展方向。然而，出席会议的马奥尼先生并没有提醒罗伯茨先生当时银行尚未采纳该建议，或在房地产开发投资政策上做进一步思考，他的会议笔记仅仅记录一切都在控制之下。而且他给出的证据表明，巴特利特信托公司董事会是一个配置完善的职业团队，可以将事情交给他们。从 1961 年起，罗伯茨先生在巴特利特信托公司每月的董事会会议上，介绍了董事会所考虑的各种发展计划，但仅仅在年度大会上透露一些他认为适宜透露给银行的有关发展计划的信息。董事会通过了一套不咨询银行的制度，也不会为银行定期提供信息，只是在年度大会之前或会上给银行提供一些信息，除非银行作为股东直接参与。巴特利特信托公司向投机性发展政策的转变没有引起银行的任何问询或向它做出任何必要的专门警示。由罗伯茨先生推进的两个开发项目一个在吉尔福德，需花费约 125 万英镑，另一个是重建伦敦老贝利街项目。董事会没有就开展这些计划咨询银行。然而，在罗伯茨先生的整个行动中，他认为这是合理的，并预计可以为信托财产带来利益。

At the November 1962 board meeting Mr. Roberts reported that details of the Old Bailey scheme were being prepared, that planning consent would "probably" be available for office user on redevelopment of the area and that a company called Far Investments Ltd ("Far") was to be incorporated to make purchases on the site. Mr. Mahony first learned of the Old Bailey scheme at a meeting with Mr. Roberts in January 1963 and despite Mr. Roberts' promise to give the bank written details of the scheme, he never did so and Mr. Mahony did not remind him to do so. An application for permission to develop the site was refused in March 1964 but the refusal was not disclosed to the bank at the 1964 annual general meeting. The disclosure by Mr. Roberts to Mr. Mahony, in January 1965, that planning consent for the site had not been obtained and that it could be ten years before development of the site could be undertaken elicited no reaction from Mr. Mahony. At the 1965 annual general meeting, at which Mr. Mahony's successor was present, it was reported that negotiations with the City of London Corporation on the Old Bailey scheme had been suspended but that the board were satisfied the scheme would eventually be carried out and would produce an adequate return. In fact prospects for the scheme were poor. No report on the scheme appeared in the bank's files in consequence of the report made at the 1965 annual general meeting. The Guildford development scheme, due to the intervention of another development company, resulted in a capital profit of £271,000.

　　在 1962 年 11 月的董事会会议上，罗伯茨汇报说已经准备好了老贝利街项目计划的细节，称"可能"获得规划同意以在该地区重建办公楼，设立了一家名为远大投资有限公司的公司来购买。马奥尼在 1963 年 1 月与罗伯茨先生的一次会议上第一次了解到老贝利街项目方案。尽管罗伯茨先生承诺给银行有关该方案的书面细节，但他从来没有这么做，马奥尼也没提醒他这么做。有关开发这一区域的许可申请在 1964 年 3 月被拒绝了，但这一被拒绝的情况在 1964 年的股东大会上未向银行披露。1965 年 1 月，罗伯茨向马奥尼透露，未获得开发该区域的规划许可，这一可能在 10 年后才能实施的区域开发计划未引起马奥尼的反应。在 1965 年的股东大会上，马奥尼的继任者出席，据汇报，在老贝利街开发计划上与伦敦城市公司的谈判已经中止，但最终董事会满意地看到该计划实施并将获得足够的回报。但实际上该项目前景很差。1965 年大会报告之后所提交给银行的文件中未提及该项目。吉尔福德的开发方案，由于另一个开发公司的介入，获得了 27.1 万英镑的投资收益。

At the 1966 annual general meeting the board reported that the Old Bailey scheme had been halted because of planning and licensing difficulties but that interim arrangements were being made to increase the present income from the scheme until it could be revived. In fact Far had decided not to buy any further properties on the site unless they would show an adequate return. At the end of 1967 BTL became a wholly owned subsidiary of Bartlett Trust Holdings Ltd ("BTH"). By the end of 1967 the Old Bailey scheme was a white elephant and the BTH board authorised Mr. Roberts to approach the City of London Corporation with a view to selling the site to the corporation.

As at 31st March 1968 BTL's loan to Far amounted to the principal sum of £245,650, and arrears of interest from Far amounted to over £49,000. No mention was made at the 1967 annual general meeting that the site was up for sale. However at the 1973 annual general meeting it was reported that further property purchases on the site were being negotiated by Far to give BTH more than 50% of the proposed development site and that BTH might put up further cash of £ 550,000 for the purchase of the properties. Further properties on the site were bought in 1973 as a result of which the loan account to Far, as shown in the 1973 accounts, increased to £1,035,750, compared with the figure of £376,000 shown in the accounts for the previous year. The end of the property boom put an end to the Old Bailey scheme, and BTH incurred substantial losses on its investment in the scheme with Far, which was probably insolvent. The venture, begun 15 years earlier, without prior consultation with the bank, and continued without any such consultation, had turned out to be an unqualified disaster.

在 1966 年的股东大会上，董事会汇报说老贝利街的开发方案因为规划许可困难已经停止，但已经做出临时安排以提高该开发项目的收入直到它被重启。事实上远大公司已经决定不购买这一区域的任何物业，除非能有充分回报。1967 年底，巴特利特信托公司成为巴特利特信托控股有限公司（简称 BTH）的全资子公司。1967 年，老贝利街方案成为一个维持费用高昂但难以获得经济效益的项目，巴特利特信托控股有限公司的董事会授权罗伯茨先生与伦敦城市公司洽谈，以期将这个区域卖给该公司。

截至 1968 年 3 月 31 日，巴特利特信托公司拖欠远大公司的贷款达到 24.565 万英镑和超过 4.9 万英镑的利息。在 1967 年度大会上，关于这一区域将被出售的事情没有被提及。在 1973 年会议上有汇报称，其正在与远大公司就该区域资产购置进行谈判，将会有一半以上的开发区域卖给巴特利特信托控股公司，巴特利特信托控股公司将筹集 55 万英镑以购买这些物业。更多的区域里的物业在 1973 年被购买了，结果就是对远大公司的负债在 1973 年的报表里增加到了 1035750 英镑，而上一年度这一财务数字是 376000 英镑。所持有资产的激增导致了老贝利街项目结束，巴特利特信托控股公司在该项目上对远大公司的投资遭受了巨大损失，远大公司可能会破产。此项投资，开始于 15 年以前，未事先征询银行的意见，接下来也未做咨询，已演变为一场绝对的灾难。

The shares in BTH were sold in September 1978 for £4,490,000. The market value of the shares in BTH would have been greater if BTH had not lost a large sum of money on its investment in Far. By how much the value would have been increased has not yet been argued.

In August 1977 a writ was issued against Barclays Bank Trust Co. The plaintiffs claim that the bank is liable to make good to the trust fund all loss accruing by reason of the various defaults specified in paras 24 to 35 of the statement of claim, broadly speaking the default of the bank in permitting BTL and BTH to engage in property development of the sort which I have indicated. They seek appropriate enquiries in order to establish their loss.

巴特利特信托控股公司的股份在 1978 年 9 月卖了 449 万英镑。如果该公司没有就在对远大的投资中遭受大额损失，该股份的市场价值应该更高。但还没有讨论会增加多少价值。

1977 年 8 月起诉巴克莱银行信托有限公司的诉状被签发了。原告诉称银行应对信托资金因上述各种过错所遭受的损失承担责任。概括地说，银行在允许巴特利特信托公司和巴特利特信托控股公司参与房地产开发方面未尽到职责。他们寻求适当的调查以便确认他们的损失。

【裁决过程与结果】（Procedure and Disposition）

By a writ dated 19th August 1977 and a subsequent statement of claim the plaintiffs, Sir Basil Bartlett Bt, Irene Theodora Bartlett, Henry David Hardington Bartlett, Sheila Bartlett, Norman Alaric Bartlett, Hazel Leslie Ellwood, Derek Bartlett and Edwina Boldero, beneficiaries under a settlement dated 23rd July 1920, claimed against the defendant, Barclays Bank Trust Co Ltd ("the bank"), the trustee of the settlement, declarations that the bank was liable to reconstitute the trust fund subject to the settlement by making good to the fund all loss which had accrued or might accrue to the fund by reason of certain alleged breaches of trust, and an enquiry as to the loss which had already accrued or might accrue to the fund by reason of the breaches of trust. Judge Brightman J of Chancery Division read the judgment which sets out the facts on July 31, 1979. Brightman J held that the bank as trustee was guilty of wilful default in certain respects by the omission to do that which a prudent trustee ought to have done and was liable to make good the loss to the trust fund caused by the breaches of trust. On January15, 1980, Brightman J issued another judgment on the question about the amount of the compensation payable by the trustee to the plaintiffs.

【裁判理由】（Reasons for Judicial Decision）

【生效判决意见】（JUDGMENT BY BRIGHTMAN J）

I turn to the question, what was the duty of the bank as the holder of shares in BTL and BTH? I will first answer this question without regard to the position of the bank as a specialist trustee, to which I will advert later. The bank, as trustee, was bound to act in relation to the shares and to the controlling position which they conferred, in the same manner as a prudent man of business. The prudent man of business will act in such manner as is necessary to safeguard his investment. He will do this in two ways. If facts come to his knowledge which tell him that the company's affairs are not being conducted as they should be, or which put him on enquiry, he will take appropriate action. Appropriate action will no doubt consist in the first instance of enquiry of and consultation with the directors, and in the last but most unlikely resort, the convening of a general meeting to replace one or more directors. What the prudent man of business will not do is to content himself with the receipt of such information on the affairs of the company as a shareholder ordinarily receives at annual general meetings. Since he has the power to do so, he will go further and see that he has sufficient information to enable him to make a responsible decision from time to time either to let matters proceed as they are proceeding, or to intervene if he is dissatisfied.

那么问题是，作为巴特利特信托公司和巴特利特信托控股公司的股东，银行的义务是什么？首先我在不考虑银行为专业受托人的情况下回答这一问题，对于什么是专业受托人我在后面会提到。银行作为受托人，应当采取与一个审慎的商人同样的方式，按照其享有的股份和所被赋予的控制地位行事。审慎的商人将采取必要的措施来保障他的投资。他将用两种方式做这件事。如果所表明的事实告诉他，公司事务不是像应该进行的那样进行，或使他产生疑问，他都会采取适当的行动。毫无疑问适当的行动在于首先开展调查并咨询董事，最后或许会召开股东大会以代替仅咨询一个或多个董事。审慎的商人将不会满足像股东从年度股东大会上获取信息一样获取公司经营事务的信息。因为他有权这样做，他将进一步获得足够的信息以使他能够不断地做出决定以让事情按照计划推进，或在不满意的情况下进行干预。

I am of opinion that a higher duty of care is plainly due from someone like a trust corporation which carries on a specialised business of trust management. A trust corporation holds itself out in its advertising literature as being above ordinary mortals. With a specialist staff of trained trust officers and managers, with ready access to financial information and professional advice, dealing with and solving trust problems day after day, the trust corporation holds itself out, and rightly, as capable of providing an expertise which it would be unrealistic to expect and unjust to demand from the ordinary prudent man or woman who accepts, probably unpaid and sometimes reluctantly from a sense of family duty, the burdens of a trusteeship. Just as, under the law of contract, a professional person possessed of a particular skill is liable for breach of contract if he neglects to use the skill and experience which he professes, so I think that a professional corporate trustee is liable for breach of trust if loss is caused to the trust fund because it neglects to exercise the special care and skill which it professes to have. The advertising literature of the bank was not in evidence (other than the scale of fees) but counsel for the bank did not dispute that trust corporations, including the bank, hold themselves out as possessing a superior ability for the conduct of trust business, and in any event I would take judicial notice of that fact. Having expressed my view of the higher duty required from a trust corporation, I should add that the bank's counsel did not dispute the proposition.

我认为，对于类似信托公司的从事信托管理业务的专业企业应适用更高程度的尽责义务。信托公司通过广告宣扬其比普通人要强。信托公司拥有受过培训的信托员和经理，随时可得到金融信息和专家建议，每天都在处理和解决各种信托问题，信托公司自称，并且也的确如此，它能够提供专门知识和技术。期待普通谨慎的人做到这一点是不现实的，而且要求他们这样做是不公平的，因为普通人很可能没有得到任何报酬，有时是碍于家庭责任感勉强接受了这一负担。这正如合同法下，具备特殊技能的专业人士如果疏于使用其拥有的技能和经验，就要承担违反合同的责任。因此我认为，专业的公司型受托人由于疏于运用其声称的特别的注意和技术导致信托财产受损，要承担违反信托的责任。银行的广告虽不能用来证明（除了收费标准），但信托公司（包括被告银行）的确给人感觉在宣扬自己有更高的能力开展信托业务，对此银行也未否认。对此事实我裁判时会有所关注。在表达了有关信托公司应负有高程度的义务的观点后，我应再补充一下，银行的律师并未对此表示异议。

I hold that the bank failed in its duty whether it is judged by the standard of the prudent man of business or of the skilled trust corporation. The bank's breach of duty caused the loss which was suffered by the trust estate. If the bank had intervened as it could and should have, that loss would not have been incurred. By "loss", I mean the depreciation which took place in the market value of the BTL and BTH shares, by comparison with the value which the shares would have commanded if the loss on the Old Bailey project had not been incurred, and reduction of dividends through loss of income. The bank is liable for the loss so suffered by the trust estate, except to the extent that I shall hereafter indicate.

我认为，无论是按照审慎商人的标准还是按照有技能的信托公司的标准，银行都未尽到其义务。银行违反义务导致信托财产遭受损失。如果银行按照其能做的和应该做的去干预，损失就不会发生。在此"损失"指的是相对于老贝利街项目没有产生损失的情况下股份应有的价值，巴特利特信托公司和巴特利特信托控股公司股份市值的减少，以及相应营业收入的损失而造成的分红的减少。银行应对信托财产遭受的损失承担责任，除非其履行职责达到我下文所表明的程度。

Since the obligation of a defaulting trustee was to effect restitution to the trust estate, and since the default continued until restitution had been made, the capital loss suffered by the three plaintiffs who became absolutely entitled in January 1974 was to be assessed as at September 1978, when the total shareholding was sold, and not as at 25th January 1974 when the settlement came to an end quoad the shareholdings of those plaintiffs.

既然未履行职责的受托人有义务将信托财产恢复原状，既然这一未履行职责的情况在完成恢复原状之前持续，在 1974 年 1 月毫无疑问地成为本案财产受托人的三个原告所遭受的损失应该以 1978 年 9 月为基准评估，此时全部的股份已经售出，而不应该以 1974 年 1 月 25日，即原告们所持股份被转让的时间为基准。

【案件影响】（Impact of the Case）

受托人义务主要包含尽责义务（duty of care 或 duty of care and skill）和忠实义务（duty of loyalty）。尽责义务，称为"恪尽职守的义务"更为贴切，是指信托关系中的受托人应当以通常的技术谨慎地运用信托财产的义务。在利罗伊德诉怀特利（1887）一案中，英国上诉法院已经指出：受托人的职责不是像一个谨慎的人为自己的利益所考虑的那样，相反，他的职责是像一个谨慎的普通人为其他人的利益（他对该人负有道德上的义务）进行投资那样小心谨慎。而本案更是提出了对专业受托人的尽责义务要求，本案法官认为，如果专业受托人自称是某方面的专家，仅仅期望他们像一般谨慎的人那样，恐怕是不现实和不合理的，必须按照他们的技能和职业标准，来判断他们的所作所为。这些专业受托人就是那些专门从事信托业务的信托公司、金融公司、银行信托部。本案实际上大大拓展了商事信托中对受托人专业能力的义务和要求。美国《信托法》也规定：受托人因具有较高的尽责能力而被委托为受托人时，应尽其较高的尽责义务及能力。

【思考问题】（Questions）

1. 民事信托和商事信托的区别是什么？民事信托制度是怎样发展成为商事信托制度的？

2. 我国商事信托相关法律制度中对受托人的尽责义务和忠实义务是怎样规定的？

十一、劳动法案例

诺顿器具公司诉特森案

Norton Tool Co. Ltd v. Tewson（1972）

【选读理由】（Selected Reason）

在劳资关系中，劳资双方的利益需求归属于不同的阶层。资方的利益是一种经营利益，属于高阶层的利益；而劳方的利益是一种生存利益，属于最低阶层的利益。因此，当劳资双方利益发生冲突时，资方可以放弃经营利益，而劳方却不能放弃生存利益。基于资本对劳动力的支配关系，资方经营利益的实现通常以牺牲劳方的生存利益为代价。在很多情况下，解雇就是资方基于对其自身经营利益的追求而牺牲劳方生存利益的行为。

英国《劳动法》在协调劳资关系、保护和救济处于弱者地位的劳动者方面所做出的努力以限制资方的管理者特权和赋予受到不公平解雇的雇员寻求平等、公平和公正的求偿权为目的，为劳动者提供了形式上的法律保障。

【案件事实】（Facts）

An employee aged 50, who had been continuously employed for 11 years, was summarily dismissed following a heated exchange of words between him and one of the employers' directors. Although the employee would normally have been entitled to six weeks' notice or six weeks' wages in lieu, he in fact received neither. The employee's net weekly wage had been £ 25.60. The employee was out of work for four weeks before he obtained other employment where he received wages slightly higher than those he had received from his former employers.

一位 50 岁的雇员在为诺顿器具公司连续工作 11 年后，由于他和雇主任命的一名经理有过激烈言辞冲突而被解雇。虽然雇员通常应享有提前六周的被通知权或六周的替代薪金，但他实际上没有享受到该项权利。该雇员的周薪为 25.60 英镑。该雇员为此失业了 4 周，才找到了一份新工作，新工作的工资略高于原雇主给予的工资。

【裁决过程与结果】（Procedure and Disposition）

Norton Tool Co. Ltd appealed against the decision of an industrial tribunal (chairman B. R. Miles Esq) sitting in London, dated 8th June 1972, that the respondent, Norman John Tewson, be awarded £ 250 by way of compensation for unfair dismissal, on the ground that the tribunal had misdirected itself in law in assessing the amount of compensation payable to the respondent. The respondent cross-appealed.

Appeal dismissed. Cross-appeal allowed. Award of £ 375 compensation substituted.

【裁判理由】（Reasons for Judicial Decision）

【原审意见】

With regard to the [respondent's] loss of wages, he was paid 64p per hour for a 40 hour week which works out at a weekly wage of £ 25.60. He was out of work for 4 weeks so that he has lost 4 weeks wages. In addition we are entitled to take into account the circumstances of his dismissal: the fact that it was abrupt, that a sacking without notice involves a degree of stigma and that furthermore the [respondent] had 11 years' service with the [appellants] and he has lost the benefit of that.

关于被告的工资损失，他时薪为 64 便士，每周工作 40 小时，周薪为 25.60 英镑。他失业 4 周，因此损失了 4 周的工资。此外，我们应考虑他被解雇的情形：该解雇是突然的，没有提前通知的解雇有着一定程度的缺陷，并且被告已为上诉人服务了 11 年，他损失了该项利益。

Section 116 of the *1971 Act* sets out the general principles to be applied in the assessment of compensation. Those principles are not solely applicable to cases of unfair dismissal, but apply to all awards of compensation in respect of unfair industrial practices of which unfair dismissal is only one. The guiding principle is set out in sub-s (1) in these terms: ... the amount of the compensation shall... be such amount as the Court or tribunal considers just and equitable in all the circumstances, having regard to the loss sustained by the aggrieved party in consequence of the matters to which the complaint relates, in so far as that loss was attributable to action taken by or on behalf of the party in default.

1971 年《劳资关系法》第 116 条设置了适用于评估赔偿的一般原则。那些原则并非仅仅适用于不公平解雇案件，而是适用于不公平劳资实践的所有情形的赔偿评估，不公平解雇仅为其中之一。第（1）款列出的指导性原则为：……赔偿金额应该……法院或审判委员会在所有情况下认为是公平合理的，已考虑了受害方由于该事件遭受的损失，只要该项损失为可归因于过错方或是由过错方的行为所致。

【生效判决意见】（Opinion by Sir John Donaldson P）

Counsel for the appellants has submitted that it is well-established that at common law in any action for wrongful dismissal, no account can be taken of injury to the plaintiff's feelings by the manner of the dismissal or, with the possible exception of the case of an actor, of the effect of the dismissal on prospects of future employment: see Addis v Gramophone Co. Ltd. The measure of damage in such a case is what the plaintiff would have earned during the period of notice, less anything which he in fact earned or, in accordance with the duty to mitigate his loss, he could have earned in that period. In counsel's submission, much clearer words than are contained in s 116 are required to vary the common law and, accordingly, the common law rules apply in relation to compensation for unfair dismissal. Alternatively, counsel for the appellants further submits that, in the context of s. 116, "loss" can only refer to financial loss and the burden is on the complaint to offer strict proof of every new penny of loss which is alleged.

上诉方律师提交了在普通法中已良好确立的规则，即不正当解雇的任何行为，都无须考虑原告方由于解雇方式或影响未来被雇用的概率而对被告造成的精神损害，演员的情况是种可能的例外。该规则可以参见 Addis v. Gramophone Co. Ltd 案例。该种情况下损失的衡量为：根据减轻损失的义务，原告在该段通知期内有可能挣到的金额，减去实际上挣到的金额。在律师提供的材料中，普通法中包含比第 116 条更明确的措辞，因此，普通法规则适用于不公平解雇赔偿。作为选择，上诉方律师进一步提出，在第 116 条的上下文中，损失仅能指财产损失，原告承担为其声称受到的损失提供严格证据的举证责任。

Counsel for the respondent, on the other hand, has relied on the fact that s 116(1) requires the court or tribunal to award such amount as it considers just and equitable in all the circumstances, the only relevance of "loss", whether financial or otherwise, being that this is one factor to which regard must be had. Accordingly, in his submission, the court or tribunal has a virtually unfettered discretion and one which is open to review on appeal only in extreme cases.

另一方面，被诉人的律师凭借第 116（1）条要求法院裁决在任何情况下认为公平合理的金额。是不是财产损失，仅是必须考虑的、同损失唯一相关的因素之一。因此，被诉人的律师在提交材料中提到，法院具有实际上不受限制的判断力，能够公开审查在极端情况下的上诉。

In our judgment, the common law rules and authorities on wrongful dismissal are irrelevant. That cause of action is quite unaffected by the *1971 Act* which has created an entirely new cause of action, namely the "unfair industrial practice" of unfair dismissal. The measure of compensation for that statutory wrong is itself the creature of statute and is to be found in the *1971 Act* and nowhere else. But we do not consider that Parliament intended the court or tribunal to dispense compensation arbitrarily. On the other hand, the amount has a discretionary element and is not to be assessed by adopting the approach of a conscientious and skilled cost accountant or actuary. Nevertheless, that discretion is to be exercised judicially and on the basis of principle.

我们认为，关于不正当解雇的普通法规则和权限同本案不相关。本案中的行为完全不受产生一种全新案由的 1971 年《劳资关系法》的影响，即不公平解雇中的"不公平劳资实践"。法定错误的补偿金的衡量本身就是成文法的本质，能在 1971 年《劳资关系法》中找到，而不能在其他地方找到。但是我们不认为议会试图让法院或审判委员会武断地做出补偿赔偿金的裁决。另一方面，补偿金额有自由裁量的因素，不能通过采取一种谨慎的、技术娴熟的成本会计或精算师的方法评估。但是，那种自由裁量权由司法机关根据基本原则做出。

But it is a corollary of the discretion conferred on the tribunals that it is their duty to set out their reasoning in sufficient detail to show the principles on which they have proceeded. A similar obligation lies on this court, when sitting as a court of first instance from which appeal lies to the Court of Appeal on questions of law alone. Were it otherwise, the parties would in effect be deprived of their right of appeal on questions of law. No great elaboration is required and the task should not constitute a burden. Indeed, the need to give reasons may well assist in the process of properly making the discretionary assessment of damages.

但是，审判委员会有责任详细列明他们的推理过程及展示推理方法，这是授予其自由裁量权的必然结果。当作为仅对法律问题质疑到上诉法院的一审法院也有类似的义务。否则的话，双方实际上将被剥夺对法律问题的上诉权。不需要详细的解释说明，该任务不能构成负担。实际上，出具理由的必要性能很好地解释在评估赔偿金过程中做出正确自由裁量的过程。

In the present case the tribunal has not made entirely clear the principles on which it has acted and to that extent has erred in law. We know that the tribunal was aware that the respondent had lost four weeks' wages at £ 25.60 per week and it is therefore probable, but not certain, that about £ 100 out of the £ 250 awarded is referable to this factor. As to the balance it must be attributable to the circumstances of the dismissal and the loss of the benefit of 11 years' service. The latter consideration is highly relevant, but the circumstances of the dismissal were only relevant if they were such as to cause or be likely to cause future loss. Injury to the respondent's pride or feelings is not loss and is irrelevant. But this faces us with the problem of not knowing how much of the compensation is attributable to the circumstances of the dismissal and whether the tribunal based itself on future financial loss or on injury to self-esteem.

该案中，审判委员会没有完全弄清评估赔偿金的原则，因此适用法律错误。我们知道审判委员会明白被诉人损失了 4 周工资，每周 25.60 英镑，因此，我们认为很有可能但不确定，在一审裁决的 250 英镑赔偿金中，大概有 100 英镑指向这项损失。至于余额，一定指的是该种解雇情形下，雇员为该雇主服务 11 年的利益损失。后一种考虑是高度相关的，但是该种解雇情形仅在很有可能导致未来损失的情况下相关。我们不认为对被诉人的自尊心或精神损害属于损害赔偿范围。但是我们并不知道赔偿金中多少数额归因于解雇的情况，也不知道审判委员会是否基于未来财产损失或精神损失确立该金额。

In these circumstances, and in the light of the request of the parties to which we have already referred, we shall substitute our own award. In our judgment the respondent is entitled to compensation in the sum of £ 375. This sum we regard as just and equitable in all the circumstances having regard to the loss sustained by the respondent. That loss falls to be considered under the following heads.

在此情况下，根据我们已经提到的双方要求，我们将转而列出我们的裁决金额。我们认为，被诉人有权获得 375 英镑。这个数额我们认为包含了被诉人所有的损失，在任何情况下都是公正合理的。该项损失由下列项目构成：

(a) Immediate loss of wages

The *Contracts of Employment Act 1963*, as amended by the *Industrial Relations Act 1971*, entitles a worker with more than ten years' continuous employment to not less than six weeks' notice to terminate his employment. Good industrial practice requires the employer either to give this notice or pay six weeks' wages in lieu. The respondent was given neither. In an action for damages for wrongful, as opposed to "unfair", dismissal he could have claimed this six weeks' wages, but would have had to give credit for anything which he earned or could have earned during the notice period. In the event he would have had to give credit for what he earned in the last two weeks, thus reducing his claim to about four weeks' wages. But, if he had been paid the wages in lieu of notice at the time of his dismissal, he would not have had to make any repayment on obtaining further employment during the notice period. In the context of compensation for unfair dismissal we think that it is appropriate and in accordance with the intentions of Parliament that we should treat an employee as having suffered a loss insofar as he receives less than he would have received in accordance with good industrial practice. Accordingly, no deduction has been made for his earnings during the notice period.

（a）因解雇直接损失的工资

被 1971 年《劳资关系法》修正的 1963 年《雇用合同法》中规定，为同一雇主连续工作 10 年以上的工人在被终止雇用时，享有不少于 6 周的提前通知的权利。良好的劳资实践要求雇主或者提前给予通知，或者给予 6 周的替代工资。被诉人没有得到其中任何一项。在不正当损害的诉讼中，同不公平诉讼相反，他可以为解雇请求 6 周工资，但是将不得不认可在通知期内他挣到的或能挣到的金额。在此情况下，他将不得不认可在最后两周挣到的工资，因此将他的诉讼请求减至大约四周的工资。但是，如果他在被解雇时已获得替代通知的 6 周工资，他在通知期内获得新的工作后，将不必返还任何金额。在补偿不公平解雇的情况下，我们认为根据议会的立法意图，一旦雇员遭受了低于良好劳资实践的待遇，应该认定该雇员已遭受了损失。因此，在通知期内我们不应该做关于他收入的任何扣减。

We have no information as to whether the £ 25.60 per week is a gross or a "take-home" figure. The relevant figure is the "take-home" pay since this and not the gross pay is what he should have received from his employer. However, neither party took this point and we have based our assessment of this head of loss on six weeks at £ 25.60 per week or £ 153.60.

我们不清楚每周 25.60 英镑是毛收入还是实发收入。相关的数额是实发收入，而不是他应该从雇主处获得的毛收入。但是，双方都没有解释这一点，我们将该项目评估为是损失了每周 25.60 英镑的收入或共计 153.60 英镑。

The respondent drew £ 3 unemployment benefit for a short period, but we were not asked to make any deduction for this and have not done so. Finally, we have taken no account of the extent to which the respondent's income tax liability may be reduced by his period of unemployment, since we consider that the sums involved will be small and that such a calculation is inappropriate to the broad common sense assessment of compensation which Parliament contemplated in the case of unfair dismissal of a man earning the respondent's level of wages.

被诉人获得了 3 英镑短期失业收益，但是我们没有被请求为此做任何扣减，因此我们没有扣减。最后，我们没有考虑被诉人的所得税义务会在失业期内减少的程度，因为我们认为该项目包括的金额非常少，按一般常识考虑，对议会在一位如同被上诉人工资水平的人被不公平解雇时所确立的赔偿金再进行如此扣减计算是不合适的。

(b) Manner of dismissal

As the respondent secured employment within four weeks of his dismissal and we have taken full account of his loss during this period, we need only consider whether the manner and circumstances of his dismissal could give rise to any risk of financial loss at a later stage by, for example, making him less acceptable to potential employers or exceptionally liable to selection for dismissal. There is no evidence of any such disability and accordingly our assessment of the compensation takes no account of the manner of his dismissal. This took place during a heated exchange of words between him and one of the directors.

（b）特定解雇方式的损失

因为被诉人在被解雇后四周内又获得了雇用，我们已完全考虑了该期间内他的损失，我们只需考虑他被解雇的方式和情形是否会在将来产生任何财产损失，例如使得被诉人对将来的雇主吸引力降低或易于被解雇的损失。没有证据显示有任何这种缺陷存在，因此我们评估赔偿金没有考虑他被解雇方式的损失。这一点经过了该雇员和其中一名经理的激烈争论。

（c）Future loss of wages

There is no evidence to suggest that the respondent's present employment is any less secure than his former employment, and we have therefore taken no account of possible future losses due to short time working, lay-off or unemployment, apart from loss of rights in respect of redundancy and unfair dismissal which are considered separately at (d) below.

（c）未来收入降低的损失

没有证据显示被诉人的现工作较之前工作有任何不稳定之处，因此我们不考虑由于短期工作、失业或失业期造成的未来可能的收入损失，此外，由于裁员和不公平解雇造成的权利损失将在下面（d）项列明。

（d）Loss of protection in respect of unfair dismissal or dismissal by reason of redundancy

These losses may be more serious. So long as the respondent remained in the employ of the appellants he was entitled to protection in respect of unfair dismissal. He will acquire no such rights against his new employers until he has worked for them for two years (see s 28 (a) of the 1971 Act). Accordingly, if he is unfairly dismissed during that period his remedy will be limited to claiming damages for wrongful dismissal which are unlikely to exceed six week's wages and may be less. Furthermore, on obtaining further employment he will be faced with starting a fresh two year period. This process could be repeated indefinitely so that he was never again protected in respect of unfair dismissal. Whilst it is impossible for us to quantify this loss, which must be much affected by local conditions, we think that we shall do the respondent no injustice if we include £ 20 in our assessment on account of it.

（d）由于不公平解雇或经济性裁员对雇员造成的保护损失

这些损失可能更严重。只要该被诉人在上诉人处工作，他就有权获得不公正解雇的保护。而他在新雇主处工作两年后才能获得该项权利（见 1971 年《劳资关系法》中第 28（a）条规定）。因此，如果在此期间，他被不公平解雇，他的救济权限于不正当解雇的请求权，不可能超过 6 周工资，甚至会少于 6 周工资。而且，在获得新的雇用时，他将面临开始一个新的两年期限。这个过程可能不确定地重复，使他不再受到关于不公正解雇的保护。虽然我们不可能量化该项损失，而且该损失必然受到当地情况影响，但是我们认为如果将该项损失评估为 20 英镑，不会对被上诉人有任何不公正。

The loss of rights under the *Redundancy Payments Act 1965* is much more serious. The claimant is aged 50 and had been continuously employed for 11 years. Accordingly, if he had been dismissed on account of redundancy he would have received about £380. In other words, he had a "paid up insurance policy" against dismissal by reason of redundancy which was worth this amount and would have increased in value at the rate of about £38 per annum, until it reached a maximum of perhaps £800. In his new job, the respondent will receive no compensation if he is dismissed on account of redundancy within the first two years and, since he is now within 15 years of his 65th birthday, can never build up to the maximum which is based on 20 years' service.

1965 年《裁员赔偿法案》中的权利损失是更严重的。原告已经 50 岁，为原雇主连续工作了 11 年。因此，如果他因为裁员被解雇，将获得大约 380 英镑。换句话说，他拥有对抗基于裁员原因解雇的"付清保险政策"，价值 380 英镑，并且在价值上约以每年 38 英镑的速度递增，直到达到大约 800 英镑的上限。在他的新工作中，被诉人在前两年内如果基于裁员原因被解雇，将不会获得任何赔偿金，而且，因为现在他距离 65 岁生日不到 15 年，再也不能积累起 20 年服务期的最高值。

We have no evidence as to whether the respondent is more or less likely to be made redundant in his new employment, but, if a redundancy situation does arise, he is clearly more likely to be selected for dismissal on the normal practice of "last in, first out", Nor have we any evidence as to the likelihood that if he had not been dismissed by the appellants when he was, he might thereafter have been dismissed by reason of redundancy. In all the circumstances, we think it just and equitable to base our award of compensation on approximately one-half of his accrued protection in respect of redundancy—say, £ 200.

关于被诉人在新工作中有多大可能会被裁员，我们没有任何证据。但是一旦裁员情况产生，很明显，根据通常的"后来者先出"的实践规则，他更容易被解雇。我们也没有任何证据证明，如果他没有被上诉人解雇，他有多大可能性会因为裁员而被解雇。考虑所有的情况，我们认为将我们的赔偿金额设定为大约他可能获得的裁员保护的一半是公正合理的，即 200 英镑。

The arithmetical sum of these sub-heads is £ 373.60, which we have rounded off at £ 375, which in our judgment represents compensation which is just and equitable in all the circumstances.

这些分项的算术总额是 373.60 英镑，我们计为 375 英镑，这个补偿金额我们认为在任何情况下都是公正合理的。

In conclusion, we wish to emphasise that it is only because the parties so requested that we have substituted our own figure for that of the tribunal. But for that request we should have remitted the matter and, so long as the correct principles were applied and shown to have been applied, would not have interfered if they had awarded a different figure which might have been higher or lower.

总而言之，我们希望强调，仅仅因为双方如此要求，我们才提出我们的裁决金额替代审判委员会的裁决金额。要不是那样要求的话，我们可能已经移交该事项。如果他们被裁决一个或高些或低些的金额，只要适用正确的原则并且显示出是正确适用、未受到干扰就可以。

【案件影响】（Impact of the Case）

该案是在 1971 年《劳资关系法》生效后做出的判决。该法为劳动者创设了一项不被不公平解雇的权利，这是英国成文法对劳资关系介入的开端。

法律救济措施对制止资方不公平行为具有充分的威慑力，在这方面，补偿将比恢复原职或重新录用更有效。诺顿器具公司诉特森案确立了补偿申请人的损失是衡量公平唯一尺度的原则。评估损失的因果关系应当是计算补偿金的首要原则，公正平等标准是评估补偿金的补充原则。英国法院和劳资关系审理委员会始终坚持：深植于补偿金中的纠正正义的观念仅仅考虑的是雇员的受伤害程度，而非雇主所表现出的过错程度。补偿金是用来赔偿雇员损失的，而不是惩罚雇主的不公平解雇行为。正如约翰·唐纳德（Sir John Donaldson）1973 年在国家劳资关系法院所说："评定补偿的目的不是表达对劳资关系政策的责难，它的目的是补偿经济的损失。"当补偿金作为对因解雇遭受损失的雇员的补偿时，它被认为是公平而公正的。

【思考问题】（Questions）

1. 经济补偿金的性质是什么？我国关于经济补偿金性质的学说有几种？
2. 我国适用经济补偿金的情形有哪些？我国是如何设计经济补偿金的计算方法的？
3. 我国经济补偿金和赔偿金适用的情形有什么区别？

十二、环境保护法案例

布默诉大西洋水泥公司案
Boomer v. Atlantic Cement Co.（1970）

【选读理由】（Selected Reason）

美国《环境法》的起源可以追溯到一些古老的衡平法原则。衡平法的一项基本原则可由这样一条格言表达："不以损害他人财产之方式使用你自己的财产。"同这条格言密切相关的另一条格言："衡平法不允许没有补偿的有害行为。"这两条格言表达了一条本案中所反映的基本原则，即任何因其行为对他人造成损害的人都负有对受害人提供补偿的义务和责任。布默诉大西洋水泥公司案（Oscar H. Boomer et al. v. Atlantic Cement Company, Inc.）就是在美国20世纪七八十年代出现的通过对环境利益和经济利益进行衡量而得出的判决。这条基本原则同样适用于当代社会环境污染对人的健康和财产损害的赔偿。

【案件事实】（Facts）

Plaintiff landowners neighbored defendant's cement factory. Defendant operates a large cement plant near Albany. These are actions for injunction and damages by neighboring land owners alleging injury to property from dirt, smoke and vibration emanating from the plant.

原告土地主们临近被告的水泥厂。被告的大型水泥厂在奥尔巴尼附近开办，附近的土地拥有者声称他们由于水泥厂产生的大量灰尘、烟雾和震动而遭受了财产损害。

【裁决过程与结果】（Procedure and Disposition）

A nuisance has been found after trial, temporary damages have been allowed; but an injunction has been denied. Plaintiffs sought review of the denial of an injunction against defendant in an action for nuisance, in the Appellate Division of the Supreme Court in the Third Judicial Department (New York).

Appeals (1) an injunction restraining defendant Atlantic Cement Company from emitting dust and raw materials and conducting excessive blasting in operating its plant in the Town of Coeymans，in such a manner as to constitute a nuisance upon plaintiffs' lands，buildings and equipment，and (2) damages sustained as a result of the nuisance so created, awarded damages to plaintiffs for the loss of rental or usable value sustained but refused to grant the injunctive relief sought by them.

The court determined permanent damages were allowed where the loss recoverable is small in comparison with the economic cost of removal of the nuisance. The court further indicated permanent damages were appropriate when there was a continuing and recurrent nuisance, as in this case. The court found it equitable to award plaintiffs permanent damages based on the theory of compensation for servitude on the land which precluded future recovery by plaintiffs or their grantees. The court granted an injunction which was vacatable upon defendant's payment of permanent damages.

【裁判理由】（Reasons for Judicial Decision）

【原审意见】

Plaintiffs sought an injunction for property damages from the factory's vibration, smoke, and dirt. The lower court found the factory a nuisance and ordered temporary damages，but denied an injunction. The court found it should not try to lay down a policy for the difficult problem of pollution elimination as the byproduct of private litigation.

原告要求颁发禁令，以补偿他们由于水泥厂产生的大量灰尘、烟雾和震动而遭受的财产损害。下级法院发现原告遭受的损害存在，并要求被告临时赔偿，但否决颁发禁令。法庭不应该通过私人诉讼来制定消除大气污染的有效政策。

【生效判决意见】（Opinion by Bergan）

The public concern with air pollution arising from many sources in industry and in transportation is currently accorded ever wider recognition accompanied by a growing sense of responsibility in State and Federal Governments to control it. Cement plants are obvious sources of air pollution in the neighborhoods where they operate.

公众关注工业和运输业中的许多大气污染源，与此同时，州和联邦政府控制大气污染的责任意识日渐增强。水泥厂显然是他们邻近社区的大气污染源。

But there is now before the court private litigation in which individual property owners have sought specific relief from a single plant operation. A court performs its essential function when it decides the rights of parties before it. Its decision of private controversies may sometimes greatly affect public issues. Large questions of law are often resolved by the manner in which private litigation is decided. But this is normally an incident to the court's main function to settle controversy. It is a rare exercise of judicial power to use a decision in private litigation as a purposeful mechanism to achieve direct public objectives greatly beyond the rights and interests before the court.

但是法庭要受理的是个人财产所有者要求一个工厂给予赔偿的私人诉讼。法庭要履行的基本功能是决定双方的权利。法庭针对个人纠纷的决议或许会大大地影响公众问题。大的法律问题经常通过解决私人诉讼的方式得以解决。但是，这是法庭解决纠纷的主要手段。掌握司法权的部门很少把私人诉讼的决议作为一种目的机制来使用，以实现权益之外直接的大众目标。

Effective control of air pollution is a problem presently far from solution even with the full public and financial powers of government. In large measure adequate technical procedures are yet to be developed and some that appear possible may be economically impracticable. It seems apparent that the amelioration of air pollution will depend on technical research in great depth; on a carefully balanced consideration of the economic impact of close regulation; and of the actual effect on public health. It is likely to require massive public expenditure and to demand more than any local community can accomplish and to depend on regional and interstate controls.

有效控制大气污染并非当前大众和政府财政部门可以解决的问题。在很大程度上，还需要开发一套完善的技术上的流程；其中有一部分看似可能实现的或许在经济上无法完成。显而易见，考虑到严密监管对经济的影响，以及大气污染对大众健康的影响，大气污染的改善离不开深层次的技术研究。大气污染的改善可能需要大规模的公共支出，需要区域性和州际间的共同控制，而并非任何一个地方社区可以完成的。

The cement making operations of defendant have been found by the court at Special Term to have damaged the nearby properties of plaintiffs in these two actions. That court, as it has been noted, accordingly found defendant maintained a nuisance and this has been affirmed at the Appellate Division. The total damage to plaintiffs' properties is, however, relatively small in comparison with the value of defendant's operation and with the consequences of the injunction which plaintiffs seek.

依据特别条款，法庭裁定被告水泥生产商损害了居住在附近的原告的财产。正如前面指出的那样，法庭因此判定被告给原告造成损害，这一点已经得到上诉法院的确认。但是，相比被告经营的价值和原告寻求禁令带来的后果，原告的财产损害总额相对较少。

The ground for the denial of injunction, notwithstanding the finding both that there is a nuisance and that plaintiffs have been damaged substantially, is the large disparity in economic consequences of the nuisance and of the injunction. The rule in New York has been that such a nuisance will be enjoined although marked disparity be shown in economic consequence between the effect of the injunction and the effect of the nuisance.

尽管发现损害存在，且原告遭受严重损害，否决禁令的依据来自损害和禁令带来的经济影响的巨大差距。纽约上诉法院的裁定如下：尽管损害和禁令带来的经济影响存在巨大差距，损害应被制止。

Although the court at Special Term and the Appellate Division held that injunction should be denied, it was found that plaintiffs had been damaged in various specific amounts up to the time of the trial and damages to the respective plaintiffs were awarded for those amounts. The effect of this was, injunction having been denied, plaintiffs could maintain successive actions at law for damages thereafter as further damage was incurred. The total of permanent damages to all plaintiffs thus found was $185,000.

尽管法庭和下级法院坚持否决禁令，但截止到审判之日，原告所遭受到不同程度的损害都得到了应有的赔偿金。结果是禁令被否决，原告可以继续上诉要求得到赔偿金来弥补未来造成的损害。原告获得的总的永久性赔偿金共 185000 美元。

This result at Special Term and at the Appellate Division is a departure from a rule that has become settled; but to follow the rule literally in these cases would be to close down the plant at once. This court is fully agreed to avoid that immediately drastic remedy; the difference in view is how best to avoid it. Respondent's investment in the plant is in excess of $ 45,000,000. There are over 300 people employed there.

上诉法院和下级法院的裁决与先前的裁决不同；但遵守先前的裁决的确意味着要立即关闭工厂。被上诉人对这个厂子的投资超过 4500 万美元。整个厂的员工超过 300 人。

One alternative is to grant the injunction but postpone its effect to a specified future date to give opportunity for technical advances to permit defendant to eliminate the nuisance; another is to grant the injunction conditioned on the payment of permanent damages to plaintiffs which would compensate them for the total economic loss to their property present and future caused by defendant's operations. For reasons which will be developed the court chooses the latter alternative.

该案的一个方案是颁发禁令，但要将执行时间推迟到将来的某一具体时间，目的是给被告时间进行技术革新以消除损害。另一方案是如果被告不支付给原告可以弥补他们现在以及将来所遭受的经济损失的永久性赔偿金，则颁发禁令。由于以下几方面的原因，法庭选择后一方案。

If the injunction were to be granted unless within a short period—e.g. 18 months—the nuisance be abated by improved methods, there would be no assurance that any significant technical improvement would occur.

如果水泥厂不能通过技术改良的方法使损害在短期内（如 18 个月）减轻，则授予禁令无法保证此期间会有任何重大的技术进步以确保水泥厂有通过较先进技术减轻污染的可能。

Moreover, techniques to eliminate dust and other annoying by products of cement making are unlikely to be developed by any research the defendant can undertake within any short period. If at the end of 18 months the whole industry has not found a technical solution a court would be hard put to close down this one cement plant if due regard be given to equitable principles.

而且水泥厂在任何短期内进行的研究中不太可能研发出消除灰尘和其他恼人的水泥生产的副产品的技术。如果在 18 个月结束时，整个工业界没有发现技术上的解决途径，而依衡平法上的原则，法庭大概也很难关闭这家水泥厂。

On the other hand, to grant the injunction unless defendant pays plaintiffs such permanent damages as may be fixed by the court seems to do justice between the contending parties. All of the attributions of economic loss to the properties on which plaintiffs' complaints are based will have been redressed. The nuisance complained of by these plaintiffs may have other public or private consequences, but these particular parties are the only ones who have sought remedies and the judgment proposed will fully redress them.

另一方面，如果被上诉人不付给上诉人法庭确定的永久损害赔偿金，将被授予禁令，这种解决方案似乎对争议双方都很公平。所有的上诉人诉请的因污染造成的财产损失将得到赔偿。被上诉人指控的污染可能有其他公共或私人的后果，但判决只会全面赔偿这些寻求补偿的上诉人。

The limitation of relief granted is a limitation only within the four corners of these actions and does not foreclose public health or other public agencies from seeking proper relief in a proper court. It seems reasonable to think that the risk of being required to pay permanent damages to injured property owners by cement plant owners would itself be a reasonable effective spur to research for improved techniques to minimize nuisance.

给予赔偿的限度是诉讼范围之内的，并没有排除因公众健康受损或其他公共机构在适当的法庭寻求适当赔偿。要求水泥厂所有者对遭受损失的财产所有者支付永久损害赔偿金的风险本身就是对其改进技术以使污染最小化的一个合理的、有效的激励——这样的认识是合理的。

【反对意见】（Dissent By Jasen）

I agree with the majority that a reversal is required here, but I do not subscribe to the newly enunciated doctrine of assessment of permanent damages, in lieu of an injunction, where substantial property rights have been impaired by the creation of a nuisance.

我同意大多数法官的观点，主张撤销判决；但是我并不赞同最新发布的永久性损害赔偿金的评估原则。这一原则取代了禁令，然而损害的产生已经严重危及原告的财产权。

It has long been the rule in this State, as the majority acknowledges, that a nuisance which results in substantial continuing damage to neighbors must be enjoined. To now change the rule to permit the cement company to continue polluting the air indefinitely upon the payment of permanent damages is, in my opinion, compounding the magnitude of a very serious problem in our State and Nation today.

众所周知，长期以来在这个州就存在对邻居造成严重的持续性损害的污染必须被制止的裁决。我认为，如今改变这一裁决，允许该水泥公司继续无限制地污染大气，虽然支付永久性损害赔偿金，但这种做法使得本来非常严重的问题在我们的州乃至国家更加突出。

In recognition of this problem, the Legislature of this State has enacted the *Air Pollution Control Act* (Public Health Law, §§ 1264-1299-m) declaring that it is the State policy to require the use of all available and reasonable methods to prevent and control air pollution (Public Health Law, § 1265).

这个州的立法机构已经意识到这个问题，颁布了《大气污染控制法案》，宣布制定州立政策，要求使用所有合理的方法防止和控制大气污染。

The harmful nature and widespread occurrence of air pollution have been extensively documented. Congressional hearings have revealed that air pollution causes substantial property damage, as well as being a contributing factor to a rising incidence of lung cancer，emphysema，bronchitis and asthma.

有关大气污染的害处和频繁发生已经被广泛记录下来。国会听证会显示大气污染造成了可观的财产损失，同时还导致肺癌、肺气肿、支气管炎和哮喘等疾病的高发。

The specific problem faced here is known as particulate contamination because of the fine dust particles emanating from defendant's cement plant. The particular type of nuisance is not new，having appeared in many cases for at least the past 60 years. It is interesting to note that cement production has recently been identified as a significant source of particulate contamination in the Hudson Valley. This type of pollution, wherein very small particles escape and stay in the atmosphere, has been denominated as the type of air pollution which produces the greatest hazard to human health. We have thus a nuisance which not only is damaging to the plaintiffs, but also is decidedly harmful to the general public.

本案面对的具体问题是被告的水泥厂释放的细小尘埃颗粒造成的微粒子污染。这种特殊的污染，在过去60年间的若干案例中均出现过，并不新奇。有意思的是，最近水泥产业被认为是哈德逊山谷最重要的微粒子污染源。这种污染涉及的细小颗粒存在于大气中，被认为是对人类最具威胁的一种大气污染。因此，本案中的污染不仅损害原告，而且毫无疑问对大众构成危害。

There are seven plaintiffs here who have been substantially damaged by the maintenance of this nuisance. The trial court found their total permanent damages to equal $ 185, 000.

这里有7名原告遭受到这种污染的巨大损害，他们的永久性损害赔偿金达到18.5万美元。

I see grave dangers in overruling our long-established rule of granting an injunction where a nuisance results in substantial continuing damage. In permitting the injunction to become inoperative upon the payment of permanent damages, the majority is, in effect, licensing a continuing wrong. It is the same as saying to the cement company, you may continue to do harm to your neighbors so long as you pay a fee for it. Furthermore, once such permanent damages are assessed and paid, the incentive to alleviate the wrong would be eliminated, thereby continuing air pollution of an area without abatement.

我看到了否决我们长期以来一直确立的对导致严重的持续性损害颁发禁令的决议所产生的危险。取消禁令，支付永久性损害赔偿金，对于大多数人来讲，就是特许一种持续性的错误。这就像对水泥公司说，只要你支付赔偿金，你就可以继续危害你的邻居。此外，一旦赔偿金确定并支付，减轻错误的动机也将荡然无存，结果就是这个地区的大气污染丝毫不会减轻。

In some cases, the court, in denying an injunction and awarding money damages, grounded their decision on a showing that the use to which the property was intended to be put was primarily for the public benefit. Here, on the other hand, it is clearly established that the cement company is creating a continuing air pollution nuisance primarily for its own private interest with no public benefit.

在某些案例中，法庭否决禁令，允许金钱赔偿，主要是为了确保大众的利益。然而，在本案中，显而易见，水泥公司为了个体利益造成了持久性的大气污染，丝毫不考虑大众利益。

The promotion of the interests of the polluting cement company has, in my opinion, no public use or benefit. Nor is it constitutionally permissible to impose servitude on land, without consent of the owner, by payment of permanent damages where the continuing impairment of the land is for a private use. This is made clear by the State Constitution which provides that "[private] property shall not be taken for public use without just compensation" (emphasis added). It is, of course, significant that the section makes no mention of taking for a private use.

我认为，造成大气污染的水泥公司的利益提高对于大众来讲毫无意义，并且宪法也不允许土地的使用权落在通过支付永久性损害赔偿金而对土地造成持续性损害的个人手里。州宪法明确规定，个人财产在没有获得公正赔偿的情况下不得转为公用。值得一提的是，这一部分根本未提到个人使用。

In sum, I would enjoin the defendant cement company from continuing the discharge of dust particles upon its neighbors properties unless, within 18 months, the cement company abated this nuisance.

综上所述，除非被告方水泥公司在 18 月内减少这种污染，否则我要求被告停止对其邻居的财产排放灰尘颗粒。

The issuance of an injunction to become effective in the future is not an entirely new concept. It is not my intention to cause the removal of the cement plant from the Albany area, but to recognize the urgency of the problem stemming from this stationary source of air pollution, and to allow the company a specified period of time to develop a means to alleviate this nuisance.

颁布在未来执行的禁令不是一个崭新的概念。让水泥厂从奥尔巴尼地区彻底消失并非是我的目的。我只是意识到这个固定大气污染源的问题的紧迫性，允许公司在指定的时间内研究出减轻污染的手段。

I am aware that the trial court found that the most modern dust control devices available have been installed in defendant's plant, but, I submit, this does not mean that better and more effective dust control devices could not be developed within the time allowed to abate the pollution.

Accordingly, the orders of the Appellate Division, insofar as they denied the injunction, should be reversed, and the actions remitted to Supreme Court, Albany County to grant an injunction to take effect 18 months hence, unless the nuisance is abated by improved techniques prior to said date.

我意识到法庭已经发现被告的厂房中安装了最现代化的防尘设施，但是这样做并不意味着将来在有限的时间内不会研发出更好、更有效的防尘设备来降低污染。

因此，上诉法院应该撤销已经颁布的否决禁令的决议。如果被告在 18 个月内未能通过技术改良减弱污染，奥尔巴尼地区法院将有权颁布禁令。

【案件影响】（Impact of the Case）

美国在 1970 年 3 月对该案做出的判决给予我们的启示是，环境保护并非是绝对的，一个社会除了环境保护目标外，还有其他多种目标，这些目标在重要性上没有先后之分。环境保护尽管十分必要，但不能不计代价，必须与其他社会目标相协调。经济效益和生态保护，二者如何取舍，是中国、美国，也是所有国家发展过程中必须面对的问题。

也许和英美法系中固有的衡平法精神存在着某种密切联系，一直以来，美国都是注重环境和经济利益平衡的典型代表。该案在审判中权衡了环境利益和经济利益，结合二者进行综合评估，通过"用永久性赔偿金购得污染权"的方案解决了本案，成为美国司法史上效用比较原则指导下的典型。利益衡量理论强调法官在民事司法中，在处理两种利益之间的冲突时，运用实质判断的方法判断哪一种利益更应受到保护。在进行判决时，不是直接通过法律规定得出结论，而是首先通过利益衡量得出结论，然后从法律条文中寻找根据，以便使结论正当化或合理化。利益衡量遭受攻击最多的地方在于它的主观性和不确定性：因为在利益调查或利益分析的过程中难以避免个人的偏好存在，其科学性值得怀疑；此外，由于利益衡量本身不能解决价值选择问题，因此在进行利益选择的过程中会出现不同的正义或公平的标准。

【思考问题】（Questions）

1. 美国法官的思路和经济学家的思路有何相近之处？
2. 美国环境侵权民事诉讼中利益衡量的适用对我国有什么启示？

十三、民事诉讼法案例

伯纳姆诉加利福尼亚高级法院案

Burnham v. Superior Court of California (1990)

【选读理由】（Selected Reason）

任何一个成熟的司法制度都必须能回答当事人一个最基本的问题，即"我可否在这里诉讼"。诉讼法的重要目的是给当事人提供公平、迅速和低成本的判决，而民事诉讼管辖权恰恰是对当事人在权利救济程序中的诉讼权利产生重要影响的一环。19 世纪和 20 世纪初的很多美国判例都表明，对出现在法院所在地的被告送达后就可以取得管辖权，并且做出判决，不管被告是居住在那里还是暂时出现。通过送达建立管辖权这个传统一直延续着。历经将近百年发展之后，多数学者都认为，在管辖权作为人权的潮流下，基于所在权力理论而发展的短暂过境管辖权可能逐渐被扬弃。在 1990 年美国联邦最高法院审理的伯纳姆诉加利福尼亚高级法院案中，传统的规则受到了挑战。

【案件事实】（Facts）

Petitioner Dennis Burnham married Francie Burnham in 1976 in West Virginia. In 1977 the couple moved to New Jersey, where their two children were born. In July 1987 the Burnhams decided to separate. They agreed that Mrs. Burnham, who intended to move to California, would take custody of the children. Shortly before that same month Mrs. Burnham departed for California, she and petitioner agreed that she would file for divorce on grounds of "irreconcilable differences."

In October 1987, petitioner filed for divorce in New Jersey state court on grounds of "desertion." Petitioner did not, however, obtain an issuance of summons against his wife and did not attempt to serve her with process. Mrs. Burnham, after unsuccessfully demanding that petitioner adhere to their prior agreement to submit to an "irreconcilable differences" divorce, brought suit for divorce in California state court in early January 1988.

上诉人丹尼斯·伯纳姆 1976 年在西弗吉尼亚州与弗朗西结婚。1977 年，这对夫妇搬到新泽西州，在那里他们的两个孩子出生了。1987 年 7 月，伯纳姆决定分居。他们决定由打算搬到加利福尼亚州的伯纳姆太太来抚养孩子。在伯纳姆太太搬往加利福尼亚州的那个月之前，她和本案的上诉人同意由她向法院以"不可调和的分歧"为由提出离婚。

1987 年 10 月，上诉人以遗弃为由申请在新泽西州法院离婚。然而上诉人没有能够让其妻子签收传票，也未能使她完成诉讼程序。伯纳姆太太在要求上诉人按照此前约定以"不可调和的分歧"为由提起离婚诉讼而未成功后，在 1988 年 1 月上旬向加利福尼亚州法院提出了离婚诉讼。

In late January, petitioner visited southern California on business, after which he went north to visit his children in the San Francisco Bay area, where his wife resided. He took the older child to

San Francisco for the weekend. Upon returning the child to Mrs. Burnham's home on January 24, 1988, petitioner was served with a California court summons and a copy of Mrs. Burnham's divorce petition. He then returned to New Jersey.

Later that year, petitioner made a special appearance in the California Superior Court, moving to quash the service of process on the ground that the court lacked personal jurisdiction over him because his only contacts with California were a few short visits to the State for the purposes of conducting business and visiting his children. The Superior Court denied the motion, and the California Court of Appeal denied mandamus relief, rejecting petitioner's contention that the Due Process Clause prohibited California courts from asserting jurisdiction over him because he lacked "minimum contacts" with the State. The court held it to be "a valid jurisdictional predicate for in personam jurisdiction" that the "defendant [was] present in the forum state and personally served with process." App. to Pet. for Cert. 5. We granted certiorari. 493 U.S. 807 (1989).

一月下旬，上诉人因公到访了加利福尼亚州南部，之后他去了北部的旧金山湾地区看望他的孩子，他的妻子也在那里居住。他带着大的孩子去旧金山度了周末。1988 年 1 月 24 日他把孩子送回伯纳姆太太的家中，接到了加利福尼亚法院的传票和一份伯纳姆太太的离婚起诉状的副本。然后，他回到了新泽西州。

当年晚些时候，上诉人专门到了加利福尼亚州高级法院，提出撤销法院诉讼程序，认为法院对他缺乏属人管辖权，因为他与加利福尼亚州的联系只是因为开展业务和看望孩子的需要来过几次。高级法院否决了他的请求，加利福尼亚州上诉法院也拒绝向下级法院发布为他提供救济的命令，反对上诉人因为他缺乏与该州的"最小联系"所以依据正当程序条款应禁止加利福尼亚州法院对其行使管辖权的观点。该法院认为这是"基于属人管辖权的有效管辖"，"被告人出现在了法院所在地州并已经参与了诉讼程序"。我们同意将本案调卷。

【裁决过程与结果】（Procedure and Disposition）

Petitioner nonresident sought review of a Court of Appeal of California, First Appellate District, decision that upheld service of process on petitioner in a divorce action and held that U.S. Const. amend. XIV did not prohibit the court from asserting in personal jurisdiction over him because he had the requisite "minimum contacts" with the state.

The Supreme Court affirmed the decision of the appeals court and held that the forum state had personal jurisdiction over petitioner nonresident in the pending divorce action in the forum because the requisite minimum contacts were satisfied by petitioner's physical presence in the forum, even if on unrelated matters. Due process was satisfied because service of process occurred while petitioner was in the forum.

【裁判理由】（Reasons for Judicial Decision）

【生效判决意见】（Opinion by SCALIA）

To determine whether the assertion of personal jurisdiction is consistent with due process, we have long relied on the principles traditionally followed by American courts in marking out the territorial limits of each State's authority. That criterion was first announced in Pennoyer v. Neff, supra, in which we stated that due process "mean[s] a course of legal proceedings according to those rules and principles which have been established in our systems of jurisprudence for the protection and enforcement of private rights," id., at 733, including the "well-established principles of public law respecting the jurisdiction of an independent State over persons and property," id., at 722. In what has become the classic expression of the criterion, we said in International Shoe Co. v. Washington, 326 U.S. 310 (1945), that a state court's assertion of personal jurisdiction satisfies the Due Process Clause if it does not violate "traditional notions of fair play and substantial justice." Id., at 316, quoting Milliken v. Meyer, 311 U.S. 457, 463 (1940). See also Insurance Corp. of Ireland v. Compagnie des Bauxites de Guinee, 456 U.S. 694, 703 (1982). Since International Shoe, we have only been called upon to decide whether these "traditional notions" permit States to exercise jurisdiction over absent defendants in a manner that deviates from the rules of jurisdiction applied in the 19th century. We have held such deviations permissible, but only with respect to suits arising out of the absent defendant's contacts with the State. See, e.g., Helicopteros Nacionales de Colombia v. Hall, 466 U.S. 408, 414 (1984). The question we must decide today is whether due process requires a similar connection between the litigation and the defendant's contacts with the State in cases where the defendant is physically present in the State at the time process is served upon him.

判断属人管辖的行使是否符合正当程序，我们长期以来所依靠的是美国法院传统的以每个州权利的地域为标记的原则。这一标准是最高院审理的彭诺耶诉内夫一案所宣告的，在该案中我们提道，"正当程序是司法系统为保护和实现个人权利而确定的推进法律诉讼的规则和原则"，还包括"在公法中建立良好的原则以尊重独立州行使对人和物的管辖权"。在已经成为标准的经典表述的1945年国际鞋业公司诉华盛顿案中，我们说到"一个州法院属人管辖权的行使满足正当程序，只要它没有违反公平公正和实质正义的传统理念"，并引用了1940年米利肯诉迈耶案。自国际鞋业公司案以后，我们只是被要求来确定这些传统理念是否允许州适用与19世纪管辖权规则有偏离的方法来对缺席的被告行使管辖权。我们已经认可这种偏离的可行性，但所适用的案件是基于缺席被告与州之间的联系本身而产生的。我们今天需要决定的问题是，如果被告在被送达时正好身处法院所在州境内的话，那正当程序是否要求该案件和该州的联系与被告和该州的联系必须是同样一种联系。

Among the most firmly established principles of personal jurisdiction in American tradition is that the courts of a State have jurisdiction over nonresidents who are physically present in the State. The view developed early that each State had the power to hale before its courts any individual who could be found within its borders, and that once having acquired jurisdiction over such a person by properly serving him with process, the State could retain jurisdiction to enter judgment against him, no matter how fleeting his visit. See, e.g., Potter v. Allin, 2 Root 63, 67 (Conn. 1793); Barrell v. Benjamin, 15 Mass. 354 (1819). That view had antecedents in English common-law practice, which sometimes allowed "transitory" actions, arising out of events outside the country, to be maintained against seemingly nonresident defendants who were present in England. See, e.g., Mostyn v. Fabrigas, 98 Eng. Rep. 1021 (K.B. 1774); Cartwright v. Pettus, 22 Eng. Rep. 916 (Ch. 1675). Justice Story believed the principle, which he traced to Roman origins, to be firmly grounded in English tradition: "[By] the common law[,] personal actions, being transitory, may be brought in any place, where the party defendant may be found," for "every nation may...rightfully exercise jurisdiction over all persons within its domains." J. Story, Commentaries on the Conflict of Laws §§ 554, 543 (1846). See also id., §§ 530-538; Picquet v. Swan, supra, at 611-612 (Story, J.) ("Where a party is within a territory, he may justly be subjected to its process, and bound personally by the judgment pronounced, on such process, against him").

美国属人管辖权的传统中最坚定的原则是一个州法院对身体出现在该州的非居民有管辖权。早期的观点认为，每个州都有权将其边界内发生的人置于其法院管辖之下，且一旦通过正当的诉讼程序建立起了管辖权，该州就可以一直保有管辖权并对其做出判决，无论他的来访有多么短暂。这一观点源于英国普通法实践，这有时候会允许短暂过境的案件产生，针对发生在国外的事情，针对曾经来过英国的非居民被告人。斯托里大法官相信这一可追溯到罗马法起源的原则构成了英国的传统，"按照普通法，个人案件，作为短暂过境管辖案件，会发生在任何被告方可以被找到的地方"，因为"每个国家都会正当地行使对处于其控制之下的所有人的司法管辖权"。参见斯托里大法官对冲突法的评论（当事人一方在境内，他会被公平地适用于其程序，会受适用这样的程序所形成的对他的判决约束）。

Despite this formidable body of precedent, petitioner contends, in reliance on our decisions applying the International Shoe standard, that in the absence of "continuous and systematic" contacts with the forum, see n. 1, supra, a nonresident defendant can be subjected to judgment only as to matters that arise out of or relate to his contacts with the forum. This argument rests on a thorough misunderstanding of our cases.

虽然有这样难以违背的先例，上诉人仍认为，按照我们适用于国际鞋业公司案的标准，在缺乏与法院所在地之间的持续和一贯的联系的情况下，非居民被告只有在争议本身源于法院或其和法院所在地相联系的情况下才受其法院管辖。这一主张是对我们案例的彻底误解。

The view of most courts in the 19th century was that a court simply could not exercise in personam jurisdiction over a nonresident who had not been personally served with process in the forum. See, e.g., Reber v. Wright, 68 Pa. 471, 476-477 (1871); Sturgis v. Fay, 16 Ind. 429, 431 (1861); Weil v. Lowenthal, 10 Iowa 575, 578 (1860); Freeman, Law of Judgments, supra, at 468-470; see also D'Arcy v. Ketchum, 52 U.S. 165, 176 (1851); Knowles v. Gaslight & Coke Co., 86 U.S. 58, 61 (1874). Pennoyer v. Neff, while renowned for its statement of the principle that the Fourteenth Amendment prohibits such an exercise of jurisdiction, in fact set that forth only as dictum and decided the case (which involved a judgment rendered more than two years before the Fourteenth Amendment's ratification) under "well-established principles of public law." 95 U.S., at 722. Those principles, embodied in the Due Process Clause, required (we said) that when proceedings "involv[e] merely a determination of the personal liability of the defendant, he must be brought within [the court's] jurisdiction by service of process within the State, or his voluntary appearance." Id., at 733. We invoked that rule in a series of subsequent cases, as either a matter of due process or a "fundamental principl[e] of jurisprudence," Wilson v. Seligman, 144 U.S. 41, 46 (1892). See, e.g., New York Life Ins. Co. v. Dunlevy, 241 U.S. 518, 522-523 (1916); Goldey v. Morning News, 156 U.S. 518, 521 (1895).

19 世纪，大多数法院认为法院不能对没有在法院所在地被送达传票的非居民行使管辖权。彭诺耶诉内夫一案，对有关第十四修正案禁止如此行使管辖权的原则做了重申，但实际上仅仅做了宣言般的阐述而以"在公法中建立的良好的原则"判决了该案（该案涉及第十四修正案通过两年之前形成的一个判决）。这些原则，体现出在正当程序条款中，要求诉讼程序"仅涉及确定被告的个人责任时，他应当在该州内通过被送达传票而被管辖，或者是他自愿出庭接受管辖"。我们在随后的一系列判决中引用该规则，将其作为正当程序的一个重要问题或管辖权的基础原则。

Later years, however, saw the weakening of the Pennoyer rule. In the late 19th and early 20th centuries, changes in the technology of transportation and communication, and the tremendous growth of interstate business activity, led to an "inevitable relaxation of the strict limits on state jurisdiction" over nonresident individuals and corporations. Hanson v. Denckla, 357 U.S. 235, 260 (1958) (Black, J., dissenting). States required, for example, that nonresident corporations appoint an in-state agent upon whom process could be served as a condition of transacting business within their borders, see, e.g., St. Clair v. Cox, 106 U.S. 350 (1882), and provided in-state "substituted service" for nonresident motorists who caused injury in the State and left before personal service could be accomplished, see, e.g., Kane v. New Jersey, 242 U.S. 160 (1916); Hess v. Pawloski, 274 U.S. 352 (1927). We initially upheld these laws under the Due Process Clause on grounds that they complied with Pennoyer's rigid requirement of either "consent," see, e.g., Hess v. Pawloski, supra, at 356, or "presence," see, e.g., Philadelphia & Reading R. Co. v. McKibbin, 243 U.S. 264, 265 (1917). As many observed, however, the consent and presence were purely fictional. See, e.g., 1 J. Beale, Conflict of Laws 360, 384 (1935); Hutchinson v. Chase & Gilbert, Inc., 45 F. 2d 139, 141 (CA2 1930) (L. Hand, J.). Our opinion in International Shoe cast those fictions aside and made explicit the underlying basis of these decisions: Due process does not necessarily require the States to adhere to the unbending territorial limits on jurisdiction set forth in Pennoyer. The validity of assertion of jurisdiction over a nonconsenting defendant who is not present in the forum depends upon whether "the quality and nature of [his] activity" in relation to the forum, 326 U.S., at 319, renders such jurisdiction consistent with "traditional notions of fair play and substantial justice." Id., at 316 (citation omitted). Subsequent cases have derived from the International Shoe standard the general rule that a State may dispense with in-forum personal service on nonresident defendants in suits arising out of their activities in the State. See generally Helicopteros Nacionales de Colombia v. Hall, 466 U.S., at 414-415. As International Shoe suggests, the defendant's litigation-related "minimum contacts" may take the place of physical presence as the basis for jurisdiction:

"Historically the jurisdiction of courts to render judgment in personam is grounded on their de facto power over the defendant's person. Hence his presence within the territorial jurisdiction of a court was prerequisite to its rendition of a judgment personally binding on him. Pennoyer v. Neff, 95 U.S. 714, 733. But now that the capias ad respondendum has given way to personal service of summons or other form of notice, due process requires only that in order to subject a defendant to a judgment in personam, if he be not present within the territory of the forum, he have certain minimum contacts with it such that the maintenance of the suit does not offend 'traditional notions of fair play and substantial justice.'" 326 U.S., at 316 (citations omitted).

然而近些年来，能够看到彭诺耶规则的影响在削弱。在 19 世纪末 20 世纪初，交通和通信技术的变化和跨州商事活动剧增，导致了适用于非居民个人和公司方面的州管辖权地域限制规则不可避免地放松。例如，州要求，非居民公司在他们境内指定一个州内的代理机构作为开展业务的条件以便送达传票，还对在州内造成伤害且在个人传票送达完成之前离开本州的非居民驾驶人员提供州内的替代送达。我们从最开始就赞成这些符合正当程序条款的法律，因为他们符合彭诺耶规则的"同意"或"现身"的严格要求。然而，正如很多人所评述的，"同意"或"现身"是假定的。我们在国际鞋业案中将这些虚构剔除，明确了这些判决的基础：正当程序条款并没有要求一州一定要恪守彭诺耶案提供的那种对州法院管辖权死板的地域性限制。对一个没有存在于法院所在州的非自愿出庭被告行使管辖权的合理性应当取决于，该被告在法院所在州境内活动的质量和特性能否使得对他实施管辖符合传统意义上的公平公正和实质正义的法律理念。之后的案例对于非居民被告所在州之外的活动引发的案件中应当遵守在法院地州被当面送达的原则。正如国际鞋业案件所建议的，被告与案件相关的"最小联系"应当发生在被告物理现身的地方，才可以作为管辖权的基础。

"历史上，对个人做出判决的法院管辖权建立在法院对被告属人的事实权力基础上。因此他现身于法院的管辖地域之内是所做出的判决对其个人产生约束力的前提条件。但现在传讯命令已经通过向个人送达传票或其他通知形式送出，正当程序仅要求，为让一个没有出现在法院所在区域内的被告人受其属人的判决约束，他要与该州有最小联系以使该案件的存在不会违背传统意义上的公平公正和实质正义。"

Nothing in International Shoe or the cases that have followed it, however, offers support for the very different proposition petitioner seeks to establish today: that a defendant's presence in the forum is not only unnecessary to validate novel, nontraditional assertions of jurisdiction, but is itself no longer sufficient to establish jurisdiction. That proposition is unfaithful to both elementary logic and the foundations of our due process jurisprudence.

然而，国际鞋业等案件并没有按照这样的原则在今天支持提出一个明显不同的主张的申请人：被告在法院所在地的现身不仅对确认假定事实这一传统上行使管辖权的基础是不必要的，而且其自身也不足以确立管辖权。这一主张不符合基本逻辑和我们所做出的有关正当程序问题分析结论的基础。

The short of the matter is that jurisdiction based on physical presence alone constitutes due process because it is one of the continuing traditions of our legal system that define the due process standard of "traditional notions of fair play and substantial justice." That standard was developed by analogy to "physical presence," and it would be perverse to say it could now be turned against that touchstone of jurisdiction.

简单说问题的实质在于，单独建立在物理现身基础上的管辖权符合正当程序，因为我们的法律体制的持续传统之一就是将公平正义和实质正义的传统观念作为正当程序的标准。这一标准是由"物理现身"推理而来的，所以我们不能说这与确立管辖权的标准相违背。

Because the Due Process Clause does not prohibit the California courts from exercising jurisdiction over petitioner based on the fact of in-state service of process, the judgment is Affirmed.

因为正当程序条款不禁止加利福尼亚州法院基于在州内送达传票的事实行使管辖权，判决予以维持。

【附合意见】（Concur by WHITE）

I join Parts, I, II-A, II-B, and II-C of JUSTICE SCALIA's opinion and concur in the judgment of affirmance. The rule allowing jurisdiction to be obtained over a nonresident by personal service in the forum State, without more, has been and is so widely accepted throughout this country that I could not possibly strike it down, either on its face or as applied in this case, on the ground that it denies due process of law guaranteed by the Fourteenth Amendment. Although the Court has the authority under the Amendment to examine even traditionally accepted procedures and declare them invalid, e.g., Shaffer v. Heitner, 433 U.S. 186 (1977), there has been no showing here or elsewhere that as a general proposition the rule is so arbitrary and lacking in common sense in so many instances that it should be held violative of due process in every case. Furthermore, until such a showing is made, which would be difficult indeed, claims in individual cases that the rule would operate unfairly as applied to the particular nonresident involved need not be entertained. At least this would be the case where presence in the forum State is intentional, which would almost always be the fact. Otherwise, there would be endless, fact-specific litigation in the trial and appellate courts, including this one. Here, personal service in California, without more, is enough, and I agree that the judgment should be affirmed.

我同意斯卡利亚大法官判决意见中的第 1、2.1、2.2、2.3 部分并同意维持原判。规则允许通过给非居民所在州法院所在地直接送达传票获得管辖权，这一规则在这个国家已经被广泛接受，无论是泛泛而谈还是在本案中，我都不可能否定这一规则，因为这样就违背了第十四修正案所保障的正当程序。虽然法院根据修正案的授权有权审查甚至在传统上已被接受的程序并宣布作废，但一般说来这种情况不会因武断和缺乏常识发生在很多案件中，如果在每个案件中都这样做就会被认为违反正当程序。另外，目前并没有显示出来，这的确也很困难，个人案件中主张这一规则适用于具体的不需要接待的非居民时是不公平的。至少现身于法院所在地州是出于其本意。否则，将会有包括本案在内的很多涉及具体事实问题的案件被呈到初审法院和上诉法院。在本案中，上诉人在加利福尼亚州被直接送达传票，没有更多，就已经足够了。我同意判决予以维持。

【案件影响】（Impact of the Case）

本案中，传统的规则虽然受到挑战，但是美国联邦最高法院仍然裁定送达完成后，法院就取得了管辖权。一直到现在，美国联邦法院和各州法院仍然以传票的送达作为对人管辖权行使的依据。甚至在 1995 年卡迪奇诉卡拉季奇案（Kadic v. Karadzic）中，第九巡回法院裁定在被告与美国没有任何实质性联系（substantial contact）的情形下，被告即使是短暂过境美国，他也可因此而被送达，法院也就取得了管辖权。

【思考问题】（Questions）

1. 长臂管辖权（Long Arm Jurisdiction）、短暂过境管辖权（Transient Jurisdiction）和接触管辖权（Tag Jurisdiction）这 3 个美国民事诉讼法中的概念有何区别？

2. 美国民事诉讼管辖权制度对我国的管辖权制度有何借鉴意义？

十四、刑法案例

女王诉达德利和斯蒂芬斯案

R v. Dudley and Stephens（1884）

【选读理由】（Selected Reason）

英国王座法庭在 1884 年 11 月 9 日做出判决的公海食人一案（R v. Dudley and Stephens）几乎是世界法学界最著名的案例之一。本案中的被害人理查德·帕克（Richard Parker）以其17 岁的生命为代价向法学界提出这样一个问题：不是你死就是大家一起死，这是一个能被法律所容忍的杀人理由么？在此案发生之后，刑法中有关正当防卫、紧急避险等行为的合法合理界限都得到了进一步的确定。

【案件事实】（Fact）

On July 5, 1884, the prisoners, Captain Dudley and Stephens, with one Brooks, all able-bodied English seamen, and the deceased, also an English boy, between seventeen and eighteen years of age, the crew of an English yacht, were cast away in a storm on the high seas, 1,600 miles from the Cape of Good Hope, and were compelled to put into an open boat. That in this boat they had no supply of water and no supply of food, except two 1lb. tins of turnips, and for three days they had nothing else to subsist upon. That on the fourth day they caught a small turtle, upon which they subsisted for a few days, and this was the only food they had up to the twentieth day, when the act now in question was committed. That on the twelfth day the remains of the turtle were entirely consumed, and for the next eight days they had nothing to eat. That they had no fresh water, except such rain as they from time to time caught in their oilskin capes. That the boat was drifting on the ocean, and it was probably more than a thousand miles away from land. That on the eighteenth day, when they had been seven days without food and five without water, the prisoners spoke to Brooks as to what should be done if no succour came, and suggested that someone should be sacrificed to save the rest, but Brooks dissented, and the boy to whom they were understood to refer was not consulted.

1884 年 7 月 5 号，被告人达德利船长和被告人斯蒂芬斯，以及另一人布鲁克斯，他们三人都是身体健壮的英国船员。死者是一个英国男孩，年龄为十七八岁，与其他三人同为英国船上的船员。他们因为遭遇风暴而漂流在距离好望角 1600 英里的公海上，不得不待在一艘敞篷的小船上。这船上没有水也没有食物，只有两罐 1 磅重的大头菜。三天的时间里他们没有吃东西。到第四天，他们抓到了一只小海龟，靠它维持了几天，这也是他们直到第二十天该被诉行动发生前的唯一食物。到第十二天，海龟被完全消耗掉了，在接下来的八天里他们没有任何东西可吃。他们没有淡水，除了下雨时他们可以不时从油布斗篷中获得一些雨水。船在海上漂流，在大概离陆地 1000 英里以外的地方。到第十八天，当他们已经七天没有进食，五天没有喝水，被告们对布鲁克斯说如果还没有获得救助就应该做些什么，并建议某人应该牺牲以拯救其他人，但是布鲁克斯不同意。他们所指的男孩没有被征询意见。

That on July 24, the day before the act now in question, the prisoner Dudley proposed to Stephens and to Brooks that lots should be cast who should be put to death to save the rest, but Brooks refused to consent, and it was not put to the boy, and in point of fact there was no drawing of lots. That on that day the prisoners spoke of their having families, and suggested that it would be better to kill the boy that their lives should be saved, and the prisoner Dudley proposed that if there was no vessel in sight by the morrow morning the boy should be killed. That next day, July 25, no vessel appearing, Dudley told Brooks that he had better go and have a sleep, and made signs to Stephens and Brooks that the boy had better be killed. The prisoner Stephens agreed to the set, but Brooks dissented from it. That the boy was then lying at the bottom of the boat quite helpless, and extremely weakened by famine and by drinking sea water, and unable to make any resistance, nor did be ever assent to his being killed. The prisoner, Captain Dudley, offered a prayer, asking forgiveness for them all if either of them should be tempted to commit a rash act, and that their souls might be saved. That the prisoner Dudley, with the assent of the prisoner Stephens, went to the boy, and telling him that his time was come, put a knife into his throat and killed him then and there. That the three men fed upon the body and blood of the boy for four days. That, on the fourth day after the act had been committed, the boat was picked up by a passing vessel, and the prisoners were rescued still alive, but in the lowest state of prostration. That they were carried to the port of Falmouth, and committed for trial at Exeter. That, if the men had not fed upon the body of the boy, they would probably not have survived to be so picked up and rescued, but would within the four days have died of famine. That the boy, being in a much weaker condition, was likely to have died before them. That at the time of the act in question there was no sail in sight, nor any reasonable prospect of relief. That under the circumstances there appeared to the prisoners every probability that, unless they then fed, or very soon fed, upon the boy or one of themselves, they would die of starvation. That there was no appreciable chance of saving life except by killing someone for the others to eat. That, assuming any necessity to kill anybody, there was no greater necessity for killing the boy than any of the three men.

那是在 7 月 24 日，即被诉行为发生前一天，被告人达德利向斯蒂芬斯和布鲁克斯提议应当抽签决定谁被处死以拯救其余的人，但布鲁克斯不同意，这一建议也并没有告之男孩，事实上也没有进行抽签。在那一天，被告人们都说他们有家庭，所以建议最好杀死男孩让他们能够活命。达德利提议如果转天早上还是看不到船只，那男孩就要被杀死。第二天，7 月 25 日，没有船只出现，达德利告诉布鲁克斯他最好去睡觉，并给斯蒂芬斯和布鲁克斯做了手势表示那男孩应该被杀死。被告人斯蒂芬斯表示同意，但布鲁克斯不同意。那男孩当时无助地躺在船底，因为饥饿和饮用海水而极度虚弱，无法做任何抵抗，也从来没有同意他的被杀。被告人达德利船长做了一个祷告，请求上帝宽恕他们所有的人，希望他们中的任何一人在诱惑之下草率行事的同时，他们的灵魂还可以被拯救。被告人达德利，在被告人斯蒂芬斯同意的情况下，走向男孩，并告诉他最后的时间到了，然后把刀插进他的喉咙，杀了他。然后，男孩的血肉被这三个男人吃了四天。在被诉行为发生后的第四天，他们的小船被一艘路过的船只救起，被告人获救时仍然活着，但处于最虚弱的状态。他们被带到法尔茅斯港，并在埃克塞特接受审判。就是说，如果这些人没有食用男孩的身体，他们极有可能在四天内死于饥饿，活不到被救的时候，而男孩因为更为虚弱非常可能死在他们前面，且当时看不到任何船只，没有任何获救的希望。这种情况下，每个被告人面前的最大的可能性就是，除非他们能够吃上东西或很快吃东西，即吃那个男孩或他们中的一个，他们就会饿死。除了杀一个人来吃以外，没有其他的明显可以挽救生命的机会。假设有必要杀死任何人，杀死男孩的必要性并不比杀死三个男人中的任何一个的必要性更大。

【裁决过程与结果】（Procedure and Disposition）

The two prisoners, Thomas Dudley and Edwin Stephens, were indicted for the wilful murder of Richard Parker on 25 July 1884, on the high seas, within the jurisdiction of the Admiralty of England. They were tried at the winter assizes at Exeter on 6 November 1884, before Huddleston, B, When, at the suggestion of the learned judge, the jury returned a special verdict, setting out the facts, and referred the matter to the Divisional Court for its decision.

The Lord Chief Justice thereupon passed sentence of death in the usual form. The prisoners were afterwards respited and their sentence commuted to one of six months' imprisonment without hard labour.

【裁判理由】（Reasons for Judicial Decision）

【原审意见】

But whether upon the whole matter by the jurors found the killing of Richard Parker by Dudley and Stephens be felony and murder the jurors are ignorant, and pray the advice of the Court thereupon, and if upon the whole matter the Court shall be of opinion that the killing of Richard Parker be felony and murder, then the jurors say that Dudley and Stephens were each guilty of felony and murder as alleged in the indictment.

尽管陪审团查明了达德利和斯蒂芬斯杀死了理查德·帕克的整个事情经过，但陪审团对这一杀害行为是否构成谋杀并不清楚，因此请求法院给予建议，并认为基于整个事实如果法院认定杀死理查德·帕克构成谋杀，则陪审团认为达德利和斯蒂芬斯已构成起诉书所指控的谋杀罪。

From these facts, stated with the cold precision of a special verdict, it appears sufficiently that the prisoners were subject to terrible temptation, to sufferings which might break down the bodily power of the strongest man, and try the conscience of the best…But nevertheless this is clear, that the prisoners put to death a weak and unoffending boy upon the chance of preserving their own lives by feeding upon his flesh and blood after he was killed, and with the certainty of depriving *him* of any possible chance of survival. The verdict finds in terms that "if the men had not fed upon the body of the boy they would *probably* not have survived," and that "the boy being in a much weaker condition was *likely* to have died before them." They might possibly have been picked up next day by a passing ship; they might possibly not have been picked up at all; in either case it is obvious that the killing of the boy would have been an unnecessary and profitless act. It is found by the verdict that the boy was incapable of resistance, and, in fact, made none; and it is not even suggested that his death was due to any violence on his part attempted against, or even so much as feared by, those who killed him. Under these circumstances the jury say that they are ignorant whether those who killed him were guilty of murder, and have referred it to this Court to determine what is the legal consequence which follows from the facts which they have found.

这一特殊的裁定冷静而准确地叙述了这些事实，充分显示被告人受到可怕的诱惑，其所遭受的痛苦可能摧毁最强壮的人的身体力量，并考验最善良的人心……但尽管如此，事实很清楚，这些被告人杀死了一个虚弱而无辜的孩子，使他们自己有机会食用他的血和肉以获得保全他们自己生命的机会，也剥夺了男孩任何可能的生存下来的机会。裁定最后说，"如果这三个男人没有食用男孩，他们极有可能无法生存下来"，并且"男孩在更虚弱的情况下可能会死在他们前面"。但他们也可能会在转天被路过的船救起，也可能根本不会被救起，在这两种情况下，杀死这个男孩显然就会成为不必要的和无益的行为。裁决认为，男孩是无法抵抗的，事实上也没有反抗，甚至没有人认为他的死亡是由于他有任何试图反对杀他的人的行为而招致的暴力或恐惧。在这种情况下，陪审团认为，他们无法确定那些杀害了男孩的人是否犯有谋杀罪，并将本案提交给上级法院，由法院基于它们所查明的事实确定相应的法律后果。

【生效判决意见】（JUDGMENTBY-1: LORD COLERIDGE CJ:）

There remains to be considered the real question in the case—whether killing, under the circumstances set forth in the verdict, be or be not murder. The contention that it could be anything else was to the minds of us all both new and strange, and we stopped the Attorney—General in his negative argument that we might hear what could be said in support of a proposition which appeared to us to be at once dangerous, immoral, and opposed to all legal principle and analogy. All, no doubt, that can be said has been urged before us, and we are now to consider and determine what it amounts to.

本案需要考虑的真正的问题是，在裁决所查明的情境下杀人是否构成谋杀。在我们看来，任何主张不构成谋杀罪的观点都很新奇。我们制止总检察长的反驳，为的就是能够听到支持那些可能对我们来说显然危险、不道德，甚至有悖所有法律原则和法律逻辑的观点。毫无疑问，所有可能的观点都在我们面前得到了极力主张，现在，我们需要考虑并判断这种观点意味着什么。

First, it is said that it follows, from various definitions of murder in books of authority—which definitions imply, if they do not state, the doctrine—that, in order to save your own life you may lawfully take away the life of another, when that other is neither attempting nor threatening yours, nor is guilty of any illegal act whatever towards you or anyone else. But, if these definitions be looked at, they will not be found to sustain the contention. The earliest in point of date is the passage cited to us from Bracton, who wrote in the reign of Henry III. It was at one time the fashion to discredit Bracton because he was supposed to mingle too much of the canonist and civilian with the common lawyer. There is now no such feeling; but the passage upon homicide, on which reliance is placed, is a remarkable example of the kind of writing which may explain it. Sin and crime are spoken of as apparently equally illegal; and the crime of murder, it is expressly declared, may be committed lingua vel facto; so that a man, like Hero, "done to death by slanderous tongues," would, it seems, in the opinion of Bracton, be a person in respect of whom might be grounded a legal indictment for murder. But in the very passage as to necessity, on which reliance has been placed, it is clear that Bracton is speaking of necessity in the ordinary sense, the repelling by violence—violence justified so far as it was necessary for the object—any illegal violence used towards oneself. If, says Bracton (Lib iii, Art De Corona, cap 4, fol 120) the necessity be "evitabilis et evadere posset absque occisione, tunc erit reus homicidii"—words which show clearly that he is thinking of physical danger, from which escape may be possible, and that "inevitabilis necessitas," of which he speaks as justifying homicide, is a necessity of the same nature.

首先，这种观点声称遵循了权威著作中有关谋杀罪的各种定义，认为这些定义即使没有明说也暗含着这样一条原则：为了挽救自己的生命，你可以合法地剥夺他人生命，即使他人没有攻击也没有威胁到你的生命，也没有任何针对你或他人的犯罪行为发生。但如果仔细审查那些权威定义，它们并不支持这种观点。在这一点上，能被我们引证的最早文献出自布莱克顿，他生活在亨利三世时代。历史上曾有一段时间，人们普遍怀疑布莱克顿，因为他把宗教学家和普通市民与普通法律师搅和在一起。当然，现在不存在这种认识了，但我们依据的关于杀人罪的论述还是一个特例，能很好地说明这一点。他认为，（宗教意义上的）罪孽和（世俗法中的）罪行显然是同等不法的，并且明确表示，谋杀罪有可能是由"语言或行动"而触犯的。所以，在布莱克顿看来，像神那样"凭借恶毒之舌致人死亡"的人好像也可以从法律上指控其犯了谋杀罪。但是，在关于紧急避险那一段，布莱克顿显然是在通常意义上谈论紧急避险——采取暴力进行反抗，只有这种暴力是反抗任何针对自己身体的非法暴力所必需的，才具有正当性。布莱克顿表示，如果紧急避险是"可避免的，他能够不受伤害地逃避，那就成了杀人"，这句话清楚表明，他分析的是身体危险，并且是有可能避免的，而他用来证明杀人行为正当性的所谓"不可避免的紧急避险"就是同一性质的紧急避险。

It is, if possible, yet clearer that the doctrine contended for receives no support from the great authority of Lord Hale. It is plain that in his view the necessity which justifies homicide is that only which has always been, and is now, considered a justification. He says (1 Hale, PC 491): "In all these cases of homicide by necessity, as in pursuit of a felon, in killing him that assaults to rob, or comes to burn or break a house, or the like, which are in themselves no felony." Again, he says that the necessity which justifies homicide is of two kinds: "(1) That necessity which is of a private nature; (2) That necessity which relates to the public justice and safety. The former is that necessity which obliged a man to his own defence and safeguard; and this takes in these inquiries: 1. What may be done for the safeguard of a man's own life;" and then follow three other heads not necessary to pursue.

可能更加清楚的是，这一原则并未能从伟大的权威黑尔勋爵那里得到支持。他的观点非常直白，不管是过去，还是现在，证明杀人行为具有正当性的唯一理由就是紧急避险。他说："在所有紧急避险的杀人案件中，诸如追捕重罪犯、杀死暴力抢劫者、杀死试图烧毁房屋或破门而入的罪犯等，这本身不构成犯罪。"他还认为，表明杀人具有正当性的紧急避险可以有两种情况：（1）关乎私人利益性质的紧急避险；（2）关系公共正义和安全的紧急避险。前者是迫使个人进行自我防卫的紧急避险，且要考虑以下要求：保护一个人的生命可能需要做什么。接着，他指出了三个不必追求的目的。

Lord Hale proceeds (1 Hale, PC 478):

"1. As touching the first of these, viz, homicide in defence of a man's own life, which is usually styled se defendendo." It is not possible to use words more clear to show that LORD HALE regarded the private necessity which justified, and alone justified, the taking the life of another for the safeguard of one's own to be what is commonly called self-defence.

然后，黑尔勋爵继续论述：

"在第一种情况下，即杀人是为了保卫自己的生命，这通常被认为是正当防卫。"黑尔勋爵的阐述再清楚不过了，他认为，通常所谓的"自卫"是能够证明——并且是唯一能够证明——为保卫自己生命剥夺他人生命正当性的私人紧急避险。

The one real authority of former time is Lord Bacon, who in his Commentary on the maxim, "Necessitas inducit privilegium quoad jura privata," lays down the law as follows: "Necessity carrieth a privilege in itself. Necessity is of three sorts: Necessity of conservation of life, necessity of obedience, and necessity of the act of God or of a stranger. First, of conservation of life. If a man steals viands to satisfy his present hunger, this is no felony nor larceny. So if divers be in danger of drowning by the casting away of some boat or barge, and one of them get to some plank, or on the boat's side, to keep himself above water, and another to save his life thrusts him from it, whereby he is drowned, this is neither as defendendo nor by misadventure, but justifiable."

There are many conceivable states of things in which it might possibly be true, but, if Lord Bacon meant to lay down the broad proposition that a man may save his life by killing, if necessary, an innocent and unoffending neighbour, it certainly is not law at the present day.

截至目前，唯一真正的权威意见来自培根勋爵。他在评论法律格言"紧急避险必须尊重私权"时，解释道："紧急避险有其自身的特权。构成紧急避险的情况有三种——保护生命、服从命令、迫于神明或他人行为。首要的是保护生命。如果一个人因饥饿偷了食物，就既不构成重罪也不构成盗窃罪。所以，如果某条小船或游船倾覆，落水者危在旦夕，其中一人得到一块木板，或是抓住船舷，使自己不至于沉底，而另一个人为了求生将他推走，致其溺亡。这既不是正当防卫，也不是意外事件，但却正当合理。"

在许多可以想到的情况下，培根勋爵的观点可能是正确的，但如果他想将这种宽泛的观点——在必要的情况下，一个人可以通过杀死无辜者或没有任何危害的邻居来保全自己的生命——规定成法律，那么在今天肯定是不可行的。

Except for the purpose of testing how far the conservation of a man's own life is in all cases and under all circumstances an absolute, unqualified, and paramount duty, we exclude from our consideration all the incidents of war. We are dealing with a case of private homicide, not one imposed upon men in the service of their Sovereign or in the defence of their country. It is admitted that the deliberate killing of this unoffending and unresisting boy was clearly murder, unless the killing can be justified by some well-recognised excuse admitted by the law. It is further admitted that there was in this case no such excuse, unless the killing was justified by what has been called necessity. But the temptation to the act which existed here was not what the law has ever called necessity. Nor is this to be regretted. Though law and morality are not the same, and though many things may be immoral which are not necessarily illegal, yet the absolute divorce of law from morality would be of fatal consequence, and such divorce would follow if the temptation to murder in this case were to be held by law an absolute defence of it. It is not so.

现在，为了讨论在所有案件中、在任何情况下，保护一个人的生命在多大程度上是绝对的、无条件的、至高无上的义务，我们不考虑所有的战争行为。我们正在讨论的是个人杀人行为，不是效忠王室、捍卫国家的义务。故意杀死这个既未挑衅也无反抗能力的男孩是不折不扣的谋杀，除非这一杀人行为能够有被法律所承认的正当合理的理由。这一点已经得到认可。还得到认可的是，在这个案件中，除了用所谓的"紧急避险"来证明谋杀行为的正当性之外，不存在法律上公认的理由。但是，本案中杀人行为的诱发因素又不是法律上所谓的紧急避险。这并不遗憾。法律与道德不同，且许多不道德的事情不一定是非法的，但是，法律绝对地与道德相分离将导致致命的后果；如果本案的谋杀诱因被法律认可为一种绝对的辩护理由，则法律与道德的分离将随之而至。事实上不应当这样。

It is not needful to point out the awful danger of admitting the principle which has been contended for. Who is to be the judge of this sort of necessity? By what measure is the comparative value of lives to be measured? Is it to be strength, or intellect, or what? It is plain that the principle leaves to him who is to profit by it to determine the necessity which will justify him in deliberately taking another's life to save his own. In this case the weakest, the youngest, the most unresisting was chosen. Was it more necessary to kill him than one of the grown men? The answer must be, No.

"So spake the Fiend; and with necessity, The tyrant's plea, excused his devilish deeds."

至于辩护人主张的观点，如果得到承认，将产生的可怕后果已无须多言。谁有权判断这种紧急避险？以什么标准来比较不同生命的价值。是体力？智力？还是其他条件？显而易见，这种原则只会让那些为了保全自己杀害他人的人获益，因为将由他来决定正当杀人的紧急状态。本案当事人选中的牺牲对象是最弱的、最小的、最无反抗能力的孩子。难道杀死他比杀死成年人中的任何一个都更必要吗？答案一定是"不"。

"魔鬼说，在必要时，暴君的要求就是他做邪恶之事的借口。"

It is not suggested that in this particular case the "deeds" were "devilish"; but it is quite plain that such a principle, once admitted, might be made the legal cloke for unbridled passion and atrocious crime. There is no path safe for judges to tread but to ascertain the law to the best of their ability, and to declare it according to their judgment, and if in any case the law appears to be too severe on individuals, to leave it to the Sovereign to exercise that prerogative of mercy which the Constitution has entrusted to the hands fittest to dispense it. It must not be supposed that, in refusing to admit temptation to be an excuse for crime, it is forgotten how terrible the temptation was, how awful the suffering, how hard in such trials to keep the judgment straight and the conduct pure.

这并不是说本案中的行为就是"邪恶"的，但很明确的是，一旦承认了这样一个原则，就可能会成为放纵激情和恶意犯罪的合法借口。法官只能尽自己最大能力查明法律，依据自己的判断伸张法律，除此之外，没有确定无疑的道路可走。如果在某种情况下，法律对个人太过严厉，那就只能呈递给国王陛下，依据宪法授予的宽宥之权，免除这项规定。我们虽然拒绝承认某种诱因能作为犯罪的借口，但我们也不该忘记此案中的诱因：环境是如此的恶劣、痛苦是多么的难以忍受，保持正当的判断与善良的行为是多么的艰难。

We are often compelled to set up standards we cannot reach ourselves, and to lay down rules which we could not ourselves satisfy. But a man has no right to declare temptation to be an excuse, though he might himself have yielded to it, nor allow compassion for the criminal to change or weaken in any manner the legal definition of the crime. It is, therefore, our duty to declare that the prisoners' act in this case was willful murder; that the facts as stated in the verdict are no legal justification of the homicide; and to say that, in our unanimous opinion, they are, upon this special verdict, guilty of murder.

THE LORD CHIEF JUSTICE thereupon passed sentence of death in the usual form. [The prisoners were afterwards respited and their sentence commuted to one of six months' imprisonment without hard labour.]

我们经常被迫确立一些我们自己都无法达到的标准，定下我们自己都无法遵守的规则。但是，人没有权利去宣称诱因是免罪的理由，即使他自己可能屈服于这种诱因；人更没有权利，因为同情罪犯，而试图去改变或削弱对于犯罪的定义。因此，我们有义务宣布被告人在本案中的行为构成故意杀人；在前面裁定中陈述的事实不能够成为其杀人的合法理由；也就是说，我们一致同意，基于前述特殊的裁决，他们构成谋杀罪。

首席法官勋爵由此宣布按照一般程序对被告人处以死刑。（被告人此后被暂缓执行，他们的刑罚被减少到 6 个月有期徒刑，无须强制劳动。）

【案件影响】（Impact of the Case）

本案经过艰难的讨论，合议庭发现无论是基于法律先例，还是基于伦理与道德，在普通法中根本没有任何针对谋杀指控所涉及的危急状态的辩护理由，法庭不得不依法判处达德利和斯蒂芬斯死刑，但建议予以宽赦。最终女王将刑期减至 6 个月监禁。后来，达德利移居澳大利亚，但始终认为对他的有罪判决是不正当的。为了纪念本案中死去的理查德·帕克，有人在其出生地附近的南安普敦市东郊梨树坪教堂立起一块墓碑。

【思考问题】（Questions）

1. 在本案中如果经过帕克同意，或者经过抽签抽中帕克，杀死帕克是否就无可厚非了？

2. 紧急避险行为人往往处于特殊情境下，法律难以做一般性的适用，但紧急避险的正当性是否仍然需要确立一些客观的衡量标准？

十五、刑事诉讼法案例

米兰达诉亚利桑那州案

Miranda v. Arizona（1966）

【选读理由】（Selected Reason）

美国刑事诉讼中的米兰达权利，也就是犯罪嫌疑人保持沉默的权利，是个具有特殊意义的法律制度。米兰达权利来自于米兰达诉亚利桑那州案，该案是美国联邦最高法院于 1966 年审理并最终以 5:4 做出判决的里程碑式的案件。在判决中，最高法院将自白任意性规则延伸到了侦查阶段，最终确立了米兰达规则。米兰达规则直接规范了国家官员在对被关押人员进行讯问时的职权行为，它的全部内容是对被告人的忠告，也是对每个警员的"忠告"。

【案件事实】（Facts）

On March 13, 1963, Ernesto Miranda was arrested, by the Phoenix Police Department, based on circumstantial evidence linking him to the kidnapping and rape of an eighteen-year-old woman ten days earlier. After two hours of interrogation by police officers, Miranda signed a confession to the rape charge on forms that included the typed statement: "I do hereby swear that I make this statement voluntarily and of my own free will, with no threats, coercion, or promises of immunity, and with full knowledge of my legal rights, understanding any statement I make may be used against me."

1963 年 3 月 13 日，一个名叫恩纳斯托·米兰达的青年男子被凤凰城警察局逮捕，警官根据一些间接证据将他与 10 天前发生的一起 17 岁少女被绑架和强奸的案件联系起来而对其展开审讯。两个小时后，米兰达在供述强奸罪的认罪供词上签了字，这份供词上有"我谨宣誓自己完全是出于自愿而做出此陈述，没有受到任何威胁、强迫或是为得到任何豁免权的交换。并且我已充分了解自己的合法权益，知晓我的任何陈述都可能对己不利"的字样。

However, at no time was Miranda told of his right to counsel. Prior to being presented with the form on which he was asked to write out the confession he had already given orally, he was not advised of his right to remain silent, nor was he informed that his statements during the interrogation would be used against him. At trial, when prosecutors offered Miranda's written confession as evidence, his court-appointed lawyer, Alvin Moore, objected that because of these facts, the confession was not truly voluntary and should be excluded. Moore's objection was overruled and based on this confession and other evidence, Miranda was convicted of rape and kidnapping. He was sentenced to 20–30 years of imprisonment on each charge, with sentences to run concurrently.

不过在这一过程中，警官并没有告知米兰达他有权保持沉默并且与律师进行商议，也没有告知其证词将会被用于指控他。在法院开庭审理时，地方检察官出示了米兰达写下的供词作为指控他犯罪的重要证据，而米兰达的公共辩护律师艾尔文·摩尔指出由于警方没有在审问前告知被告的宪法权利，因此这些证据应该被排除，但法庭没有接受这一意见。米兰达被陪审团认定强奸和绑架罪名成立，法官判处他每项罪名 20 至 30 年有期徒刑，两罪刑期同时执行。

Moore filed Miranda's appeal to the Arizona Supreme Court, claiming that Miranda's confession was not fully voluntary and should not have been admitted into the court proceedings. The Arizona Supreme Court affirmed the trial court's decision to admit the confession in State v. Miranda, 401 P.2d 721 (Ariz. 1965). In affirmation, the Arizona Supreme Court emphasized heavily the fact that Miranda did not specifically request an attorney.

摩尔将案件向亚利桑那州最高法院上诉，声称米兰达的认罪并非完全自愿，因此不应为法庭所接受。而亚利桑那州最高法院则在亚利桑那州诉米兰达案中同意了之前法院的意见，并特别强调米兰达并没有主动要求要有律师。

On certiorari, the Supreme Court of the United States reversed in a 5-4 majority. The Court held that both inculpatory and exculpatory statements made in response to interrogation by a defendant in police custody will be admissible at trial only if the prosecution can show that the defendant was informed of the right to consult with an attorney before and during questioning and of the right against self-incrimination before police questioning, and that the defendant not only understood these rights, but voluntarily waived them. This had a significant impact on law enforcement in the United States, by making what became known as the Miranda rights part of routine police procedure to ensure that suspects were informed of their rights. The Supreme Court decided *Miranda* with three other consolidated cases:Westover v. United States, Vignera v. New York, and California v. Stewart.

美国联邦最高法院以 5:4 做出判决推翻了上诉判决。在判决中，联邦最高法院规定在实施逮捕和审讯嫌犯时，警方必须及时提醒被告以下事项：1.有权保持沉默，拒绝回答警方提出的问题；2.如果回答了警方的问题，这些供词将会用来起诉和审判他们；3.可以请律师，并且可以要求审问时有律师在场给予帮助；4.如果他请不起律师，法庭将免费为之指派一位。这四条内容就是著名的"米兰达告诫"。同时判决中还规定，警方在告知嫌疑人其拥有以上权利后，还必须确定他们的确已经明白了其中的意义，如果他们仍然自愿放弃这些权利配合警方，那么之后的供词以及根据这些供词所获得了其他任何证据就能在法庭审判中呈庭，否则就都是无效的。联邦最高法院对这一案件的判决是和另外三个案件一起做出的，另外三个案件分别是韦斯托弗诉美国案、弗吉尼拉诉纽约州案和加利福尼亚州诉史都华案。

【裁决过程与结果】（Procedure and Disposition）

At the trial in an Arizona state court, at which the confession was admitted in evidence, Miranda was convicted of kidnapping and rape. On appeal, the Supreme Court of Arizona affirmed. On certiorari, the Supreme Court of the United States reversed in a 5-4 majority.

【裁判理由】（Reasons for Judicial Decision）

【生效判决意见】（Opinion by WARREN）

Chief Justice Earl Warren delivered the opinion of the Court, ruling that due to the coercive nature of the custodial interrogation by police (Warren cited several police training manuals which had not been provided in the arguments), no confession could be admissible under the Fifth Amendment self-incrimination clause and Sixth Amendment right to an attorney unless a suspect had been made aware of his rights and the suspect had then waived them.

美国首席大法官厄尔·沃伦撰写了判决书中的多数意见，认为由于被警方强制性关押和审讯环境肯定会对被告产生胁迫性的效果（沃伦在判决书中以多个之前庭审辩论过程中并没有作为证据出现过的警察培训手册作为证明），因此除非犯罪嫌疑人清楚地知道自己的权利并且主动选择放弃这些权利，否则根据美利坚合众国宪法第五条修正案中的自证其罪条款和第六条修正案中的律师权条款，其所做的任何供词都将是无效的。

The person in custody must, prior to interrogation, be clearly informed that he has the right to remain silent, and that anything he says will be used against him in court; he must be clearly informed that he has the right to consult with a lawyer and to have the lawyer with him during interrogation, and that, if he is indigent, a lawyer will be appointed to represent him.

任何被羁押的人在受审前，必须被明确告知其有权保持沉默，他的任何供词都将被用在法庭上作为证据指控他；他必须被明确地告知自己有权在受审前与律师商讨，并要求律师于审问时在场，并且如果他请不起律师，也将会有一位律师被指派给他。

Thus, Miranda's conviction was overturned. The Court also made clear what had to happen if the suspect chose to exercise his or her rights: If the individual indicates in any manner, at any time prior to or during questioning, that he wishes to remain silent, the interrogation must cease... If the individual states that he wants an attorney, the interrogation must cease until an attorney is present. At that time, the individual must have an opportunity to confer with the attorney and to have him present during any subsequent questioning.

因此，米兰达的定罪被推翻。判决书中还明确规定了如果犯罪嫌疑人要求行使其权利时的应有程序：如果犯罪嫌疑人在审问开始前或正在受审时的任何时间以任何方式表示自己希望保持沉默，则审讯必须马上停止……如果他表示自己需要律师，审问也必须马上停止直到律师到场后。并且嫌疑人有足够的时间与律师进行商议，并在之后任何问话中都要有律师在场。

Warren pointed to the existing practice of the Federal Bureau of Investigation(FBI) and the rules of the *Uniform Code of Military Justice*, both of which required notifying a suspect of his right to remain silent; the FBI warning included notice of the right to counsel.

沃伦还指出当时联邦调查局和《统一军事法典》中都已经有了类似的规定，两者都要求告知嫌犯有权保持沉默，而联邦调查局的告诫用语中还包括明示对方有权与律师进行商议。

However, the dissenting justices accused the majority of overreacting to the problem of coercive interrogations, and anticipated a drastic effect. They believed that, once warned, suspects would always demand attorneys, and deny the police the ability to gain confessions.

不过，对这一判决投下反对票的另外4位大法官认为这一决定是多数派对刑讯逼供问题的过度反应，并且将最终导致非常严重的后果。他们相信，所有犯罪嫌疑人一经警告，肯定都会要求律师帮助并拒绝给予警方口供。

【部分同意和部分反对意见】（Clark's concurrence in part, dissent in part）

In a separate concurrence in part, dissent in part, Justice Tom C. Clark argued that the Warren

Court went "too far too fast." Instead, Justice Clark would use the "totality of the circumstances" test enunciated by Justice Goldberg in Haynes v. Washington. Under this test, the court would: consider in each case whether the police officer prior to custodial interrogation added the warning that the suspect might have counsel present at the interrogation and, further, that a court would appoint one at his request if he was too poor to employ counsel. In the absence of warnings, the burden would be on the State to prove that counsel was knowingly and intelligently waived or that in the totality of the circumstances, including the failure to give the necessary warnings, the confession was clearly voluntary.

汤姆·C. 克拉克对判决表示了部分同意和部分异议并写出了相应的意见。他认为多数派的决定有些"操之过急"，相反，他认为应该根据实际加以区别，具体案件具体分析，并根据海恩斯诉华盛顿案（Haynes v. Washington）中大法官亚瑟·戈德伯格所提出的测试方案，法院可以根据具体案件判断是否需要让警察在开展审讯前告知犯罪嫌疑人他可以与律师商议，并且告知他如果雇不起也将被指派到一位免费律师。在没有告知嫌犯这些权利时，各州有义务证明被告是在明确知道自己可以与律师商议的情况下仍然决定放弃这一权利，或是被告显然是自愿做出供述的，因此没有对其给予这样的警告。

【反对意见 1】（Dissent by Harlan）

In dissent, Justice John Marshall Harlan II wrote that "nothing in the letter or the spirit of the Constitution or in the precedents squares with the heavy-handed and one-sided action that is so precipitously taken by the Court in the name of fulfilling its constitutional responsibilities." Harlan closed his remarks by quoting former Justice Robert H. Jackson: "This Court is forever adding new stories to the temples of constitutional law, and the temples have a way of collapsing when one story too many is added."

在其不同意见中，大法官约翰·马歇尔·哈兰二世写道："宪法中没有任何文字和精神或是有过任何的先例来允许一个应该履行其宪法职责的法院做出这样越俎代庖的单方面决定。"人人皆知，如果没有嫌犯口供，有些案件很可能永远无法破案，众多专家的证据表明，这对减少犯罪非常关键。"由于犯罪行为将会导致社会付出极大的代价，这种新的程序只能视为是一种高风险的实验"，他还在意见的最后引用了其前任大法官罗伯特·H. 杰克逊的话："这个法院总是在宪法的圣殿中增加新的案例，但是当一类案例增加得太多时，这个圣殿是有可能倒塌的。"

【反对意见 2】（Dissent by White）

Justice Byron White took issue with the court announcing a new constitutional right when it had no "factual and textual bases" in the Constitution or previous opinions of the Court for the rule announced in the opinion. He stated: "The proposition that the privilege against self-incrimination forbids in-custody interrogation without the warnings specified in the majority opinion and without a clear waiver of counsel has no significant support in the history of the privilege or in the language of the Fifth Amendment." Nor did Justice White believe it had any basis in English common law. White further warned of the dire consequences of the majority opinion: I have no desire whatsoever to share the responsibility for any such impact on the present criminal process. In some unknown number of cases, the Court's rule will return a killer, a rapist or other criminal to the streets and to the environment which produced him, to repeat his crime whenever it pleases him. As a consequence, there will not be a gain, but a loss, in human dignity.

拜伦·怀特大法官认为法院在没有明确的相应宪法规定并且也没有相关先例的情况下宣布了一种新宪法权利的存在。他表示："无论是在第五修正案或是历史上的先例中，都没有这种禁止未经警告而进行审讯来防止自治其罪的多数意见。"并且他认为在英国普通法中也没有相应的根据。他还对多数意见将会产生的后果给予了警告："我实在不想承担这种会给目前执法程序带来巨大冲击的责任。"在无数案件中，（最高）法院的规则将把杀人犯、强奸犯或其他罪犯放回到大街上或是其他产生这些犯罪行为的环境中，放任其在任何时候重复自己的罪行。其结果是，这不但不会有助增强，反而会削弱人的尊严。

【案件影响】（Impact of the Case）

"米兰达权利"的规定出台后，美国警察怨声载道。警察们好不容易抓住嫌犯，还要宣读大段的"米兰达告诫"，后来，警方干脆把"米兰达告诫"印制成卡片发给每一名警官，让他们办案时照本宣科读一遍。根据美国司法部统计，"米兰达权利"出台后，美国的破案率降低了10%左右，但因警方刑讯逼供而造成的冤假错案也因此大大减少。至于米兰达，他的案子被发回重审后，尽管之前的"证言"不作为证据使用，但最终还是因其他证据而被判有罪。1972年，米兰达获假释出狱，通过给警方的"米兰达卡片"签字谋生。4年后，他在酒吧的一次斗殴事件中被刺身亡。警察逮捕了一名嫌犯，在获悉了"米兰达权利"后，嫌犯选择保持沉默，警察终因无法得到其他有力证据将其释放。

对米兰达案判决的批评之声至今不绝，但不可否认的是这一判决对美国社会产生了深刻的影响。美国联邦最高法院现任首席法官兰奎斯特2000年在宣判迪克森一案时说："米兰达权利已经深深植根于警察的日常工作中，成为美国民族文化的一部分。"

【思考问题】（Questions）

1. 在我国法律视角下思考下列"米兰达告诫"体现了对犯罪嫌疑人的何种权利的保障？

You have the right to remain silent and refuse to answer questions. Anything you do say may be used against you in a court of law. You have the right to consult an attorney before speaking to the police and to have an attorney present during questioning now or in the future. If you cannot afford an attorney, one will be appointed for you before any questioning if you wish. If you decide to answer questions now without an attorney present you will still have the right to stop answering at any time until you talk to an attorney. Knowing and understanding your rights as I have explained them to you, are you willing to answer my questions without an attorney present?

2. 即便在美国，在任何情况下都要求警察执行"米兰达告诫"是不现实的，米兰达权利的例外规则有哪些？

十六、国际私法案例

巴贝科克诉杰克逊案

Babcock v. Jackson（1963）

【选读理由】（Selected Reason）

巴贝科克诉杰克逊交通事故损害赔偿案是美国冲突法改革的标志性案例之一，该案的出现，为美国国内冲突法规则的改革者提供了一个良好的机遇。该案摒弃了侵权行为地法这一确定侵权行为准据法的传统做法，突破了萨维尼"法律关系本座说"的桎梏，引入了"最密切联系说"。至此，"最密切联系说"攻入了冲突法中最坚固的侵权法领域，使原本僵化、教条的侵权行为地法规则更富于灵活性，从而使法院在解决涉外侵权行为时拥有更大的自由裁量权，可以从一个更广泛、更综合的角度看待侵权行为准据法的确定问题。"最密切联系说"是对传统的侵权行为地法的一次重大调整和修正，更有利于平衡双方当事人之间的权利义务关系，从而使争议得到更加公平、公正的解决。

【案件事实】（Facts）

On Friday, September 16, 1960, Miss Georgia Babcock and her friends, Mr. and Mrs. William Jackson, all residents of Rochester, left that city in Mr. Jackson's automobile, Miss Babcock as guest, for a week-end trip to Canada. Some hours later, as Mr. Jackson was driving in the Province of Ontario, he apparently lost control of the car; it went off the highway into an adjacent stone wall, and Miss Babcock was seriously injured. Upon her return to this State, she brought the present action against William Jackson, alleging negligence on his part in operating his automobile.

1960 年 9 月 16 日星期五，巴贝科克女士及其朋友杰克逊夫妇乘坐杰克逊先生的汽车前往加拿大度假，他们都是纽约州罗切斯特市居民。当他们行驶到加拿大境内安大略省时，杰克逊先生的汽车突然失控，脱离高速路，撞到路边的石墙上。巴贝科克女士严重受伤，回到美国后，她立即向法院起诉杰克逊先生，声称他在驾驶过程中存在严重的过失。

【裁判过程与结果】（Procedure and Disposition）

The court at Special Term, agreeing with the defendant, granted the motion and the Appellate Division, over a strong dissent by Justice Halpern, affirmed the judgment of dismissal without opinion. The plaintiff appealed the case to Supreme Court of New York, and the Court reversed the case and the motion to dismiss the complaint denied.

【裁判理由】（Reason for Judicial Decision）

【原审反对意见】

The question of whether a guest should be barred from recovering from his host for the host's negligence in theoperation of his automobile is a question of policy to be decided by the appropriate legislative body. NewYork's policy is in favor of allowing a recovery by the gratuitous passenger. The New York Legislature has repeatedlyrefused to enact a statute denying or limiting the right of a guest to recover from his host (for the latest attempt, seeSenate Introductory No. 3662, Pr. No. 3967, 1960 Session, which died in Committee). Ontario's policy, since 1935 (ch.26, § 11, Statutes of 1935), has been contrary to that of New York, denying recovery to a gratuitous passenger even forgross or wanton negligence. The Ontario statute is sweeping in its terms. No other Province of Canada has such asweeping statute and no State in this country has a guest statute in terms as broad as those of the Ontario statute. Indeed, it has been held in this country that a statute couched in such terms is unconstitutional (*Stewart v. Houk*, 127Ore. 589; see Ann. 111 A.L.R. 1011).

免费搭乘者能否因为司机在驾驶过程中的过失而获得赔偿的问题是由相关立法机关所决定的政策性问题。纽约州允许免费搭乘者基于驾驶者的过失而造成的损失获得赔偿，同时立法机关也多次拒绝制定否认或限制搭乘者获得赔偿权利的法律。而自 1935 年开始，加拿大安大略省的政策就与纽约州相左，该省的法律拒绝承认免费搭乘者享有获得赔偿的权利，即使驾驶者存在重大或完全的过失。在这方面，安大略省的法律规定是彻底的免责，加拿大其他各省以及美国各州的法律都没有规定得如此彻底。

The primary purpose of the Ontario statute was stated by an academic commentator, shortly after its enactment, asfollows: "Undoubtedly the object of this provision is to prevent the fraudulent assertion of claims by passengers,in collusion with the drivers, against insurance companies." (Survey of Canadian Legislation, 1 U. Toronto L.J. 358, 366[1935]) In the light of this purpose, it is apparent that the interest of Ontario in the enforcement of its legislativepolicy is limited to accidents involving Ontario residents. Ontario is concerned only with the adverse effect of guest-host recoveries upon Ontario insurance premiums. Ontario insurance premiums would not be affected by a recovery chargeable against an insurance policy issued in a foreign jurisdiction covering a foreign car. At any rate, the interest of Ontario in having its policy apply to nonresidents traveling through Ontario is a minimal one.

安大略省法律制定后不久，一名学术评论家如此评价这部法律的主要目的："毫无疑问，该条款的目的是为了防止乘客针对驾驶者提出欺诈性的要求，从而要求保险公司进行赔偿。"鉴于这个目的，很明显，在实施立法政策方面，安大略的利益仅限于涉及安大略居民的事故。安大略只关注搭乘者与驾驶者之间产生的索赔关系对安大略保险费产生的不利影响。安大略保险费不应该受到其他国家保险政策的影响。无论如何，在将其政策适用于旅行经过安大略的非居民方面，安大略涉及的利益非常小。

The problem in this case can be stated as a question of characterization or classification, the answer to which may determine the selection of the choice-of-law rule to be applied. The question in this case is not one of ordinary tort law, dealing with rules of conduct, as to which, under the traditional view, the law of the place of the wrong is controlling. The question is rather one of State policy with respect to the incidents to be attached to therelationship of guest and host. As to this question, the policy of the State in which the relationship was created should be held to be controlling, even under the traditional view (cf. *Dyke v. Erie Ry. Co.*, 45 N.Y. 113).

本案中的焦点问题是定性或分类的问题，其答案将决定适用的法律规则的选择。本案中的问题不是一个涉及行为规则的普通的侵权法问题。在传统观点看来，这类问题适用侵权行为地法，是一个政策选择问题。而本案的问题涉及免费搭乘者与驾驶者之间发生的事故。关于这个问题，即使是从传统观点来看，搭乘者与驾驶者之间关系成立时所属国家的政策应该起到决定作用。

The law of Ontario will undoubtedly be controlling, in determining whether the defendant was guilty of negligence in the manner in which he operated his automobile. The State in which the accident occurred has the most significant contacts with, and the dominant interest in, issues of that kind. The rules of conduct laid down by the laws of each State (sometimes referred to as admonitory laws) must be obeyed, not only by the permanent residents of the State but also by persons temporarily residing in the State or traveling through it. Conversely, all the persons within the State have the right to rely upon the rules of conduct laid down by the laws of the State as guide lines for their behavior. Therefore, the question of whether the defendant's conduct was wrongful or innocent must be determined by the law of the place of the alleged wrong. But that law is not necessarily controlling with respect to other questions of law or policy which may be involved in the case. Once it is determined by the law of the State in which the accident occurred that the defendant's conduct was wrongful, the question of the availability of a remedy for the wrong and the extent of the remedy and its collateral incidents may well be determined by the law of some other State. The law and policy of the State having the most significant contacts and the dominant interest with respect to the particular issue should govern.The leading illustration of the application of this principle in New York State is the Kilberg case. It was there held that the limitation of damages in a death action fixed by the law of the place of the occurrence of the accident would not be applied to an action in the courts of this State brought against an airline company for the death of a resident of this State which occurred upon a trip originating in this State, but that the New York law and policy would be applied instead.

毫无疑问，在确定被告驾驶汽车是否存在过失的问题上，应该适用安大略省法律。事故发生地所在国与事故有着最密切的联系，从而有着重大的利益。不仅国家的永久居民，而且临时居住在一国境内或只是途经一国的人也必须遵守该国的行为规则。与此相较，一国境内的所有人都有权利将国家制定的行为规范作为自身行为的指导性规则并按其行事。因此，被告的行为是否存在过失应该由事故发生地的法律予以确定，但是在确定案件可能涉及的其他法律或政策问题上，该法并不必然适用。由事故发生地所在国的法律确定被告人的行为是否存在过失，救济的可获得性、可获得救济的范围以及附带发生的事件则可能由其他国家的法律确定，应适用在某一特定方面有最密切联系和重大利益的国家的法律和政策。该原则在纽约州适用的最好例证是 Kilberg 案。该案确定，在涉及死亡事件的诉讼中，根据事故发生地法律确定的损失限额，在本州法院审理的对航空公司提起的另一州公民人身伤亡案件中并不必然适用，尽管该航班是从公民所在的州出发，但仍然依据纽约州的法律和政策加以确定。

In other States, the principle has been applied to many other issues of substantive law in tort actions. Thus it has been held that the question of the survival of a personal injury claim upon the death of the tort-feasor should be determined by the law of the tort-feasor's domicile rather than by the law of the fortuitous place of the happening of the accident.

在其他各州，这一原则也在侵权诉讼中被适用于实体法的诸多问题之中。因此，人身伤亡案件中幸存者基于侵权行为而提出的主张应由侵权行为人的继承人住所地的法律而非偶然的侵权行为地的法律确定。搭乘人从驾驶者处获得赔偿的权利应该由当事人之间的法律关系形成时的住所地的法律确定，而不是由偶然产生的侵权行为地的法律确定。

【生效判决意见】

The traditional choice of law rule, embodied in the *Original Restatement of Conflict of Laws*, and until recently unquestioningly followed in this court has been that the substantive rights and liabilities arising out of a tortious occurrence are determinable by the law of the place of the tort. It had its conceptual foundation in the vested rights doctrine, namely, that a right to recover for a foreign tort owes its creation to the law of the jurisdiction where the injury occurred and depends for its existence and extent solely on such law. Although espoused by such great figures as Justice Holmes and Professor Beale, the vested rights doctrine has long since been discredited because it fails to take account of underlying policy considerations in evaluating the significance to be ascribed to the circumstance that an act had a foreign situs in determining the rights and liabilities which arise out of that act. "The vice of the vested rights theory", it has been aptly stated, "is that it affects to decide concrete cases upon generalities which do not state the practical considerations involved." More particularly, as applied to torts, the theory ignores the interest which jurisdictions other than that where the tort occurred may have in the resolution of particular issues. It is for this very reason that, despite the advantages of certainty, ease of application and predictability which it affords, there has in recent years been increasing criticism of the traditional rule by commentators and a judicial trend towards its abandonment or modification.

体现在《第一次美国冲突法重述》中的传统意义上的法律选择规则，以及本法院直至现在仍毫无疑问地适用的一项规则是，由侵权行为而产生的当事人之间的实体权利和义务应由侵权行为地的法律加以确定。该规则的理论基础是既得权利原则，即从发生在国外的侵权行为获得赔偿的权利是基于损害发生地的法律而产生的，其存在和获得赔偿的范围是完全基于该法律的。尽管该项规则得到了像霍尔姆斯大法官和比尔教授这样著名人物的支持，但是在确定由涉外侵权行为而产生的当事人之间的权利和义务关系方面，该规则未能考虑其中隐含的政策性因素。"既得权利理论的不足之处在于它将具体案件大而化之，而并未能表明涉及的具体因素。"特别是，在适用于侵权案件时，该理论忽略了行为地之外的国家对于案件的解决有着重大的利益关系。也正是由于这些原因，尽管既得利益原则有着确定性、适用简易以及可预见性强的优势，但是近年来，这项传统的规则遭到了强烈的批判，而且在司法实践中也出现了要求抛弃或修改该项规则的趋势。

The "center of gravity" or "grouping of contacts" doctrine adopted by this court in conflicts cases involving contracts impresses us as likewise affording the appropriate approach for accommodating the competing interests in tort cases with multi-State contacts. Justice, fairness and "the best practical result" may best be achieved by giving controlling effect to the law of the jurisdiction which, because of its relationship or contact with the occurrence or the parties, has the greatest concern with the specific issue raised in the litigation. The merit of such a rule is that "it gives to the place 'having the most interest in the problem' paramount control over the legal issues arising out of a particular factual context" and thereby allows the forum to apply "the policy of the jurisdiction 'most intimately concerned with the outcome of [the] particular litigation.'"

本法院在涉及合同争议的案件中适用的 "重力中心地" 或 "联系聚集地" 原则也可以为侵权案件提供协调各种利益关系的适当方法。正义、公平以及 "最佳实际结果" 的要求可以通过适用与诉讼中具体争议问题有最密切联系的国家的法律而达到。这一规则的优势在于 "它赋予了 '与争议问题有最密切的利益关系的' 国家的法律对基于特定事实而产生的法律问题最高的控制权，由此，允许审理案件的法院适用 '与特定诉讼案件结果有着最密切联系' 的国家的法律。"

Comparison of the relative "contacts" and "interests" of New York and Ontario in this litigation, vis-a-vis the issue here presented, makes it clear that the concern of New York is unquestionably the greater and more direct and that the interest of Ontario is at best minimal. The present action involves injuries sustained by a New York guest as the result of the negligence of a New York host in the operation of an automobile, garaged, licensed and undoubtedly insured in New York, in the course of a week-end journey which began and was to end there. In sharp contrast, Ontario's sole relationship with the occurrence is the purely adventitious circumstance that the accident occurred there.

通过将本案中纽约州和安大略省的相关 "联系" 和 "利益" 与本案提出的问题进行对比即可发现，毫无疑问，纽约州的利益和联系更重大、更直接，而安大略省的利益则微乎其微。本诉讼涉及的是在一次从纽约州启程并返回纽约州的周末旅行中，一位纽约州公民由于在驾驶汽车过程中的疏忽而导致汽车上一名乘客受伤，由此而产生的人身损害赔偿，该辆汽车通常停放在纽约州，由纽约州许可，同时在纽约州投保。而与此形成鲜明对比的是，安大略省与该事件唯一的联系只是该事故发生在其境内，这是非常偶然的。

Although the traditional rule has in the past been applied by this court in giving controlling effect to the guest statute of the foreign jurisdiction in which the accident occurred, it is not amiss to point out that the question here posed was neither raised nor considered in those cases and that the question has never been presented in so stark a manner as in the case before us with a statute so unique as Ontario's. Be that as it may, however, reconsideration of the inflexible traditional rule persuades us, as already indicated, that, in failing to take into account essential policy considerations and objectives, its application may lead to unjust and anomalous results. This being so, the rule, formulated as it was by the courts, should be discarded.

尽管本法院过去适用的传统规则是适用侵权行为发生地的法律，但仍要指出在之前审理的案件中，法院从未遇到过如安大略省的法律这般独特的法律，并以这样一种极端和明显的方式展现出来。然而，对这一僵化的传统规则的重新审视使我们确信，正如上文所述，由于未能考虑关键性的政策因素和目标，该规则的适用可能导致不公平和令人费解的后果。因此，尽管该规则是由法院形成并适用的，但在本案中它应不予适用。

In conclusion, then, there is no reason why all issues arising out of a tort claim must be resolved by reference to the law of the same jurisdiction. Where the issue involves standards of conduct, it is more than likely that it is the law of the place of the tort which will be controlling but the disposition of other issues must turn, as does the issue of the standard of conduct itself, on the law of the jurisdiction which has the strongest interest in the resolution of the particular issue presented.

综上所述，在侵权案件中，没有理由仍然适用侵权行为地的法律。当争议问题涉及行为标准时，侵权行为地法更可能被适用，但是其他问题的解决很可能依赖于与特定问题的解决有最密切联系的国家的法律，甚至行为标准本身都适用该法律。

【案件影响】（Impact of the Case）

侵权行为法是国际私法领域涉及侵权行为的准据法，其理论依据是萨维尼提出的著名的"法律关系本座说"，而国际私法中侵权行为准据法的确定问题为萨维尼"法律关系本座说"提供了一个绝佳的适用领域。然而，在适用过程中，侵权行为地法僵化、教条的适用往往会产生一些极为不公的后果。本案就是一个很好的例证。

在本案之前，美国国际私法学界对于萨维尼"本座说"适用于侵权行为而导致的不公平甚至荒谬的结果已经有所非议，要求采用更加灵活和公平的方法来确定准据法。对此，美国学者提供了两种改良和变革的进路：一种是以本案终审法官富尔德为首的"最密切路径"，另一种是柯里开创的"利益分析之路"。这两条路径的共同特点之一都是要打破侵权行为地法在侵权准据法中的独占地位，要求对僵化和不变通的萨维尼主义进行方法论上的改革和修正。而本案正是为美国国际私法的改革者们提供了一个绝佳的"竞技场"。本案摒弃了国际私法中传统的侵权行为地法而将"最密切联系原则"引入了侵权法这一萨维尼主义根深蒂固的领域，打破了侵权行为地法在该领域的垄断性地位，从而使其适用出现了松动，为"最密切联系原则"的适用扫清了障碍。

【思考问题】（Questions）

1. 法院在适用"最密切联系原则"时应考虑的因素主要有哪些？如何保证法院的自由裁量权控制在法律规则的范围之内？

2. 为何"最密切联系原则"适用于侵权法领域时遭到诸多学者的反对？

十七、国际经济法案例

美国虾和海龟案

United States — Import Prohibition of Certain Shrimp and Shrimp Products（1998）

【选读理由】（Selected Reason）

1997 年 1 月，印度、马来西亚、巴基斯坦和泰国等四国认为美国以未采用"海龟隔离装置"为由禁止海虾进口的做法违背了世界贸易组织（WTO）的规定，并向 WTO 争端解决机构提出起诉，从而形成美国禁止进口某些海虾及其制品案件（WT/DS58, United States — Import Prohibition of Certain Shrimp and Shrimp Products，又称第一虾和海龟案）。WTO 上诉机关在 1998 年做出最终裁决。本案所涉及的不仅是用司法手段协调立法难以解决的 WTO 贸易体制与环境保护政策的关系问题，而且也给 WTO 司法机制的运作树立了一个成功的范例，从而成为国际贸易界、环境保护界以及国际司法界讨论的一个经久不息的热点问题。

【案件事实】（Facts）

Pursuant to the United States Endangered Species Act (ESA) of 1973, all sea turtles that occur in US waters are listed as endangered or threatened species. In 1987, the United States issued regulations pursuant to the ESA that required all United States shrimp trawlers to use Turtle Excluder Devices ("TEDs") or tow-time restrictions in specified areas where there was a significant mortality of sea turtles associated with shrimp harvesting. Developed over the past two decades in the southeast shrimp fisheries of the United States, TEDs are considered to be an effective way in which to exclude by-catch during shrimp trawling. The 1987 Regulations became fully effective in 1990 and were modified to require the use of TEDs at all times and in all areas where shrimp trawling interacts in a significant way with sea turtles.

按照 1973 年美国《濒危物种法》，所有在美国海域出现的海龟都被列入濒临灭绝的物种名单。1987 年，美国按照《濒危物种法》颁布了政府规章，要求所有美国用拖网捕海虾的渔民在因为捕虾而造成海龟大量死亡的特定区域使用"海龟隔离装置"或限制使用拖网的时间。经过 20 多年在美国东南部捕虾区的使用和发展，"海龟隔离装置"被认为可以在捕虾时有效地阻止海龟入网。1987 年的行政规章在 1990 年变为全面有效，并进行修订，要求在拖网捕虾会对海龟造成重大影响的所有时间和区域将都要使用"海龟隔离装置"。

This case concerns section 609 of the *United States Public Law* 101-162 relating to the protection of sea turtles in shrimp trawl fishing operations enacted in 1989 pursuant to the ESA and its implementing measures. Section 609 calls upon the US Secretary of State, in consultation with the US Secretary of Commerce, inter alia, to initiate negotiations for the development of bilateral or multilateral agreements for the protection and conservation of sea turtles, in particular with governments of countries engaged in commercial fishing operations likely to have a negative impact on sea turtles. Section 609 further provides that shrimp harvested with technology that may adversely affect certain species of sea turtles protected under US law may not be imported into the United States, unless the President annually certifies to the Congress: (a) that the harvesting country concerned has a regulatory programme governing the incidental taking of such sea turtles in the course of such harvesting that is comparable to that of the United States, and that the average rate of that incidental taking by the vessels of the harvesting country is comparable to the average rate of incidental taking of sea turtles by United States vessels in the course of such harvesting; or (b) that the fishing environment of the harvesting country does not pose a threat of incidental taking to sea turtles in the course of such harvesting.

本案主要涉及《美国公共法律》第 101－162 节第 609 条有关在海虾捕捞作业中保护海龟的法律规定。该法依照《濒危物种法》及其实施措施在 1989 年制定。该 609 条款要求美国国务院协同商务部"尽快发起与其他国家进行保护海龟的双边或多边谈判",尤其是要与那些从事的商业捕捞可能对海龟有危害的国家进行谈判。第 609 条还要求,采用对美国法律所保护的具体类型的海龟有危害的捕捞技术所捕捞的海虾不能进口到美国,除非美国总统向美国国会证明:(a) 相关捕虾国家有防止意外捕龟的经常性措施,该措施可与美国措施相媲美,并且这些国家的捕虾船偶获海龟数应与美国渔船平均捕龟率相当;或者(b)这些捕虾国的捕虾作业过程不会产生偶然捕龟的威胁。

The 1996 Guidelines define shrimp or shrimp products harvested in conditions that do not affect sea turtles to include:(a) shrimp harvested in an aquaculture facility;(b) shrimp harvested by commercial shrimp trawl vessels using TEDs comparable in effectiveness to those required in the United States;(c) Shrimp harvested exclusively by means that do not involve the retrieval of fishing nets by mechanical devices or by vessels using gear that, in accordance with the US programme, would not require TEDs; and (d) species of shrimp, such as the pandalid species, harvested in areas in which sea turtles do not occur.

The 1996 Guidelines provided that certification could be granted by 1 May 1996, and annually thereafter to harvesting countries other than those where turtles do not occur or that exclusively use means that do not pose a threat to sea turtles "only if the government of [each of those countries] has provided documentary evidence of the adoption of a regulatory programme governing the incidental taking of sea turtles in the course of commercial shrimp trawl harvesting that is comparable to that of the United States and if the average take rate of that incidental taking by vessels of the harvesting nation is comparable to the average rate of incidental taking of sea turtles by United States vessels in the course of such harvesting."

1996 年的修正指令将"在不伤害海龟条件下所捕捞的海虾及海虾制品"界定如下:1.在设备齐全的养殖场捕捞的虾;2. 商业拖船捕捞的虾,该拖船使用相当于美国所要求的效率的"海龟隔离装置";3. 使用专门方法捕捞的虾,其捕捞时不使用机械设备或拖船上的齿轮回收渔网,在此情况下按照美国方案无须使用"海龟隔离装置";4. 一些特殊品种的虾,例如有一种长额虾,是在没有海龟出没的海域捕捞的。

1996 年的指令要求在 1996 年 5 月 1 日前获得认证,对于捕虾国而言今后每年都要获得认证。那些海龟不会出现的国家或使用不会伤害海龟的方法的捕虾国不办理认证的条件是:

每个国家的政府提供书面证明表明已制定实施了监管方案以监管商业拖网渔船捕虾过程中对海龟的意外捕捞，这一监管方案与美国方案类似，且拖网渔船对海龟的平均意外捕获率与美国拖网渔船捕虾时对海龟的平均意外捕获率相当。

【裁决过程与结果】（Procedure and Disposition）

Following a joint request for consultations by India, Malaysia, Pakistan and Thailand on 8 October 1996 22 , Malaysia and Thailand requested in a communication dated 9 January 1997 23 , and Pakistan asked in a communication dated 30 January 1997 24 , that the Dispute Settlement Body (DSB) establish a panel to examine their complaint regarding a prohibition imposed by the United States on the importation of certain shrimp and shrimp products by Section 609 and associated regulations and judicial rulings.

On 25 February 1997, the DSB established two panels in accordance with these requests and agreed that these panels would be consolidated into a single Panel, pursuant to Article 9 of the Dispute Settlement Understanding (DSU), with standard terms of reference.

On 10 April 1997, the DSB established another panel with standard terms of reference in accordance with a request made by India in a communication dated 25 February 1997 26 , and agreed that this third panel, too, would be merged into the earlier Panel established on 25 February 1997.

The Report of the consolidated Panel, United States – *Import Prohibition of Certain Shrimp and Shrimp Products*, was circulated to WTO Members on 15 May 1998.

On 13 July 1998, the United States appealed certain issues of law and legal interpretations in the Original Panel Report. The Appellate Body issued its Report on 12 October 1998.

Appellate Body Report found that the United States measure at issue, Section 609, qualified for provisional justification under Article XX(g), but that it failed to meet the requirements of the chapeau of Article XX, as it was applied in a manner that constituted arbitrary and unjustifiable discrimination.

【裁判理由】（Reasons for Judicial Decision）

【原审意见】（Report of the Panel）

Therefore, we find that the United States admits that, with respect to countries not certified under Section 609, the measures imposed in application of Section 609 amount to "prohibitions or restrictions" on the importation of shrimp within the meaning of Article XI:1 of GATT 1994. Even if one were to consider that the United States has not admitted that it imposes an import prohibition or restriction within the meaning of Article XI:1, we find that the wording of Section 609 and the interpretation made of it by the CIT are sufficient evidence that the United States imposes a "prohibition or restriction" within the meaning of Article XI:1. We therefore find that Section 609 violates Article XI:1 of GATT 1994.

因此我们确认，美国承认对那些没有能够基于第 609 条的规定获得认证的国家所采取的适用第 609 条规定禁止或限制虾进口的措施，属于关贸总协定 1994 第 11 条（普遍取消数量限制条款）第 1 款的措施。即使人们认为美国不承认它采取了第 11 条第 1 款规定的进口禁止或限制措施，我们发现第 609 条文字及美国国际贸易法院对该条的解释都足以充分证明美国实施了第 11 条第 1 款的禁止或限制。因此我们确认第 609 条违反了关贸总协定 1994 第 11 条第 1 款的规定。

The relevant parts of Article XX provide as follows: Article XX General exceptions Subject to the requirement that such measures are not applied in a manner that would constitute a means of arbitrary or unjustifiable discrimination between countries where the same conditions prevail, or a disguised restriction on international trade, nothing in this Agreement shall be construed to prevent the adoption or enforcement by any contracting party of measures: ...(b)necessary to protect human, animal or plant life or health; ...(g)relating to the conservation of exhaustible natural resources if such measures are made effective in conjunction with restrictions on domestic production or consumption.

关贸总协定 1994 第 20 条相关部分内容为：第 20 条 一般例外   本协定的规定不得解释为阻止缔约国采用或实施以下措施，但对情况相同的各国，实施的措施不得构成武断的或不合理的差别待遇，或构成对国际贸易的变相限制：

......

（b）为保障人民、动植物的生命或健康所必需的措施；

......

（g）与国内限制生产与消费的措施相配合，为有效保护可能用竭的天然资源的有关措施。

The arguments of the parties raise the general question of whether Article XX(b) and (g) apply at all when a Member has taken a measure conditioning access to its market for a given product on the adoption of certain conservation policies by the exporting Member(s). We note that Article XX can accommodate a broad range of measures aiming at the conservation and preservation of the environment. At the same time, by accepting the WTO Agreement, Members commit themselves to certain obligations which limit their right to adopt certain measures. We therefore consider it important to determine first whether the *scope* of Article XX encompasses measures whereby a Member conditions access to its market for a given product on the adoption of certain conservation policies by the exporting Member(s).

争议各方提出的普遍问题是，当一个成员根据某类产品出口国采取某种环境保护政策的情况而决定是否允许该产品进入本国市场时，第 20 条 b、g 款是否适用。我们注意到，该第 20 条所能够包容的旨在保护环境的措施的范围广泛。与此同时，通过接受 WTO 协定，成员方承诺他们有义务限制其自身采取某些措施的权利。因此，我们认为重要的是要首先确定，第 20 条包含的措施是否包括成员方根据某类产品出口国采取某种环境保护政策的情况而决定是否允许该产品进入本国市场的措施。

In reaching our conclusions, we based ourselves on the current status of the WTO rules and of international law. As far as the WTO Agreement is concerned, we considered that certain unilateral measures, insofar as they could jeopardize the multilateral trading system, could not be covered by Article XX. Our findings with respect to international norms confirm our reasoning regarding the WTO Agreement and GATT. General International Law and *International Environmental* Law clearly favour the use of negotiated instruments rather than unilateral measures when addressing transboundary or global environmental problems, particularly when developing countries are concerned. Hence a negotiated solution is clearly to be preferred, both from a WTO and an international environmental law perspective. However, our findings regarding Article XX do not imply that recourse to unilateral measures is always excluded, particularly after serious attempts have been made to negotiate; nor do they imply that, in any given case, they would be permitted. Nevertheless, in the present case, even though the situation of turtles is a serious one, we consider that the United States adopted measures which, irrespective of their environmental purpose, were clearly a threat to the multilateral trading system and were applied without any serious attempt to reach, beforehand, a negotiated solution.

We therefore find that the US measure at issue is not within the scope of measures permitted under the chapeau of Article XX. In the light of the findings above, we conclude that the import ban on shrimp and shrimp products as applied by the United States on the basis of Section 609 of Public Law 101-162 is not consistent with Article XI:1 of GATT 1994, and cannot be justified under Article XX of GATT 1994. The Panel recommends that the Dispute Settlement Body request the United States to bring this measure into conformity with its obligations under the WTO Agreement.

在得出结论时，我们充分考虑了世贸组织规则和国际法的现状。就世贸组织协定而言，我们认为，某些单方面措施可能会危及多边贸易体制，不能被第 20 条所涵盖。我们对国际规则的研究结果与我们按照 WTO 协定和关贸总协定的规定进行推理得出的结论是一致的。一般国际法和《国际环境法》明确赞成在解决跨界或全球环境问题，特别是在与发展中国家有关的问题时，使用谈判的方式而不是采取单方面措施。因此，通过谈判解决问题的方案显然是优先适用的，无论是从世贸组织还是从国际环境法的角度。然而，我们关于第 20 条的研究结果并不意味着诉诸单方面措施总是被排除在外，特别是在对谈判进行认真的尝试之后；也不意味着在任何情况下这些单方措施都会被允许。在本案中，虽然海龟面临着严峻的情势，尽管是以保护环境为目标，我们仍然认为美国所采取的措施很明显构成了对多边贸易体制的威胁，在执行之前未进行以谈判方式解决问题的认真的尝试。

因此我们认定，所争议的美国措施不在第 20 条前言所允许的措施范围内。基于上述认定，我们的结论是美国基于美国公法101—162节第609条对虾及虾产品采用的禁止进口措施，不符合关贸总协定 1994 第 11 条第 1 款，也不能被认为是关贸总协定第 20 条中的例外。专家组建议争端解决机构要求美国调整这项措施以与其在世贸组织协定项下的义务保持一致。

【生效判决意见】（Report of the Appellate Body）

Clearly, the United States negotiated seriously with some, but not with other Members (including the appellees), that export shrimp to the United States. The effect is plainly discriminatory and, in our view, unjustifiable. The unjustifiable nature of this discrimination emerges clearly when we consider the cumulative effects of the failure of the United States to pursue negotiations for establishing consensual means of protection and conservation of the living marine resources here involved, notwithstanding the explicit statutory direction in Section 609 itself to initiate negotiations as soon as possible for the development of bilateral and multilateral agreements. The principal consequence of this failure may be seen in the resulting unilateralism evident in the application of Section 609. As we have emphasized earlier, the policies relating to the necessity for use of particular kinds of TEDs in various maritime areas, and the operating details of these policies, are all shaped by the Department of State, without the participation of the exporting Members. The system and processes of certification are established and administered by the United

States agencies alone. The decision-making involved in the grant, denial or withdrawal of certification to the exporting Members, is, accordingly, also unilateral. The unilateral character of the application of Section 609 heightens the disruptive and discriminatory influence of the import prohibition and underscores its unjustifiability.

显然，美国在出口至其国内的海虾的谈判中认真对待某些成员方，而对于其他成员方（包括被上诉人）则不然。其效果是明显具有歧视性的，在我们看来，是毫无道理的。在我们考虑"美国没有在涉及海洋资源的保护和养护方面为了达成共识而寻求谈判"的累积影响时，尽管 609 条有明确的法律规定要尽快启动谈判的双边和多边协定，这种歧视呈现出明显的不合理。没能积极谈判的主要后果就是导致了 609 条款执行中的单边主义。正如我们前面强调的，在不同的海域使用具体类型的海龟隔离装置的必要性的相关政策，以及这些政策的操作细节，均是由美国国务院所制定的，出口成员方没有参与。认证系统和流程是由美国机构单独设置和管理的。相应地，对出口成员方做出认证的许可、拒绝或撤销的决策也是单方的。第 609 条执行中的单边特征，使进口限制措施被赋予了破坏性和歧视性，从而构成了其不合理性。

We find, accordingly, that the United States measure is applied in a manner which amounts to a means not just of "unjustifiable discrimination", but also of "arbitrary discrimination" between countries where the same conditions prevail, contrary to the requirements of the chapeau of Article XX. The measure, therefore, is not entitled to the justifying protection of Article XX of the GATT 1994. Having made this finding, it is not necessary for us to examine also whether the United States measure is applied in a manner that constitutes a "disguised restriction on international trade" under the chapeau of Article XX.

我们发现，美国措施在执行中采取的方式，按照第 20 条前言的要求，在情况相当的国家之间不只是构成"不合理的差别待遇"，还构成"武断的差别待遇"。这些措施，不能得到关贸总协定 1994 第 20 条的正当性的保护。得出这一认识后，我们没有必要再去审查美国措施的执行方式是否构成第 20 条前言中规定的"对国际贸易的变相限制"。

What we have decided in this appeal is simply this: although the measure of the United States in dispute in this appeal serves an environmental objective that is recognized as legitimate under paragraph (g) of Article XX of the GATT 1994, this measure has been applied by the United States in a manner which constitutes arbitrary and unjustifiable discrimination between Members of the WTO, contrary to the requirements of the chapeau of Article XX. For all of the specific reasons outlined in this Report, this measure does not qualify for the exemption that Article XX of the GATT 1994 affords to measures which serve certain recognized, legitimate environmental purposes but which, at the same time, are not applied in a manner that constitutes a means of arbitrary or unjustifiable discrimination between countries where the same conditions prevail or a disguised restriction on international trade. As we emphasized in United States – Gasoline, WTO Members are free to adopt their own policies aimed at protecting the environment as long as, in so doing, they fulfill their obligations and respect the rights of other Members under the *WTO Agreement*.

我们在上诉中所认定的事情大致如下：虽然上诉所争议的美国措施是为 GATT 1994 第 20 条第 g 款通过立法确认的保护环境的目标服务的，但美国政府执行这一措施的方式，对照第 20 条前言的要求，构成了在 WTO 成员方之间武断的不合理的差别待遇。基于所有在本报告中列出的具体原因，这项措施不符合 GATT 1994 第 20 条提供的措施的例外条件。这些措施服务于特定的环境保护目的，但同时，其适用方式不能在具有大致相当情况的成员方之间构成武断的或不合理的歧视或构成对国际贸易的变相限制。正如我们在美国汽油案中所强调的，世界贸易组织成员可以自由地通过自己的政策保护环境，只要在这一过程中他们履行 WTO 协议中的义务并尊重其他成员的权利。

For the reasons set out in this Report, the Appellate Body: (a) reverses the Panel's finding that accepting non-requested information from non-governmental sources is incompatible with the provisions of the DSU; (b) reverses the Panel's finding that the United States measure at issue is not within the scope of measures permitted under the chapeau of Article XX of the GATT 1994, and (c) concludes that the United States measure, while qualifying for provisional justification under Article XX(g), fails to meet the requirements of the chapeau of Article XX, and, therefore, is not justified under Article XX of the GATT 1994.

基于报告中的理由，上诉机构：1.推翻专家组有关从非官方来源接收未经请求的信息不符合《争端解决规则与程序的谅解》条款的裁决；2.推翻专家组关于美国的争议措施不属于 GATT 1994 第 20 条前言所允许的措施范围的裁决；3.认定美国措施符合第 20 条 g 款的正当性，不满足第 20 条前言的条件，因此，不能依据 GATT 1994 第 20 条确认其正当性。

【案件影响】（Impact of the Case）

WTO 通过本案的解决进一步宣示了它对环境问题的关注，并再次确认主权国家采取本国认为适当的环境措施的权利。本案上诉机构认定了美国 609 条款根据 GATT 第 20 条(g)款所取得的合法性，再次扩大解释了"可用竭自然资源"的范围，指出不应单纯拘泥于矿物或其他非生命资源，应该包括海龟等濒危物种。

到 2000 年马来西亚诉美国虾与海龟案中，专家组适用上诉机构在"第一虾与海龟案"审查第 20 条引言性质时所做的裁定："在成员援引第 20 条例外规定的权利和其他成员根据 1994 年 GATT 各种实体规定享有的权利之前进行精巧地平衡时，解释和适用序言是至关重要的。"裁定认为，由于保护迁徙物种最好通过国际合作实现，并已经将这条平衡线向双边或多边谈判解决的方向推动，因此诉诸单边措施是不被接受的。专家组裁定，美国的义务是谈判的义务，而不是缔结国际协定的义务。它还裁定，美国已经做出诚信的努力以缔结国际协定。上诉机构支持了专家组的裁定，拒绝了马来西亚关于美国在实施进口禁令之前应当"谈判"并"缔结"一项保护和保育海龟的国际协定的主张。这样使得"第二虾与海龟案"成为继"石棉案"后第二个成功援引 GATT 第 20 条的案例，并使美国首次以第 20 条 g 款"保护可能耗竭的天然资源"为依据全面胜诉。

【思考问题】（Questions）

1. 从贸易与环境的关系来看，允许采用的有效的环境保护措施和禁止实施的以 GATT 第 20 条为借口的贸易保护措施，这两者之间的界限如何确定？
2. 争端解决机构做出的裁决报告如何执行？

十八、中外法制史案例

斯科普斯诉田纳西州案
John Thomas Scopes v. The State of Tennessee（1925）

【选读理由】（Selected Reason）

在美国法制史、科学史和教育史上，发生于 1925 年的斯科普斯诉田纳西州案是一个里程碑式的案例。为了抗议部分保守州禁止学校讲授达尔文进化论，田纳西州中学教师约翰·斯科普斯在美国公民自由联盟组织的授意下，故意违反本州禁止中学讲授与《圣经》冲突的理论的法案，并成功地将此事诉诸法庭，因进化论常被称为"人由猴子变来"的理论，故历史上称此案为"猴子审判"（Monkey trial）。斯科普斯在法庭上败诉，但通过新闻媒体对法庭审理过程的报道，支持进化论一方取得了舆论胜利，上诉后田纳西州高等法院在程序上推翻了原判，直到 20 世纪 80 年代，科学生物进化论教育才在美国逐步取得合法教学地位。

【案件事实】（Facts）

John Scopes, a twenty-four-year old general science teacher and part-time football coach, was convicted of a violation of chapter 27 of the *Acts of 1925* for that he did teach in the public schools of Rhea county a certain theory that denied the story of the divine creation of man, as taught in the Bible, and did teach instead thereof that man had descended from a lower order of animals. Scopes argued that the Tennessee *Anti-evolution Act*, 1925 Tenn. Pub. Acts ch. 27, violated various provisions in the state and federal constitutions including the U.S. Const. amend. IV, § 1, and the Due Process Clause of the United States Constitution. After a verdict of guilty by the jury, the trial judge imposed a fine of $ 100, and Scopes brought the case to this court by an appeal in the nature of a writ of error.

约翰·斯科普斯，一个 24 岁的普通科学课老师和兼职教练，因违反 1925 年第 27 号法案而被定罪，因为他在里厄县公立中学教学中用"人是某种低等动物的后代"取代《圣经》中的人被上帝创造的说法。斯科普斯认为田纳西州 1925 年《反进化论法》第 27 章违反了联邦和州宪法的大量条款，包括美国宪法第四修正案第 1 款，以及美国宪法中规定的正当程序原则。经陪审团裁定有罪后，主审法官对其处以 100 美元的罚款。斯科普斯向本庭提起上诉。

【裁决过程与结果】（Procedure and Disposition）

Defendant was convicted of teaching the theory of evolution in the public schools in violation of the Tennessee *Anti-evolution Act*, 1925 Tenn. Pub. Acts ch. 27 in the Circuit Court of Rhea County (Tennessee).The trial court denied his motion for a new trial and granted him 30 days in which to prepare, perfect, and file his bill of exceptions. He appealed this judgement. The conviction was upheld by the Supreme court of Tennessee (Knoxville). Defendant appealed to the

Supreme court of Tennessee (Nashville), the court reversed the judgment.

【裁判理由】（Reasons for Judicial Decision）

【原审判决意见】（Opinion by Green）

The plaintiff in error has been convicted of a violation of chapter 27 of the *Public Acts* of 1925, known as the *Anti-Evolution Act*, and has appealed in error to this court. A motion has been made by the State to strike from the record the bill of exceptions on the ground that it was not seasonably filed.

Plaintiff in error was tried at a special term of the circuit court of Rhea county beginning on July 10, 1925. The minutes of the court, of date July 21, 1925, show that a motion for a new trial was made and overruled on that day, and this minute entry further recites: "Upon motion, the court is pleased to grant defendant thirty days from July 21, 1925, in which to prepare, perfect, and file his bill of exceptions.Thereupon court adjourned until court in course."

上诉人因违反 1925 年公共法案第 27 章，即《反进化法》而被判决有罪。他向本庭提出上诉。州检察机关提出动议要求直接驳回抗辩状，因为该抗辩状未及时提交。

上诉人在里厄县巡回法庭自 1925 年 7 月 10 日开始以特殊庭审程序被初审，1925 年 7 月 21 日的庭审笔录显示，上诉人曾提出要求重审的动议，但当天被驳回了，这份庭审笔录还提及"基于该动议，法庭给予被告人自 1925 年 7 月 21 日起 30 天的时间以准备、完善和提交他的抗辩状。法庭休庭直到重新开庭"。

The thirty days allowed by order of the court in which plaintiff in error was entitled to file his bill of ex-ceptions expired August 20th. The bill of exceptions herein appears to have been signed September 14th, and to have been filed September 16th.

法院裁定许可上诉人递交抗辩状的 30 天时间在 8 月 20 号到期，但抗辩状显示签署的日期是 9 月 14 号，是在 9 月 16 号递交的。

In his discretion the trial judge restricted the time for filing a bill of exceptions to thirty days after July 21st, as appears from an order of that date and thereupon adjourned his court. The time in which a bill of exceptions might be authenticated thus became fixed. The discretion of the court in the matter had been exercised and exhausted. Upon the expiration of the thirty days the authority of the judge in the matter ceased. He could not on September 14th, fifty-five days after adjournment, sign a bill of exceptions or change his former order respecting same. Such an act was at that time beyond his jurisdiction. Consent of counsel could not then avail. Jurisdiction of subject-matter cannot be conferred upon a court by consent.

The motion to strike the bill of exceptions must accordingly be sustained.

初审法官在其自由裁量权范围内将递交抗辩状的时间限制在 7 月 21 日之后的 30 天，并将此做出裁定并予以休庭。抗辩状的递交时间因此确定下来。法庭对此的裁量权已经行使和用尽。在 30 天期限届满后法官对此事的权利即终止，他不能在 9 月 14 日，即休庭 55 天以后，签收抗辩状或改变此前对此问题的裁定。这一行为在该时间已超出其裁量范围。双方律师同意也没有用，关于实体问题的裁量权不能基于同意而被授予法庭。

因此驳回抗辩状的动议应得到支持。

【生效判决意见】（Opinion by Green）

While the Act was not drafted with as much care as could have been desired, nevertheless, there seems to be no great difficulty in determining its meaning. It is entitled "An Act prohibiting the teaching of the evolution theory in all the Universities, Normals and all other public schools of Tennessee, which are supported in whole or in part by the public school funds of the State, and to provide penalties for the violations thereof."

Thus definding evolution the Act's title clearly indicates the purpose of the Statute to be the prohibition of teaching in the Schools of the State that man has developed or descended from some lower type or order of animals.

When the draftsman came to express this purpose in the body of the Act he first forbade the teaching of "any theory that denies the story of the divine creation of man as taught in the Bible"— his conception evidently being that to forbid the denial of the Bible story would ban the teaching of evolution. To make the purpose more explicit he added that it should be unlawful to teach "that man has descended from a lower order of animals."

Supplying the ellipsis in section 1 of the Act, it reads that it shall be unlawful for any teacher, etc., "to teach any theory that denies the story of the divine creation of man as taught in the Bible, and to teach instead (of the story of the divine creation of man as taught in the Bible) that man has descended from a lower order of animals."

尽管法案并非起草得尽善尽美，然而，我们不难理解其含义。该法案的标题是"禁止在田纳西州所有由州财政提供全部或部分财政支持的大学、中学和其他公立教育机构讲授进化论并对违者实施处罚的法案"。

该法案的标题已经清楚表明，禁止公立学校讲授的是"人从某种低等动物进化而来"。

法案的起草者在法案中表达其目的时表示，他首先要禁止"任何否定《圣经》中人是由上帝创造的理论"——他的构想显然是通过禁止讲授进化论来禁止否定《圣经》。为了更清楚地表明目的，他补充说，讲授"人是由低等动物演变而来的"是非法的。

该法案的第一条的摘要为，任何教师"讲授下述理论——否定《圣经》中上帝创造人类，并（把上帝创造人类的学说）替换为人类是由低等动物演变来的"都是非法的。

It is contended that the Statute violates section 8 of article 1 of the Tennessee Constitution, and section 1 of the Fourteenth Amendment to the Constitution of the United States--the Law of the Land clause of the State Constitution, and the Due Process of Law clause of the Federal Constitution, which are practically equivalent in meaning.

We think there is little merit in this contention. The plaintiff in error was a teacher in the public schools of Rhea county. He was an employee of the State of Tennessee or of a municipal agency of the State. He was under contract with the State to work in an institution of the State. He had no right or privilege to serve the State except upon such terms as the State prescribed. His liberty, his privilege, his immunity to teach and proclaim the theory of evolution, elsewhere than in the service of the State, was in no wise touched by this law.

抗辩认为，《反进化论法》违反了田纳西州宪法第1条第8节，以及美国宪法第十四修正案——美国宪法的基础条款，和联邦宪法正当程序原则的条款，两者含义几乎完全相同。

　　我们认为这项抗辩没什么意义。原审原告是里厄县公立学校的教师，是田纳西州市政单位的雇员，他要根据与州政府签订的合同为政府工作。除此之外，他并没有权利或特权为政府工作。只要是在他为政府服务之外，他讲授进化论的自由、特权或豁免权与《反进化法》无关。

The Statute before us is not an exercise of the police power of the State undertaking to regulate the conduct and contracts of individuals in their dealings with each other. On the other hand it is an Act of the State as a corporation, a proprietor, an employer. It is a declaration of a master as to the character of work the master's servant shall, or rather shall not, perform. In dealing with its own employees engaged upon its own work, the State is not hampered by the limitations of section 8 of article 1 of the Tennessee Constitution, nor of the Fourteenth Amendment to the Constitution of the United States.

　　我们面前的《反进化论法》，不是让州政府的警察权去调整私人之间相互关系的合同。相反，法案中的州政府是以公司、雇主的身份出现的。法案是工作意义上的雇主要求工作意义上的雇员可做或不可做某种行为的宣告。在要求自己的雇员完成本职工作方面，州政府并不受田纳西州宪法第 1 条第 8 节，以及美国宪法第十四修正案的限制。

The last serious criticism made of the Act is that it contravenes the provision of section 3 of article 1 of the Constitution, "that no preference shall ever be given by law to any religious establishment or mode of worship."

　　最后，一个对《反进化论法》的严肃的批评意见是，这部法案违反了田纳西州宪法第 1 条第 3 节："法律不应对任何宗教有所偏颇。"

We are not able to see how the prohibition of teaching the theory that man has descended from a lower order of animals gives preference to any religious establishment or mode of worship. So far as we know there is no religious establishment or organized body that has its creed or confession of faith any article denying or affirming such a theory. So far as we know the denial or affirmation of such a theory does not enter into any recognized mode of worship. Since this cause has been pending in this court, we have been favored, in addition to briefs of counsel and various amici curiae, with a multitude of resolutions, addresses and communications from scientific bodies, religious factions, and individuals giving us the benefit of their views upon the theory of evolution. Examination of these contributions indicates that Protestants, Catholics, and Jews are divided among themselves in their beliefs, and that there is no unanimity among the members of any religious establishment as to this subject. Belief or unbelief in the theory of evolution is no more a characteristic of any religious establishment or mode of worship than is belief or unbelief in the wisdom of the prohibition laws. It would appear that members of the same churches quite generally disagree as to these things.

　　我们不认为，阻止讲授"人是某种低等生物后代"的进化论就是偏向于某种官方宗教或信仰。据我们所知，没有任何宗教机构或组织将其教义建立在否认或支持进化论的基础之上。支持或否定进化论也不会影响任何信仰。在法庭审理期间，各种来自科学机构、宗教组织和个人的辩护律师和法庭之友以决议、声明、邮件等方式表达自己对进化论的观点。对捐款的审查表明，新教徒、天主教徒和犹太教徒彼此的信仰存在分歧，各教内部也并无统一意见。因此，是否相信进化论，并不比是否相信禁令是明智的更构成一种宗教或信仰的特征。甚至同一个教堂内部都无法统一。

Our school authorities are, therefore, quite free to determine how they shall act in this state of the law. Those in charge of the educational affairs of the State are men and women of discernment and culture. If they believe that the teaching of the Science of Biology has been so hampered by chapter 27 of the *Acts* of 1925 as to render such an effort no longer desirable, this course of study may be entirely omitted from the curriculum of our schools. If this be regarded as a misfortune, it must be charged to the Legislature. It should be repeated that the *Act* of 1925 deals with nothing but the evolution of man from a lower order of animals.

It is not necessary now to determine the exact scope of the Religious Preference clause of the Constitution and other language of that section. The situation does not call for such an attempt. Section 3 of article 1 is binding alike on the Legislature, and the school authorities. So far, we are clear that the Legislature has not crossed these constitutional limitations. If hereafter, the school authorities should go beyond such limits, a case can then be brought to the courts.

然而，学校当局有权自由决定如何执行法律。州教育立法的目标是培养男女公民的洞察力和文明程度。如果学校认为生物科学被 1925 年 27 号法案限制，可以将全部课程从学校的课程表中删除。如果有人认为这是不幸的，可以向立法机构请愿。应该再强调一遍，1925 年法案是关于人起源于低等动物的进化论的。

要求现在精确界定州宪法中的宗教优先条款和其他法条中用语的含义是没有必要的。这种情况下无须进行这样的尝试。第一条第三节对立法机构和学校方面都有约束力，因此，我们认为立法机构没有违反州宪法的限制是很清楚的，如果未来学校违反了这方面的限制，法院会受理这方面的诉讼。

Much has been said in argument about the motives of the Legislature in passing this Act. But the validity of a Statute must be determined by its natural and legal effect, rather than proclaimed motives. Some other questions are made but in our opinion they do not merit discussion, and the assignments of error raising such questions are overruled.

大量争论在立法机关通过该法案的时候已经讨论过。但反进化论法案在自然法和实在法意义上的有效性必须确认，就像其宣称的那样。还有一些问题，本庭看来不值得讨论，此类问题均被驳回。

This record discloses that the jury found the defendant below guilty but did not assess the fine. The trial judge himself undertook to impose the minimum fine of $ 100 authorized by the Statute. This was error. Under section 14 of article 6 of the Constitution of Tennessee, a fine in excess of $ 50 must be assessed by a jury. The Statute before us does not permit the imposition of a smaller fine than $ 100.

Since a jury alone can impose the penalty this Act requires and as a matter of course no different penalty can be inflicted, the trial judge exceeded his jurisdiction in levying this fine and we are without power to correct his error. The judgment must accordingly be reversed. *Upchurch v. The State*, 153 Tenn. 198, 281 S.W. 462.

The court is informed that the plaintiff in error is no longer in the service of the State. We see nothing to be gained by prolonging the life of this bizarre case. On the contrary we think the peace and dignity of the State, which all criminal prosecutions are brought to redress, will be the better conserved by the entry of a nolle prosequi herein. Such a course is suggested to the Attorney-General.

法庭记录表明，陪审团认定被告有罪，但没有被征收的罚款。主审法官承诺将按照该法案规定的最低限额征收 100 美元的罚款。这是错误的。田纳西州的宪法第 6 条第 14 节规定，超过 50 美元的罚款必须由陪审团进行。法案不允许超过 100 美元的罚款。

既然陪审团可以单独判处本案要求的刑罚，而且也不会造成不同的惩罚，主审法官超越其司法管辖权征收的罚款，我们无权予以直接纠正其错误，但判决相应地应予以撤销。

法庭知悉，上诉人不再是政府雇员，继续延长审理本案已经没有意义。相反，我们认为撤销本案的起诉可以维持本州的安宁与尊严，这正是刑事诉讼的意义所在。以上建议，已提交本州的总检察长。

【反对意见】（Dissent by Mckinney）

"That the terms of a penal statute creating a new offense must be sufficiently explicit to inform those who are subject to it what conduct on their part will render them liable to its penalties is a well-recognized requirement, consonant alike with ordinary notions of fair play and the settled rules of law; and a statute which either forbids or requires the doing of an act in terms so vague that men of common intelligence must necessarily guess at its meaning and differ as to its application violates the first essential of due process of law. *International Harvester Co. v. Kentucky,* 234 U.S. 216, 221, 34 S. Ct. 853, 58 L. Ed. 1284; *Collins v. Kentucky,* 234 U.S. 634, 34 S. Ct. 924, 58 L. Ed. 1510."

Applying the foregoing rule to the statute here involved, I am of the opinion that it is invalid for uncertainty of meaning. I, therefore, respectfully dissent from the contrary holding of my associates.

"用于定义一个新罪行的刑事法案的内容必须足够清晰地向那些违犯了该罪行的人表明，他们所犯下的罪行使得他们容易受到惩罚。这种清晰表述是对刑事法案的公认要求。必须考虑公平竞争以及法律确定性的观念。一项禁止或者要求做某事的法律，应避免使用模糊的以至于正常人的智慧必须猜测其含义和差异的用语，这是正当程序原则的首要含义（国际联合公司诉肯塔基州，柯林斯诉肯塔基州案）"。

按照上述原则，我认为本案中含有不确定的含义。故我与我的同事持相反的意见。

【案件影响】（Impact of the Case）

斯科普斯诉田纳西州案，最终州高等法院 5 位法官以 3:1（一人弃权）做出了判决，表面上是撤销了一审判决，并推动检察机关撤销公诉。但该判决并未否认《反进化论法》的合法性，因此斯科普斯试图以司法诉讼推翻田纳西州《反进化论法》的意愿失败了，直到后来联邦最高法院才在另案中判决《反进化论法》违背联邦宪法的精神。"猴子审判"为日后进化论的继续发展开拓了道路，不失为美国法制史上一个影响巨大的案例。此外，法官对正当程序原则与司法中立原则，科学、道德与宗教，立法机构和司法机构之间的关系的阐述，也对日后的美国法律发展有着深刻的影响。

【思考问题】（Questions）

1. 法院对科学与宗教之间的冲突应该持何种立场？
2. 司法制度如何在科学观念不断进步的时代维持社会的稳定性？

本书的英美案例判决书大多可以从 Lexis 或 Westlaw 等法律数据库下载，经过数据服务商整理的判决书在体例上一般由以下部分构成：

一、标题部分

这一部分主要包括案件名称、判决法院、索引出处、判决时间。例如 New York Times Co.v.Sullivan 一案的判决原文标题如下：

NEW YORK TIMES CO. v. SULLIVAN

No. 39

SUPREME COURT OF THE UNITED STATES

376 U.S. 254; 84 S. Ct. 710; 11 L. Ed. 2d 686; 1964 U.S. LEXIS 1655; 95 A.L.R.2d 1412; 1 Media

L. Rep. 1527

January 6, 1964, Argued

March 9, 1964, Decided

（一）案件名称

列出诉讼双方当事人的名称，有时会注明当事人在诉讼中的法律地位，例如：Helen Palsgraf, Respondent, v. The Long Island Railroad Company, Appellant。刑事案件的一方通常是政府，上诉或申诉程序中，上诉或申诉方的名称往往位于左边，v. 是 versus 的缩写，在刑事诉讼里可以读为 versus 或 against；在民事诉讼里宜读为 and。

（二）判决法院

是出具本判决的法院全称。案例名称与判决法院之间的编号为法院内部对案例的编号，也可能并没有该编号。

（三）索引出处

是对该判决文件原始文献出处的缩写。例如 376 U.S. 254，是指本判决文件出自《美国案例汇编》第 376 卷第 254 页；有时一个案件会注明多个出处，例如 84 S. Ct. 710，是指《最高法院案例汇编》第 84 卷第 710 页；1964 U.S. LEXIS 1655 是 Lexis 数据库内部的编码；95 A.L.R.2d 1412 指《美国法律报告》第二辑第 95 卷第 1412 页。这些缩写代表的汇编主要包括：

1. 官方汇编，包括 United States Reports（简写为 U.S.，《美国案例汇编》），收录美国最高法院判例；另外美国的各个州法院也有自己的官方正式判例汇编。例如 Boomer v. Atlantic Cement Co.一案注明的索引出处为：26 N.Y.2d 219；257 N.E.2d 870；309 N.Y.S.2d 312；1970 N.Y. LEXIS 1478；1 ERC (BNA) 1175；40 A.L.R.3d 590，其中 26 N.Y.2d 219 是指纽约州法院自己的官方判例汇编。

2. 非官方的汇编，以西方出版公司（West Publishing Corporation）的美国全国判例汇编系统（National Reporter System）为例，包括：

S. Ct. 即 Supreme Court Reporter（《最高法院案例汇编》）；

F. 即 Federal Reporter（《联邦判例汇编》）；

F. 2d. 即 Federal Reporter, 2d Series（《联邦判例汇编第二辑》）；

F. 3d. 即 Federal Reporter, 3d Series（《联邦判例汇编第三辑》）；

F. Supp. 即 Federal Supplement（《联邦判例补编》）；

F. Supp. 2d 即 Federal Supplement, Second Series（《联邦判例补编第二辑》）；

F.R.D. 即 Federal Rules Decisions（《联邦诉讼规则判例汇编》）；

F. Cas. 即 Federal Cases（《联邦判例汇编》）；

Fed. Appx 即 Federal Appendix（《联邦判例附录汇编》）；

A. 即 Atlantic Reporter（《大西洋地区判例汇编》）；

A. 2d. 即 Atlantic Reporter, 2d Series（《大西洋地区判例汇编第二辑》）；

A. 3d. 即 Atlantic Reporter, 3d Series（《大西洋地区判例汇编第三辑》）；

N. E. 即 Northeastern Reporter（《东北地区判例汇编》）；

N. E. 2d. 即 Northeastern Reporter, 2d Series（《东北地区判例汇编第二辑》）；

N. W. 即 Northwestern Reporter（《西北地区判例汇编》）；

N. W. 2d. 即 Northwestern Reporter, 2d Series（《西北地区判例汇编第二辑》）；

S. E. 即 Southeastern Reporter（《东南地区判例汇编》）；

S. E. 2d.即 Southeastern Reporter, 2d Series（《东南地区判例汇编第二辑》）；

S. W. 即 Southwestern Reporter（《西南地区判例汇编》）；

S. W. 2d. 即 Southwestern Reporter, 2d Series（《西南地区判例汇编第二辑》）；

S. W. 3d. 即 Southwestern Reporter, 3d Series（《西南地区判例汇编第三辑》）；

So. 即 Southern Reporter（《南方地区判例汇编》）；

So. 2d. 即 Southern Reporter, 2d Series（《南方地区判例汇编第二辑》）；

So. 3d. 即 Southern Reporter, 3d Series（《南方地区判例汇编第三辑》）；

P. 即 Pacific Reporter（《太平洋地区判例汇编》）；

P. 2d. 即 Pacific Reporter, 2d Series（《太平洋地区判例汇编第二辑》）；

P. 3d. 即 Pacific Reporter, 3d Series（《太平洋地区判例汇编第二辑》）；

N. Y. S. 即 New York Supplement（《纽约判例补编》）；

N. Y. S. 2d. 即 New York Supplement, 2d Series（《纽约判例补编第二辑》）；

Cal. Rep. 即 California Reporter（《加利福尼亚州判例汇编》）；

Cal. 2d. Rep. 即 California Reporter, 2d Series（《加利福尼亚州判例汇编第二辑》）；

Cal. 3d. Rep. 即 California Reporter, 3d Series（《加利福尼亚州判例汇编第三辑》）。

3. 美国律师合作出版公司出版的相关判例汇编主要有：

A.L.R. 即 American Law Reports（《美国法律报告》）；

A.L.R. Fed. 即 American Law Reports, Federal（《美国联邦法律报告》）；

L. Ed. 即 U.S. Supreme Court Reports，Lawyers' Edition（《美国最高法院判例汇编律师版》）；

L. Ed. 2d. 即 U.S. Supreme Court Reports, Lawyers' Edition, 2d Series（《美国最高法院案例汇编律师版第二辑》）。

（四）判决时间

是判决做出的时间，有时还会注明辩论时间，如果判决做出时间与判决成文时间不一致，有时会另行注明判决书提交时间。

二、首部信息

除在标题中提供的判决信息外，在判决意见正文之前，判决书还会在首部对判决书的一些相关信息加以注明，这些首部信息通常并不是判决文件的原有组成部分，而是由出版公司委托专业人士精心整理的，通常包括以下项目：

（一）案件历史（Prior History）及程序状况（Procedural Posture）

案例历史主要介绍这一判例在此前经历过的审理程序，大多时候会注明原审判例的索引出处；程序状况主要介绍本次审判程序的启动依据。从这两部分材料里通常能够简要看清楚这一案件的来龙去脉及各级法院的先前裁判结果。在数据库中有时还能够进一步链接到与本案有关的所有程序的文件数据。

（二）处置情况（Disposition）和判决结果（Outcome）

案例的处置情况主要是说明对本案之前的程序是如何在本判决中做出处置的，例如对上诉的案件通常会有 affirmed、reversed、reversed and remanded 三种情况。判决结果主要是说明本判决自身所得出的最终结论。

（三）案例总结（Case Summary）、案情概览（Overview）和判决要旨（Syllabus）

案例总结对本案判决涉及的事实与法律问题要点做出整理；案情概览较多阐述事实与处理程序；判决要旨主要概括案例适用的法律原则。这些都不是法院原始判决的构成部分，而是由案例汇编的编撰者编写的，以便于让读者在阅读原始判决前就能很快了解案例内容概要。

（四）法官（Judges）和律师（Counsels）

主要说明参与案件审理的法官以及代理各方当事人的律师信息。

（五）关键词（Core Terms）和法律摘要（Headnotes）

关键词是对本案涉及的重要法律术语的概括整理；案例的法律摘要在案例总结部分之后由案例出版商总结编辑，是对判决之中法律观点的引述或总结，会将其纳入不同的分类标题之下，以表明该摘要内容涉及何种法律问题。

三、判决意见

这是判决书的正文部分，通常由主审法官或受法庭委托的法官或法官助理起草，有时还会注明是法官的口头意见或由谁宣读。由法庭经投票做出的多数意见，即法庭意见是具有法律拘束力的意见，但同时根据案件情况也允许载明同案法官的附合意见和反对意见。

附合意见（Concur），也译为协同意见，是指同意法庭决定，但对法庭推理有不同看法的意见。这充分体现了英美国家法官的独立性。协同意见不具有法律拘束力，但里面体现的思想往往会与法庭意见互为映照，甚至进一步解释了法庭规则。反对意见（Dissent）是不同意法庭意见的意见。反对意见亦无法律拘束力。如同附和意见一样，反对意见往往也会孕育新思想、新规则。在一个案件中的反对意见，有时会在后来的案件中成为正面意见在判决中作为论据被引述。

四、附录

除判决意见正文中会出现大量文献引用和注释外，判决书的最后有时还会出现附录（Reference），以注明与判决有关的信息或案情资料。

参考文献与案例索引

【参考文献】

[1]高尔森. 英美合同法纲要. 天津：南开大学出版社，1984.

[2]任东来等. 美国宪政历程：影响美国的 25 个司法大案. 北京：中国法制出版社，2005.

[3]何主宇. 最新法律专业英语读写全程点拨. 北京：机械工业出版社，2003.

[4]何主宇. 英美法案例研读全程指南. 北京：法律出版社，2007.

[5]朱伟一. 美国经典案例解析. 上海：上海三联书店，2007.

[6]朱伟一. 法学院. 北京：北京大学出版社，2014.

[7]李长栓. 非文学翻译理论与实践. 北京：中国对外翻译出版公司，2004.

[8]罗国强. 涉外法律实训教程. 武汉：武汉大学出版社，2009.

[9]理查德·拉撒路斯，奥利弗·哈克编著. 曹明德等译. 中国律师实训经典·美国法律判例故事系列：环境法故事. 北京：中国人民大学出版社，2013.

[10]李小年. WTO 法律规则与争端解决机制. 上海：上海财经大学出版社，2000.

[11]王锴译. 美国联邦最高法院马伯里诉麦迪逊案判词. http://www.dffyw.com/sifashijian/ jj/201403/35287.html.

[12]海伦·帕尔斯格莱芙（被上诉人）诉长岛铁路公司（上诉人）案. http://blog.163.com/likedarcy@126/blog/static/58565772200955104739689/.

[13]王春燕. 作品中的表达与作品之间的实质相似——以两组美国著作权判例为线索. 中外法学，2000（5）.

[14]孟军，陈建萍译. 微软垄断案判决书. 电子知识产权，2000（9、10）.

[15]李松锋. 女王诉杜德利和斯蒂芬斯案. 苏州大学学报（法学版），2014（1）.

[16]蔡红. 英国劳动法的不公平解雇及其法律救济. 欧洲研究，2002（2）.

[17]方杰，黄共兴. "贝科克诉杰克逊"案件研究. 南阳师范学院学报，2014（4）.

【案例索引】

[1] New York Times Co. v. Sullivan, 376 U.S. 254; 84 S. Ct. 710; 11 L. Ed. 2d 686; 1964 U.S. LEXIS 1655; 95 A.L.R.2d 1412; 1 Media L. Rep. 1527 (1964)

[2] Marbury v. Madison, 5 U.S. 137; 2 L. Ed. 60; 1803 U.S. LEXIS 352; 1 Cranch 137（1803）

[3]Hadley v. Baxendale, [1843-1860] All ER Rep 461（1854）

[4]Palsgraf v. Long Island Railroad Co., 248 N.Y. 339; 162 N.E. 99; 59 A.L.R. 1253（1928）

[5]Nichols v. Universal Pictures Co., 45 F.2d 119; 1930 U.S. App. LEXIS 3587（1930）

[6]Walkovszky v. carlton, 18 N.Y.2d 414; 223 N.E.2d 6; 276 N.Y.S.2d 585（1966）

[7]Leyland Shipping Co. v. Norwich Union Fire Insurance Society Ltd., [1918-1919] All ER Rep 443（1918）

[8]United States v. Microsoft Corp., 97 F. Supp. 2d 59; 2000 U.S. Dist. LEXIS 7582（2000）

[9]United States v. O'Hagan, 139 F.3d 641; Fed. Sec. L. Rep. (CCH) P90,178（1996）

[10]Bartlett v. Barclays Bank Trust co., [1980] CH 515, [1980] 2 All ER 92（1980）

[11]Norton Tool Co.Ltd v. Tewson, [1973] 1 All ER 183, [1973] 1 WLR 45, [1972] ICR 501, 13 KIR 328, [1973] ITR 23.（1972）

[12]Boomer v. Atlantic Cement Co., 26 N.Y.2d 219; 257 N.E.2d 870; 309 N.Y.S.2d 312; 1970 N.Y. LEXIS 1478; 1 ERC (BNA) 1175; 40 A.L.R.3d 590（1970）

[13]Burnham v. Superior Court of California, 495 U.S. 604; 110 S. Ct. 2105; 109 L. Ed. 2d 631; 1990 U.S. LEXIS 2700; 58 U.S.L.W. 4629(1990)

[14]R v. Dudley and Stephens, [1881-1885] All ER Rep 61（1884）

[15]Miranda v. Arizona, 384 U.S. 436; 86 S. Ct. 1602; 16 L. Ed. 2d 694; 1966 U.S. LEXIS 2817; 10 Ohio Misc. 9; 36 Ohio Op. 2d 237; 10 A.L.R.3d 974 (1966)

[16]Babcock v. Jackson, 12 N.Y.2d 473; 191 N.E.2d 279; 240 N.Y.S.2d 743; 1963 N.Y. LEXIS 1185; 95 A.L.R.2d 1 (1963）

[17]United States — Import Prohibition of Certain Shrimp and Shrimp Products, WT/DS58/R、WT/DS58/AB/R（1998）

[18]John Thomas Scopes v. The State of Tennessee, 154 Tenn. 105; 289 S.W. 363; 1926 Tenn. LEXIS 109; 1 Smith (Tenn.) 105; 53 A.L.R. 821 (1926)

编者的话

本书选取了英美法系法律发展历史上具有重要影响的 18 个经典案例，并对案件的原始判决书及相关法律文件进行整理、翻译和编排。本书编写初衷是撰写一本能在具有涉外法律培养特色的法学本科教学课堂上使用的英美司法案例选读课程教材。由于英美普通法系的案例数量巨大，本书具有以我国部门法观念为主，结合普通法系法律部门区分的特点，在宪法、行政法、合同法等各类法律，以及与美国有关的世界贸易组织（WTO）争端解决报告、中外法制史等领域内各选取了一个案例。这些案例或者本身创设了该法律领域的重要先例，或者通过判决取得了良好的社会效果，也可能判决意见略有争议，但均具有历久弥坚的法律实践价值。

由于这些法律判决本身风格不一，或古奥难懂，或简洁明快，或文采斐然，或繁冗无味，在编译过程中因编者水平所限难以一一体现，但都注重对照判决原文尽量直白阐明判决含义，力求准确运用法律术语。由于部分案例在国内已为诸多学者引证甚至做了译介，编者充分参考借鉴了可以检索到的研究成果，在这些成果的基础上，编者大都又重新对照原文补充了细节或进行了突出要点的整理。考虑行文整洁，本书在案例正文中未对引用文献和法律术语做逐一注明，仅在文末列出参考文献与案例索引，且还有一些论文及网络资料未能列出，在此一并表示感谢。

本书无意对这些经典案例本身进行更深入的研究和解读，但本书所做的工作补充了当前对英美司法案例进行准确而直观介绍的国内资料的不足。如果读者希望再进一步获得案例判决书原文，可通过 LEXIS 等法律数据库进一步检索获取。编者相信，深入研读这些案例，对于准确了解英美国家的法律规则和法律思维、做好国际法律规则接轨工作、增益当今法治中国建设都有着重要意义。

本书案件的编写分工为：陈桂华教授编写第 4 个案例，王岩华副教授编写第 9 个、第 15 个案例，黄影博士编写第 2 个、第 16 个案例并参与编写第 8 个案例，白明华博士编写第 11 个、第 12 个案例，严飞行老师和翟文喆老师分别编写第 5 个、第 18 个案例，其余案例与附录的编写和统稿工作由焦洪宝副教授完成。

本书可以作为各类高校开设英美司法案例选读课程的教材使用，也可供法学专业本科生、研究生和英语专业学生，以及对英美国家法律文化有兴趣者和从事涉外法律实务的人士阅读、学习、研究使用。

因编者水平所限，书中难免有疏漏之处，欢迎读者不吝赐教，以便更正。如有任何问题，敬请通过以下电子邮箱联系：229882121@qq.com。

编 者
2016 年 10 月 1 日